DON'T ASK THE PRICE

MARCUS SIEFF

Don't ask the price

THE MEMOIRS OF

THE PRESIDENT

OF MARKS & SPENCER

WEIDENFELD AND NICOLSON

LONDON

First published in Great Britain by
George Weidenfeld & Nicolson Limited
91 Clapham High Street, London SW4 7TA

Copyright © by Lord Sieff of Brimpton, 1986

ISBN 0 297 78714 4

Printed and bound in Great Britain by
Butler & Tanner Ltd, Frome and London

TO

MY WIFE

LILY

FOR HER PATIENCE AND

ENCOURAGEMENT

CONTENTS

ILLUSTRATIONS

All photographs are from the author's collection

ACKNOWLEDGEMENTS

Nothing that I have done well in my seventy-three years has been accomplished without the support of my family and friends, and the help and co-operation of my colleagues at Marks & Spencer. If some of them are not mentioned by name in the following pages, I hope they will forgive me and understand that this does not reflect any lack of affection or respect for them; it is merely due to the restrictions of space.

I would like to thank also the many friends and colleagues who have been so helpful in reminding me of and confirming events of long ago – again too many to name individually. However, I am particularly grateful to my wife , my children David, Amanda and Daniela, and the rest of my family for their encouragement; to Kenneth Harris, whose advice and help have been most valuable; to Roger Saoul and Paul Duncan for their research and constructive criticism; to Jeffrey Archer, who gave me sensible advice; and my editor Alex MacCormick. Lastly I would like to thank my secretary Margaret Bartlett, without whose patience, perseverance and hard work this book would not have been finished.

CHAPTER ONE

I AM and have been a very fortunate man. I was born into a remarkable family; my two grandfathers came to this country as young Jewish immigrants from Poland and, starting virtually without a penny in their pockets, founded companies which made their heirs into wealthy men. These heirs, my father and my uncle Simon Marks, made a valuable contribution to life in Britain. They were also Zionists, disciples and helpers of Chaim Weizmann and thus, with many others, involved in the creation of the State of Israel. Through them and the outstanding women they married there came to me many privileges and opportunities. It is partly out of a sense of gratitude, therefore, that I write these observations. There are three other motives. President Navon, an Israeli friend and colleague, said last year, 'Marcus, all the great Jews we worked with, you and I, to bring the State of Israel into being after the Second World War — Weizmann, Ben Gurion, Golda Meir — are dead; many of our own generation have also gone. One day you must make a record of those times.' I promised that I would. The second reason for this book is that I would like my family to know of my gratitude for having been born into it and for having been able to live a life for which I am very thankful. And last but not least, my daughter, Daniela, said to me two years ago, 'Daddy, if you were to write your memoirs once and for all, you would stop telling us the same stories over and over again, wouldn't you?' She is probably right.

Soon after the great wave of pogroms in the early 1880s my grand-father, Ephraim Sieff, decided, along with hundreds of thousands of Russian, Polish and Lithuanian Jews, to emigrate. He had been brought up in the village of Eiregola in Lithuania, well inside the Pale of Settlement, the area ceded to Russia after the series of partitions of Poland which began in 1772. Ephraim's father was a rabbi; his mother owned the village cornmill; their income came from grinding the villagers' corn. Ephraim had no desire to be a rabbi and thought he could do better than grind the village corn. So, having saved about £50, he obtained a permit to live in Königsberg in Germany, at the house of a cousin who had a small cloth business. Drawing on what he had learned in the village mill, he bought hemp, flax and barley across the Russian border and sold it on the German side. He also helped his cousin in his business and in particular started buying scraps from local tailors, separating wool from hemp, linen from cotton – recycling, as we would call it now. Within a couple of years he had a small business of his own and was doing well.

Then came a major Russian pogrom. This was followed by an agreement between Germany and Russia that all Russian Jews living in Germany should be forcibly repatriated so that they could be conscripted into military service; the Germans wanted no Jews and the Russians wanted soldiers. My grandfather was compelled to sell his business in Königsberg almost overnight for far less than it was worth and to return to Eiregola with the prospect of compulsory service in the Russian army; for Jews conscription could mean twenty years. On the way home he decided that he would try to get out of Russia as soon as possible. His parents endeavoured to persuade him to change his mind, but soon saw that he was resolved. Because he was eligible for call-up, he could not leave Russian soil legally and therefore had to smuggle himself out. His mother took all the responsibility for helping him; if his father had been discovered doing so, the penalty would have been death. The corn trade across the frontier continued and the mill's covered wagon often crossed the line with dozens of chalk markings to show that it had been cleared by the frontier guards. Early one morning, in winter, when the light was not too good, my grandfather curled up in the wagon and his parents heaped sacks of corn around him. Then his mother took the reins and drove him over the frontier. The guards stopped the wagon and, as usual, prodded the outside sacks with their bayonets before letting it proceed.

Once my grandfather was on German soil he made his way to Stettin, a port from which it was possible to sail to New York, where he had some relations. However, a rascally ticket-seller took his money, but gave him a ticket valid only as far as Hull, on the northeast coast of England. Many other Jewish immigrants were apparently swindled in this way. When the ship reached Hull, it was met by a crowd of Jews who came to see if any of their relatives were on board. One of these, seeing my grandfather standing there lost and unable to speak English, took pity on him and spoke to him in

Yiddish. He must have been a saintly fellow, for he not only took grandfather home but also gave him lodging for some weeks. From there my grandfather moved on to Manchester, where, his benefactor advised him, there was a large and secure settlement of Jews. Here he had the good luck to encounter a woman who had known him in Eiregola and was now married to a master tailor, also a Litvak immigrant; they, too, took him to their house and befriended him.

In the course of his work the master tailor produced a number of cuttings which he regarded as waste and paid to have removed. My grandfather asked if he could take away the cuttings without payment. He aimed to sell them, and a few days later, having sorted the waste, about which he was extremely knowledgeable, and having borrowed some sacks and hired a handcart, he pushed his cargo through Manchester to the warehouse of Beaumont & Company. He was able to find it only by showing passers-by cards on which the master tailor had written the names of the connecting streets.

The Beaumont manager was impressed by the thoroughness with which the scrap had been sorted, paid my grandfather well, and promised to take as many loads as he cared to bring, provided they were up to the same standard. That was the beginning of a business which by the time he died had made my grandfather a wealthy man. Two years later he was able to use horse vans instead of barrows and had a small warehouse of his own near Manchester's Victoria Station. Six years after that he bought Beaumont & Company, which, just before the First World War, became Sieff & Beaumont Limited. The war gave the business a great opportunity because of a demand for gun cotton, and white cotton waste was also required for the manufacture of paper when the enemy shipping blockade cut off our cotton imports.

My father, Israel, and his younger brother, Edward, who inherited this prosperous business, would probably have continued to own and manage Sieff & Beaumont for the rest of their lives, but, when they became deeply involved in Marks & Spencer in the mid-1920s, they felt it only fair to the company and its staff to sell Beaumont's to the men then running it; the managers thus became the owners. My father was always very proud of what his father had done in acquiring Beaumont's and making it an efficient and successful firm. He often used to say of Ephraim, 'It all began with the cuttings on the basement floor. He did nothing new; he did what other people were doing but did it better. There is always room for people like him.' What was true then is even more true today.

In some respects the history of my other grandfather, Michael Marks, was similar. He was born in a village near Bialystok, a city within the Pale in what was then Russian Poland. From what we can gather, his family lived in circumstances very much like my Sieff grandfather, except that they were not so well off. His mother died giving birth to him and so he was brought up with many brothers and sisters by a devoted eldest sister. Michael too was driven out by the pogroms, coming to England when he was nineteen, but, unlike Ephraim, he landed where he intended to, in Hartlepool. From there he went to Stockton-on-Tees and then to Leeds, where he had heard there was a large Jewish community and where a philanthropic firm called Barran's was good to Jewish refugees. What happened to him there has been recorded by Alistair Dewhirst, the present chairman of I. J. Dewhirst Ltd, a firm from which Marks & Spencer has bought goods for more than a hundred years.

One morning in 1884 Alistair's grandfather, Isaac, a well-known Leeds wholesale merchant who sold goods to cheap shops and market stalls, was standing outside his warehouse in Kirkgate in the centre of the city. Suddenly he was accosted by a striking-looking red-haired youth who kept repeating the name 'Barran's', the only word he seemed able to say. Isaac was accompanied by his general manager, Charlie Backhouse, who, because of his dealing with the shopkeepers and stallholders, some of whom were Jewish immigrants, knew a little Yiddish. They soon had the gist of my grandfather's story. As a result, Isaac offered to lend him £5, a substantial sum in those days; my grandfather said he would buy the equivalent amount of goods from Isaac's warehouse and peddle them in the villages around Leeds. He did well, but it was hard physical work and his health was not good; as soon as he had saved enough money, he hired a pitch in the Leeds open-air market, his stall consisting of a trestle table six feet by three. The market was only a hundred yards from Dewhirst's warehouse, which he visited daily to buy goods, and he became known to the Dewhirst staff. He was well thought of by them, particularly by the cashier, Tom Spencer. Each of the towns around Leeds had its own market open one or two days a week, the stall owner frequently moving from one site to another during the course of a week. His experience as a pedlar had taught Michael what people wanted. Two days a week he sold from his stall in Leeds, where he soon had two tables, and on other days he was in the markets of Castleford and Wakefield. It wasn't long before he asked Dewhirst's if they could supply him with staff. They provided him with two girls, who continued to work for him for many years. Soon he was leaving them in charge in Leeds so that he himself could go elsewhere, thus selling in two markets on the same day.

At this time some open-air markets were superseded by covered ones. A permanent market hall was built in Leeds and was open six days a week. Michael was conscious that shopping was difficult for him because he knew so little English. It struck him that in this respect he had something in common with many of his customers, who were partially or completely illiterate. Even in the days when his stall consisted of only one trestle table he drew a chalk line down the middle, putting on one side goods which were variously priced and on the other a great variety of goods with a big poster above them saying, 'Don't ask the price, it's a penny.' When he graduated to a large permanent stall in the market hall, he put up another: 'M. Marks: the original Penny Bazaar.' Within two years he had opened up penny bazaars in covered market halls in several towns in Yorkshire and Lancashire and as far off as Cardiff.

A chain of stores soon appeared in the cities and larger towns throughout England and Wales bearing the legend, 'M. Marks — Originator of the Penny Bazaar.' The fronts of these were open during shopping hours and the counters stood along the rear wall and two sides. This meant that customers did not have to ask for goods to be brought out from cupboards, a request they might have been shy of making but which was how most shopkeepers kept their goods in those days. When they had chosen what they wanted, all they had to do was hand over the money. Out of this developed two of the most important principles of retail distribution today, self-selection and self-service — and the store was designed for the purpose.

In 1886, when Michael was twenty-two, he married a girl of twenty-one called Hannah. In 1891 they moved to Wigan, set up a stall in the market and lived in Caroline Street. Wigan was then a town of poor people with simple needs and Michael's assortment met their requirements. Three years later he took three major decisions. Firstly, he opened what was for him at this stage a big shop in Manchester and moved his home there. Secondly, he began to buy some of his goods, not from wholesalers, but direct from manufacturers, something which the organization he founded has tried to do ever since. Thirdly, he asked Isaac Dewhirst if he would come in with him as a partner because he needed someone to share the responsibility for a rapidly expanding business. Dewhirst, since his own business was prospering, refused, but he suggested that Tom Spencer would be interested in improving his lot. Marks knew Spencer well and in 1894 the partnership of Marks & Spencer was established, Spencer investing £300 in the business. By 1903 they had thirty-six market bazaars and shops, including three in London, and formed a limited company. In 1908 there were sixty units, two thirds of them shops, the rest permanent market bazaars.

Both my grandfathers married outstanding women. Michael died at the age of forty-seven; it was fortunate for him that he met Hannah, because she helped him enormously throughout their married life and was a wonderful mother to their five children after she was widowed. She was not a robust woman, being small, slight and delicate-looking, yet she had vast energy and dominated her husband and her family. My father described her as an outstanding dressmaker with a shrewd sense of design and a good head for figures. My Sieff grandmother was different; she hadn't the same commercial sense though she was shrewd and, when she was young, she was beautiful.

In 1902, when my father was twelve, my grandfather moved house to 408 Bury New Road. Socially, this was quite a step up in the world. My father liked to tell people, 'I was born on top of a fish and chip shop.' It was quite true; theirs was a two-room flat above the shop and the neighbourhood was rough and noisy. From there they went to a tiny house in Elsworth Street, not far from Stock Street, where they had first met. Other moves followed, social progress being marked almost by the distance traversed from the environs of Victoria Station in a north-westerly direction up Bury New Road. Indeed, No. 408 was located in the Borough of Salford. Though the house was one of four joined together, the Sieffs had gone up in the world; so had the Marks family — farther up, in fact. That same year Michael had a house built for him on the site of an older one about fifty yards away from the Sieffs' house. He called it Knoll House and it was comparatively grand, with a front lawn, eight bedrooms and a summerhouse in the back garden.

According to Father, the contact between the two families came about through him. One cold Saturday he was walking in Cheetham Hill Road when he saw three little girls walking smartly in step, in line abreast. They were of different heights but were dressed identically in winter coats and carried muffs. He noticed that the tallest girl had very pretty legs and decided that he would like to see if she had a face to match. He discovered, when he overtook them, that she had, but soon the trio turned into a house in the same street. The following Saturday he was introduced to the girl at a birthday party; her name was Rebecca Marks (Becky), and she was to become my mother.

My father talked to Becky for most of the afternoon. A few days later he met her brother, Simon, who was just about to go out to play cricket in the field behind the house. 'Shall I come out and play with you?' Father asked. 'Yes,' said Simon, 'come on.' And so out they went. In his memoirs, Father had this to say, looking back on that memorable afternoon:

I remember the first game well. It was like so many we played on the field behind his father's house. He was not dictatorial and he did not abuse his power. But he did not conceal the fact that he was in control of the game and the players. If there was any doubt about whether a boy was stumped, leg before, or run out, Simon was the arbitrator. If a player refused to accept his judgement he ordered the offender off the field. The culprit inevitably had to go, otherwise he would not be invited to the game the following week. Our friendship began that Saturday afternoon. It lasted sixty-two years, up to his death in 1964. All through it he remained the one who possessed the bat, ball and wickets, and I was happy and fulfilled under his captaincy.

Father was always inclined to be self-deprecating where Simon was concerned, but certainly an intimate, lifelong friendship began as a result of that game of cricket, a friendship unclouded by a frown or cross word, personal or professional, which, as boys, youths and men, both took for granted for the rest of their lives. They shared a school desk, went on holidays together, went to the films and the theatre together, shared an office for a while and each married the other's sister. As boys, they read the same books. When they were youths, Father in Britain, Simon on the Continent, they wrote long letters to each other after the manner of the Goethe–Schiller correspondence. Sometimes they showed almost telepathic knowledge of each other's thoughts or whereabouts. Despite all this, they were very different personalities, which may be why they got on so well. Certainly the way they complemented each other had beneficial consequences for Marks & Spencer.

Throughout their schooldays, Israel and Simon assumed that they would each go into their family businesses. But whereas Simon did so, after some years abroad, my father, on the insistence of his father, went to the University of Manchester, where he read business economics. He was soon followed there by Becky; they were inseparable. From the university Father went into my grandfather's flourishing business. My grandfather was by then exporting high-quality waste to several European countries and to the United States. As well as sending his son around the United Kingdom, he sent him to Europe four or five times a year. My father learned a great deal about cloth in all its forms and conditions and also about trading in Europe, knowledge which later was to become very useful to Marks & Spencer.

While my father went up to university, Simon was living in France and Germany for more than two-and-a-half years. His father, who loved him dearly ('My Prince', he used to call him), being torn between wanting him to learn all he could abroad and wanting him at home, asked him to return in 1907. His decision may have been influenced by a presentiment of his own death. At all events, Michael died at the end of that year and at seventeen Simon became head of a family comprising his widowed mother and four sisters.

There now began a struggle for control of Marks & Spencer which nearly resulted in its becoming Steel & Chapman. This led to my father's joining the board and beginning his long professional association with Simon. Tom Spencer, much older than Michael Marks, had already retired, his place being taken by a friend of the Spencers, a handkerchief-maker called William Chapman. When Michael died, Chapman was left as sole director. Two weeks later Bernard Steel, a friend of Michael Marks and an executor of his estate, was appointed to the board. The business made good progress; after a couple of years Chapman and Steel proposed to increase the firm's capital from £30,000 to £70,000, for those days a very large financial outlay, which Chapman and Steel could afford but which the Marks &

Spencer families certainly could not. The Marks family, who held a majority of the shares, resisted this attempt by Chapman and Steel to take control, and, to protect the Marks interest, they pressed for and obtained the election to the board of two more directors, Simon and Tom Spencer's son, Thomas. In 1912, after disagreements with Chapman, Steel resigned and died the following year.

Chapman, who was chairman, refused to elect a successor. Marks & Spencer therefore was, in effect, now William Chapman. There followed five very troubled years; there was great tension between the Marks family and Chapman. Simon and his family, as did mine, looked on Marks & Spencer as a way of life. Chapman, however, was ready to sell it as soon as he received a good offer. There was bound to be conflict; Chapman was determined to have the Marks family out. He took his stand on an article of the company which said that, if anybody wanted to elect a new director against the wishes of his colleagues, he must have the support of at least seventy-five per cent of the shareholders. Simon therefore had to try to buy back enough shares to reach the requisite level. Chapman put an exorbitant price on them. Mrs Marks and other relatives put up their savings; Grandfather Sieff contributed and my father, by now married to Becky, put in all his savings and, unknown to his father, who would have worried, borrowed another £2500 from the bank. The issue was resolved in 1917, but only after the Marks family won an action in the Court of Chancery which left them in sole control, with Simon as chairman. That was the beginning of Marks & Spencer as it is today.

CHAPTER TWO

I WAS born in 1913 in Didsbury, which is now a suburb of Greater Manchester but in those days was a village, though only a mile or two from the outskirts of the city proper. It had its grocer, its butcher, its baker, and a few other shops. Our house in Belfield Road was a comfortable detached property in its own garden. Michael was the oldest of the children; I came next, then Daniel and Judith.

I don't have many early memories. My first is of being taken by Father, at the age of four, in November 1917 to a meeting at the Free Trade Hall, Manchester, to celebrate the announcement of the Balfour Declaration. Chaim Weizmann, years later to become the first President of Israel, was the principal speaker. Father said it was a joyous occasion, but I saw that a lot of people were crying. I asked him why were they crying if it was a joyous occasion. He replied, 'They are weeping tears of joy.' I didn't understand what he meant.

My mother and father and my uncles, Simon Marks and Harry Sacher (Harry had married my aunt, Miriam Marks), were already working with Dr Weizmann. Dr Weizmann was a statesman, a man of prophetic vision and an eminent scientist. He had experienced the Russian pogroms and was a tireless worker on behalf of his fellow Jews. He left Russia and eventually settled in England, though he nearly settled in Germany. His wife Vera was a doctor, an accomplished and soignée woman. Weizmann's objective was the establishment of a Jewish State. He was a brilliant leader who inspired loyalty and affection in, and received enormous support from, his followers. It was he who in 1917 negotiated with Mr Balfour, then the Foreign Secretary, the Balfour Declaration, under which His Majesty's Government took it upon itself to establish a national home for the Jews in Palestine. Another famous Englishman connected with the Balfour Declaration was the late Leo Amery. To help and support first the Jewish national home in Palestine and then the State of Israel were to be an important purpose of my life; of that, more later. At the age of four I hadn't a notion what it was all about.

I just made the hansom cab age. When I was five my parents took me to London. The city didn't seem to a little boy that much different from Manchester, but I remember vividly when I got out of the train at Withington station, the last stop before Manchester, going home in a hansom cab. I talked through a little trap door to the driver sitting up on the roof. I didn't want to get out. It was a curious contrast: the two-wheeled hansom cab clip-clopping through the semi-rural road, only three miles away from Manchester, a metropolis with its world-renowned cotton industry, its stock exchange and its great cultural life. The *Manchester Guardian* was one of the most famous papers in the world, the Hallé Orchestra perhaps the best British orchestra of its day.

Grandfather Marks died six years before I was born. He had always worked hard and smoked too many cigars, and, when people asked how he died, the reply was often 'from Twofahs Disease'. What was 'Twofahs Disease'? In those days Marks & Spencer stocked cigars, which they sold at two for tuppence: they were nicknamed 'Twofahs'. They didn't sell well, so my grandfather smoked them in large numbers, too many for the good of his health.

Grandmother Marks had died before I was old enough to remember her, but I remember my Sieff grandparents well. I got on very happily with Uncle Simon (Marks) and his wife, Miriam, my father's sister. They lived about a mile away and I treated their house, which was rather imposing by our standards, as a second home.

My other Aunt Miriam, my mother's younger sister, was married to Harry Sacher; he was a barrister and leader-writer of the *Manchester Guardian*, later to become a director of Marks & Spencer, and father of the late Michael Sacher, until recently joint-vice-chairman and managing director of the firm.

Both my mother and father were strong characters, but they got on well together. My mother was not very tolerant of men, Father and Simon being about the only two she respected. For her my father could hardly ever do wrong. Father inherited from his father a love of music and in his early days had taken up the violin. He continued his violin playing into married life; he was never much good and became worse. My mother finally protested against the sounds he produced and insisted that, whenever he played his fiddle, there should be at least two doors shut between her and him. There was one other outburst – about Father's spats. The wearing of spats was fashionable in those days and he was a bit of a dandy. One Saturday, about midday, a large parcel was delivered and my mother opened it to find it full of spats. The following day at lunch she exploded. 'I'm going to throw the whole bloody lot out,' she shouted. Mother's wrath was always shortlived; Father kept his spats, though he did not add to his collection.

My father was diplomatic by nature. He used to say, 'Give way on little things and you may get your way with big things.' He practised what he preached; he had a wonderful way of turning away wrath, not with a soft answer but with one which immediately appealed to the better nature of the other person. My older brother Michael and I were good friends, but I sometimes felt that he was getting better treatment than I was; one day, feeling this strongly, I went to Father and said, 'Father, you favour Michael more than you do me,' to which he replied, 'Of course I do. He needs it more.' What could I say? My mother both loved and admired my father. She had never thought about marrying anyone else and my father has related the story of how, several years before he had thought of proposing to her – though he too had never thought of marrying anyone else – at the age of fifteen she said to him when they were out walking one day, 'Israel, what are we going to do about bringing up children?' My father's answer was, 'Don't worry, we'll bring them up as our parents brought us up.'

Beautiful, dynamic, extremely intelligent, at times imperious, and somewhat wilful, my mother believed that women were the equals of men. Nobody could tell her that she could not make a speech or run a business as well as any man; they would have had to prove it to her before she would have accepted it. Early in life she had shown that she could in fact make a fine speech and run an efficient organization. As well as her work for Zionism, she did much in the movement for the extension of women's rights and, because she was sincere, direct, outspoken and attractive, she enlisted in her cause people who might have been put off by a more doctrinaire woman. (In December 1984 I received a letter from the Pankhurst Trust appealing for support to restore and preserve the Emmeline Pankhurst home in Nelson Street, Manchester, 'in memory of the part played by your mother in the suffragette movement'.)

Though for many years the background of our family – and of the Marks family – was essentially simple, it was comfortable. We lived well. Both families lived close enough to the early days of the grandfathers to have no thoughts of social class or aspiration to social status. They wanted only to enjoy their lives, to be grateful, and to do what they could for those less fortunate. We junior Sieffs got a great kick when my father bought a big secondhand touring Daimler which had belonged to the Prince of Wales. It was a striking vehicle and stood out a mile among the motor cars of Didsbury. We saw it as a jolly and exciting method of transport rather than as a status symbol – a kind of private bus.

Our income in those early years of my life was not constant. Even in the days when we had a nanny and two maids, Father's earnings varied, so that one year we were conscious of having a smart holiday and another an economical one. In the early 1920s, when business was good, we went off to Lytham St Annes, then the Biarritz of Lancashire. When business was disappointing, we hired a small charabanc to take all of us to Chapel en le Frith and disported ourselves in lodgings. The village was surrounded by impressive peaks and valleys, and had health-giving breezes, but was far from donkeys, sands and sea.

Ours was a Jewish house, but in no way orthodox; I always knew I was a Jew, but I was never conscious of anti-Semitism because in my school and university days I never experienced it personally. I suppose it was there at the back of my mind; I heard a little in my younger days of what happened in Russia, but I only became really conscious of anti-Semitism with Hitler's rise to power in Germany, and subsequently when Sir Oswald Mosley and his Fascists adopted an anti-Semitic policy here. We had many non-Jewish as well as Jewish friends. In Manchester the total Jewish population was about 30,000, small enough to be absorbed easily into the life of the city as a whole, yet large enough to give that comparative lack of racial consciousness which comes from a sense of security. We only went to synagogue on the high holidays. However, I became an active young Zionist after my first visit to Palestine in 1929.

Grandfather Sieff was moderately orthodox, but Grandmother was unorthodox and, though a woman of high moral standards, was not religious. Food was frequently eaten in her house that would not have been allowed in even a mildly orthodox home. Despite the lack of orthodoxy in our home, my parents made Kiddush on Friday, the grace before the Sabbath, and went to synagogue on the high holidays, Rosh Hashanah, the New Year, and Yom Kippur, the Day of Atonement. They also held annually a family Seder, a festive service at home celebrating the first night of Passover, which commemorates the Exodus from Egypt. Lily, my wife, and I keep up these traditional Jewish practices to this day.

The Marks family also were not religious minded, but for both families Zionism was a different matter, and I was conscious of its existence before I had much idea of what the Jewish religion was about. This developed to a great extent because of the relationship which Father and Simon developed while still young men with Dr Weizmann, and the role they played in the genesis of the Balfour Declaration and the foundation of the Jewish homeland.

Though not religious, I probably went to synagogue more than any other member of either family. There was a reason for this. While still a small boy, I became a passionate supporter of Manchester United football team. Second to them in my affections came Manchester City. Even today, when I read the sports page of the Sunday newspapers, I turn at once to see how the Manchester teams got on the previous day. Neither Father nor Uncle Simon was free enough, or interested enough, to take me regularly to the matches, but one day I discovered that my great-uncle Noah Laski, who attended synagogue assiduously on Saturday mornings, went to see Manchester United play on Saturday afternoons. Thereupon I too became a regular attender at the synagogue, sat close to Uncle Noah – and went to the match with him in the afternoon. My keen new interest in religion was widely noted and some of my cousins thought I might become a rabbi.

In 1926, when I was thirteen, I went on a school trip to Newfoundland, a great adventure in those days. Because my parents were away and there was no one at home, I was sent to spend the night before I was to leave for embarkation in Liverpool at the house of my Aunt Elaine (Marks), then married to Norman Laski. As I lay in bed, I was reading the latest Dracula novel and became more and more nervous. Dracula was one of my favourite characters, but I suddenly remembered that my garlic to keep out the vampires was hanging above my bedroom window back in Didsbury. I crept downstairs and ransacked the house for garlic, but couldn't find so much as a pickled onion. I don't know how I got to sleep that night. Actually my reading was not confined to morbid literature and I was as much a fan of Billy Bunter as I was of Dracula – indeed there was scarcely anything which came out in those coloured-cover periodicals that I did not read with gusto.

The trip to Newfoundland was one of the most exciting events of my boyhood. It came about under the auspices of John Lewis Paton, perhaps the most famous and respected High Master of Manchester Grammar School. Paton was a brilliant classical scholar at Cambridge and, if he hadn't devoted himself to teaching, could have become world-famous. He was a very modest man; for instance, he would not sit for his portrait, and he destroyed all his personal papers so that no biography of him could be written. His pupils, who included Father and Simon, loved him. He retired in 1924 at the age of sixty, but continued his interest in education by becoming the first president of the Memorial University College (since 1949 the Memorial University, St John's, Newfoundland). When the war broke out he returned to Britain, aged seventy-six, and worked in a prep school almost to the day of his death at eighty-three. It was a privilege to have known him.

Forty Manchester Grammar School boys, of whom I was the youngest, sailed from Liverpool on board a small passenger ship of 7000 tons. For three days we were battered by storms and I was continuously seasick. In Newfoundland we camped out; it was mid-summer, and warm. We were welcomed by the Governor-General, Sir William Allardyce, and as the youngest boy in the party I had to reply on their behalf to the Governor-General's words of welcome — my first public speech. I could see even then that economic conditions in Newfoundland were poor. In 1979, fifty-three years later, I went there for the second time to visit a store that Marks & Spencer Canada had opened in St John's; it had not changed much.

The year 1926 saw a great change in my family's circumstances, which was to influence my life. My father became a full-time director of Marks & Spencer and moved the family to London. What led to this and how it came about is a part of the history of Marks & Spencer as well as of my story. Father used to say that the first great period of Marks & Spencer was the penny bazaar period; the second, for convenience, could be called the five shilling period. The first took place before the First World War; the second began in the late 1920s. Michael Marks was the pioneer of the first, Simon the creator of the second, when a chain of bazaars was converted into a national network of stores. Allowing for the over-simplification which takes place in conversation, I think Father summed it up well, though as usual he gave all the credit to Simon and did less than justice to himself.

The penny bazaar period came to an end because, during the First World War, Marks & Spencer could not limit itself to goods priced a penny; there were too few of them about and, in order to have enough goods for sale to attract customers into the shops, articles at a wide range of prices were displayed. After the war Marks & Spencer was retailing goods at prices varying from 1d to £3; Woolworth, on the other hand, maintained their 3d and 6d price range, expanding their business rapidly and doing much better than Marks & Spencer. Simon came to the conclusion that, if Marks & Spencer could not meet this challenge, the firm might be pushed out of the market. He was conscious of his own lack of experience; he had never worked in a shop, never stood behind the counter, and had not been given a business training. Though he had grasped the importance of price range and of converting bazaars into stores – bigger, brighter, modernized premises – he felt that he needed to learn more.

In 1924 he went to the United States, where the chain store was more developed. Later he described his sojourn as 'my first serious lessons in the chain-store art'. He learned a good deal there about sophisticated administration, about statistical control of stocks in relation to sales, and that modern accounting machines could produce in hours information that was taking Marks & Spencer weeks to collect. The most important lesson of all was, to use his own words, 'the value of counter footage; that is that each counter foot of space had to pay wages, rent, overhead expenses, and earn a profit. There could be no blind spots on the counters so far as goods were concerned. This meant a much more exhaustive study of the goods we were selling and of the demands of our customers; it meant that the staff had to be re-educated and re-trained; it meant new people.'

My father used to say that Simon, in recalling what he had learned in America, was unduly modest; that what Simon had seen and heard in America only confirmed what he had already found out for himself. Even if that were so, the experience strengthened Simon's confidence in himself and it provided him with three working policies: firstly, nothing should be priced over five shillings; secondly, an extensive programme of enlarging and improving our shops should be introduced; thirdly, it was vital to have fortnightly stock-checking lists which could help control the production and flow of goods from factory to shop. It also strengthened his belief that business should be conducted on a moral basis. Marks & Spencer has always tried to treat its staff, its customers and its suppliers decently. It was in this relatively early period that Simon learned that many customers were concerned with quality and value, not just cheapness, and that as the standard of living improved this would be the basis for a sound and growing business.

His success over the next two years was modest. First of all he set about increasing the size of his stores; the policy of substituting superstores on the scale of Woolworth's for penny bazaars was going to be costly and he found he could not finance these developments himself; Marks & Spencer would have to go public. With the support of the Prudential Assurance Company he was able to achieve this in 1926, and the close relationship between that great institution and Marks & Spencer continues to this day. Nevertheless, when the problem of capital had been alleviated by going public, there were still obstacles in the way of Simon's progress, the main one being the conservatism of his colleagues on the board and of his senior executives. They were not keen on change and thought Simon's views on human relations worthy but impracticable.

In the early 1920s Simon had moved his headquarters from Manchester to Chiswell Street in the City of London. Father became a director of the company in 1917 after the ownership issue had been resolved, but he had his own business to run. In the early 1920s he usually saw Simon only when he attended the regular board meetings and stayed with him for one or two nights. On one visit in 1926 he found Simon tense and uncommunicative. He asked if there was anything wrong. 'No,' Simon replied, 'nothing.' But he continued silent and ill at ease. Before Father left he determined to get to the bottom of this and once again asked what was the matter. Simon poured his heart out: he could get no support for his ideas and plans for change and development; his colleagues were not interested. When Simon erupted, he could use strong language. He ended his outburst with, 'I've nobody to talk to. I'm surrounded by a lot of morons.' 'Oh, you want somebody to talk to,' said Father. 'Well, that's all right. I'll join you for six months and sit in the next room so that you'll have somebody to talk to.' I have often chuckled over

Simon's response to this offer: 'But what will your mother say?'

Later in 1926 – actually on the first day of the General Strike – Father and Mother came down to London. Simon had put my father's desk in his own office so that they sat side by side, and Father remained in London for the rest of his life, first as joint managing director and vice-chairman, and then after Simon's death as chairman.

My brother Michael was keen to go to London, and was sent to St Paul's School. My youngest brother Daniel and my sister Judith were too young for education to be a problem; I wasn't. I was due to spend the next school year preparing to sit the matriculation examination, which I needed to pass to qualify for university entrance. I wasn't much good at games, whereas Michael, who was not very academic, was good at any sports – particularly soccer, tennis and cricket, at which he was a big hitter. So, at my own urging, when the family moved I was left with my Sieff grandparents to work for my matriculation. It was a happy year, partly because I was fond of my grandparents and enjoyed their home, and partly because I was doing what I had chosen to do. We ate very well; my grandmother spoiled me and my grandfather was a charming companion. The year passed quickly and I worked hard. In the holidays I went to London, though my parents also came to see me in Manchester. I gained in self-confidence when I passed my matric just before I was fourteen. This was a good performance, as most people did it when they were a year or eighteen months older.

Father's decision to go to London, initially for six months, to spend time with Simon gave me a sense of how important the Marks & Spencer business was to both sides of the family. I had already come to think of it as more than a business; I suppose I dimly perceived it as a way of life, and Father's move from Manchester, like Simon's move before it, made me realize this all the more. I knew that we did not have stores the size of the department stores like Lewis or Kendal Milne, and I knew that we were small compared with Woolworth, but I used to hear Simon and Father talking about our business, what it stood for and what they were going to do with it. They discussed what its role in society should be and I felt there was something special about it that had nothing to do with size and that it stood for more than making money.

I was most impressed by Simon, who was its leader. He was energetic, observant, imaginative, self-critical. He was good to me when I was a small boy. Sometimes when he came to Manchester he would take me round the local store and talk to me as if I were reasonably grown up. I went with him when I was eleven to our store in Oldham Street. I watched him looking around, picking up articles for sale, scrutinizing them and making notes. That day I caught sight of a pair of knitting needles which had no knobs on their ends and held them up to him. 'Uncle Simon, how can you knit if the needles don't have proper ends?' 'Good,' he said, 'that's one lesson you've learned. Those are lousy goods; they should never have been allowed to leave the factory. They should never have been delivered here, they should never have been accepted and they should never have been put on display. Everything we sell must be of good quality. Quality, Marcus, is all-important.'

I understood what he meant when he used to encourage me to become a businessman and often thought of it again, as boy, youth and grown man, but at first I was not sure what quality meant. I found the answer a few weeks later when Simon again came up to Manchester and stayed for a few days at the Midland Hotel, which then boasted one of the best restaurants in the country. He invited me to breakfast and ordered a kipper. It arrived under an impressive silver cover, but when he tasted it he said, 'It's not good,' and asked the waiter to take it back. He was served with another kipper; that wasn't good either and back that one went. A third kipper arrived; Simon took a mouthful and his face relaxed into a smile. 'This', he stated, 'is good to eat — it is "quality".'

So, with the move of my family to London and the passing of my matric examination, the days of my childhood came to an end. They had been easy and uneventful. Shortly after moving to London Father bought a house in St John's Wood, on the corner of Marlborough Place and Loudon Road. In addition to his many British friends, he entertained there a number of people connected with the Zionist movement, including Dr Weizmann, Selig Brodetsky, then a famous professor of mathematics at Leeds, later president of the Hebrew University in Jerusalem, and Nahum Sokolow, who was chairman of the Zionist Executive from 1921 to 1931. I got to know them quite well and learned a good deal about Zionism from them.

My first experience of working in Marks & Spencer was in the two weeks before Christmas 1927. During the school holidays I worked in our store in Brewer Street, Soho, a large shop employing seven or eight assistants and run by Mrs Kelly, a widow, and her daughter. The store no longer exists. Soho then was a very different place from what it is today, noted for its charming, inexpensive restaurants, not for its pornographic bookshops and sex parlours. I did not stand and serve behind the counter; I wasn't considered to be up to that. Odd jobs of a manual nature were my lot at that time, the main tasks being to carry goods in from the delivery lorry and unpack parcels of clothing or crates of china and toys, and take them to the counter. On Fridays and Saturdays I escorted from the premises the occasional drunk who wandered in from the pubs with which Soho was well provided. I was large enough at fourteen to look convincing as a novice bouncer. We worked long hours in the weeks before Christmas, but I enjoyed it. Life in the streets around was colourful and bustling, all very novel, and the young ladies in the store were nice to me and regarded me as something of a curiosity on the premises. My only complaint was that I was not paid. When I look back half a century later, I am glad I worked in the Brewer Street store because it was one of the last of a type between the original penny bazaar and the larger stores which Marks & Spencer began to open in the late 1920s: on two floors, it had a frontage of about twenty feet and was quite shallow; there were narrow counters along the three walls and one large counter in the middle.

It was at about this time that I first went to an opera at Covent Garden, where I had the privilege of hearing the great Chaliapin singing the title role in *Boris Godunov*. He was still singing superbly and made a tremendous impression on me. That experience gave me a taste for opera which has persisted throughout my life. I have seen some very good productions of *Boris Godunov* with fine singing, but I still recall Chaliapin's magnificent performance and the sight of him lying distraught on the throne.

One of the major events of my teenage years took place in our St John's Wood house. At the end of the house, where my sister Judith and I slept, was a kind of little tower with two storeys. I slept on the first floor, Judith on the second; a staircase led down outside our doors into the main part of the house. I had flu and one night at about 3.00 am — it was 28 February 1929 and one of the coldest winters ever recorded in Europe — I awoke with a feeling of congestion. It seemed to me that my flu had become worse and I had difficulty in breathing, so I switched on the lights. When they did not come on, I thought a fuse had blown, but under the door I saw a red glow. Opening it I saw flames and thick black smoke pouring up the stairs and into my room. I started down to the main part of the house, then heard Judith, aged eight, crying in the room above. I went up to fetch her, but by the time we reached the stairs the smoke was impenetrable, so we went back into Judith's bedroom and opened the window to call for help. At first I was restrained by the foolish thought that calling out would be undignified but, as the flames at ground-floor level increased, I changed my mind and shouted for help as loudly as I could. There was no response. There was an iron bar across Judith's window to prevent her falling out. I decided to knot some sheets together, tie them to the bar, lower her down, and then follow myself. I dashed all the glass out of the window on to the courtyard below and started to knot the sheets — it sounds easy, but I was surprised how difficult it was. Meanwhile I kept shouting. In the house down the road a woman had just come in from a nightclub with her husband, and, hearing the clatter of the glass shattering on the courtyard, she said to him: 'There's someone throwing bottles about, you'd better go and look.' He said — he told me the tale afterwards — 'I'm not going out at this time of night. We're going to bed.' Then his wife heard Judith crying and my loud shouts, which she misinterpreted. She said, 'There's a man beating up a child. You've got to do something.' All this in the middle of St John's Wood at three o'clock in the morning, but nobody answered my cries except this man. Fortunately he was soon followed by the police and the fire brigade, who got us down safely. Mother and Father were in the house all the time, but were sleeping on the far side and heard nothing until the fire brigade arrived. The tower side of the house was gutted and much of the rest was badly burned.

The next day, in the absence of more important news, the evening paper printed a short account of the fire with the highly exaggerated, but to me very pleasing, sub-headline, 'Boy Hero of St John's Wood Fire'. Soon afterwards the Society for Protection of Life from Fire awarded me a certificate 'in testimony of distinguished conduct while engaged in the rescue of life at a fire on 28th February 1929'; equally exaggerated but equally pleasing. This description of my behaviour on the night of the fire taught me that, whatever you do, if people want to describe something in the way that suits them, that is what they will do. I had done nothing heroic; I had yelled for help. I do not know to this day if I could have lowered Judith to the ground on the sheets without killing her, let alone slid down the sheets myself.

The night of the fire also taught me once again that one good thing doesn't necessarily lead to another. As a reward for my fire-rescuing exploits, and because I had a further bad attack of flu from standing around outside in my pyjamas in the bitterly cold weather, my parents decided I should have a holiday in Palestine; it was my first visit. My Aunt Miriam and Uncle Harry Sacher were living in Jerusalem at the time. While I was there, a small group of us were loaned a new motor launch by Mr Novomieski, the man who had founded and developed the Palestine Electric Corporation on the Dead Sea. We spent the night at a hotel at the northern end of the Dead Sea at a place called Kallia. We were to spend the following day going around the sea, on which there was hardly another boat, returning in the evening. We were thirteen in all: three crew and ten passengers, including Hadassah and Edwin Samuel, who was the son of Herbert Samuel, Home Secretary in Lloyd George's government and first High Commissioner in mandated Palestine; Max Nurock, later to be one of Israel's ambassadors; Louis Green, the chief engineer of the Mandatory Government; and Elsie Graff, who was about my age and whose brother was our doctor in London; as well as Harry and Miriam Sacher.

We started off down the east coast of the Dead Sea, the Transjordan side, and stopped for lunch at the mouth of a small river, the Arnon, half way down the coast. As we were leaving to cross from the east to the west coast we hit a rock, but there was no hint of serious damage and we continued to cross the sea, which at that point was about ten miles wide. A few miles out there was a considerable thudding under the hull. The crew, which consisted of one Arab and two Jews, didn't really have a clue but assured us there was nothing to worry about. Gradually the noise grew louder and suddenly, in the middle of the Dead Sea, several planks burst up and the water poured in, flooding the small engine-room.

When we struck the rock the collision had bent the propeller shaft which went fore and aft under the hull, and every time the bend in the revolving shaft came uppermost it hammered into the plates until they were forced up and the water poured in. We began to sink. I believed that the Dead Sea water was so salty that nothing could sink, but found I was wrong. At first we could not locate the hole, but Edwin Samuel, a good swimmer, dived under the boat and found it. Using our clothing, towels and anything else we could lay our hands on, we managed to plug the hole. Several of us baled frantically to keep the water at a manageable level while we rowed to the western shore with the aid of four oars. It was a painfully slow journey: we reached shore at about eight o'clock that night.

The question now was what to do. After our frightening experience at sea, we wanted to get back by land and decided that the best place to make for would be Hebron, about thirty miles away over some small mountains. However, the three women in the boat, Miriam Sacher, Hadassah Samuel and Elsie Graff, had lost their shoes and it would really have been impossible for them to have made their way on foot to Hebron. So we had to think again. At the time there was a good southerly breeze and the Arab boatman said that, with the emergency sail he could rig, we would be back in Kallia in about six hours. We started at dawn; after a few minutes the breeze died down and we rowed and baled all day Saturday, hoping we might sight another vessel, but saw none. At most places the cliffs came down sheer into the water, but we did find a place on the Saturday night where we went ashore, but we had no sleep because we were bitten to death by massed mosquitoes. At dawn we heard a plane. We still had some petrol in the launch but, though we lit a fire, the plane went on in the direction of Jerusalem. We were utterly despondent; someone said it must be the new Jerusalem air service. In actual fact the plane had been sent out to look for us but, though it had spotted us, it could find nowhere to land. Our failure to return had been reported and there had been much speculation about our fate; some thought we had been drowned, others that we had been killed by Arabs. The British papers reported that 'hope had been given up for the party lost on the Dead Sea'.

We finally arrived back in Kallia on Sunday evening under our own steam, or more exactly three oars, as one rowlock had broken, to find the town packed with officials, journalists, sightseers, and the Governor-General of Transjordan, Lt-Col. Sir Charles Cox. We had only had the leftovers of our Friday lunch to eat on Saturday and Sunday; I had been one of the rowing team and lost just under a stone. So during the first three months of 1929 I experienced a fire and a shipwreck. We were thirteen in the launch and we set off on Friday 13 April; yet we all survived and, despire the thirteens, we could say we were lucky!

It was some time in 1928 or 1929 that I took out a leading débutante for the first time; her name was Stella Coke, and she was a charming, attractive and bright girl, older than I was. We went to see Matheson Lang, one of the most famous actors of the day, in a play called *Such Men are Dangerous* at the Duke of York's theatre. The best known restaurant for supper was the Savoy Grill, so I decided we should go there. This was the first time I had been host in such a restaurant and I ordered expensive dishes, and thought that we must have champagne. I remember being worried about the bill, but in the end, including a good tip, the total cost for the two of us came to about thirty-five shillings.

It was at this time, too, that I met Freddie Brisson, who was the son of the well-known Danish actor Carl Brisson, a great favourite on the London stage in pre-war days. He starred in many musicals. I had a charming, extrovert dentist called Nico Bartman, who was both good-looking and sociable. One day, just after I'd had a session with him, very unpleasant at that time with the heavy and painful drilling, he introduced me to Freddie, who drove me back home feeling very sorry for myself. Freddie and I were the same age and he drove me in his father's great Isotta Fraschini car with a fitted bar in the back; it was the first time I had seen anything like this in a motor car and I was impressed. This was the beginning of a lifelong friendship. Freddie followed his father into the theatre, not as an actor but as a producer. In the 1930s he emigrated to America, eventually settling in Hollywood, where he met and married Rosalind Russell, a very attractive and lovely lady of immense ability, great charm and considerable intellectual capacity; she was a good actress. We became close friends and, after the war, I stayed on a number of occasions with them in their home in Los Angeles; they were immensely hospitable and Ros was a marvellous hostess. Lance, Freddie and Ros's son, was a small boy when I stayed with them. Every evening he said his prayers, which ended with, 'God save Mummy and Daddy and Uncle Marcus.' He told me later that he did this regularly even when I wasn't there. That someone was praying for me gave me a feeling of security. Alas, both Ros and Freddie are dead, but I saw

Lance recently; he is involved in improving what I call 'human relations' in industry.

When I moved to London in 1927 I had followed Michael to St Paul's, which was not all that different from Manchester Grammar School; both, by chance, were ruled by High Masters rather than mere headmasters. The High Master at St Paul's was John Bell. I did not do well scholastically, but got on better at games. I did not exactly overexert myself academically at St Paul's and the fact that I was admitted to Corpus Christi College, Cambridge, was due less to my achievements than to my deficiencies. I was bored in my last year and did little work. One day I decided to explore the school premises and, while examining the roof, fell through a glass dome on to a master taking a senior class. My poor showing that term and this incident resulted in a summons to the High Master, with whom up to then I had got on well. I knew I was in trouble when he addressed me as 'Sieff' instead of 'Marcus'. He pointed out that I had always mixed with the older boys, all of whom would be leaving at the end of July; he felt that I would be bored and it would be best if I left with them; he did not actually expel me. I pointed out to him that I could not leave because I was sitting for an exhibition to Cambridge in the late autumn and really had to do some more work. He replied, 'Marcus,' − then I knew things were getting better − 'Cambridge must not miss you. What college are you trying for?' I told him it was Corpus Christi. 'Well,' he said, 'let's see what we can do. Will Spens is the Master of Corpus and he happens to be a friend of mine.'

Spens also happened to be a friend of Sidney Dark, the well known editor of the *Church Times*, who was a close friend and good drinking companion of Father; as a result of the combined efforts of the High Master of St Paul's and the editor of the *Church Times*, I found myself admitted to Corpus Christi in October without taking an entrance examination, my admission being based on my matriculation and, I suspect, the High Master's eagerness to see the back of me.

I enjoyed Cambridge very much. Because I had already made up my mind I was going into Marks & Spencer, I read economics. I worked hard and took a First in Part I of the Tripos, when the college awarded me an exhibition. However, during my second year, I contracted an illness which meant that I missed two out of three terms; I got a Second in my finals. I was fortunate in having as a tutor Humphrey Mynors, now knighted, who had great ability and was most helpful. It is in no small measure due to him that I did reasonably well academically. Humphrey was not only my tutor but we also became friends.

However, for a long time, through no fault of mine, a number of people were under the impression that I got a Double First, which, when it was mentioned, I had to deny. Many years later I learned how this false accolade had come about when I asked Humphrey Mynors, then deputy governor of the Bank of England, to the opening of a new Marks & Spencer store in Hereford, near where he lived. At the pre-opening party with the city and county notables he asked if he could make a few remarks. He said he was delighted, after such a long time, to see his star pupil at Cambridge, implying that I had got a Double First. When I told him afterwards that I did not get a Double First, he said, 'I always thought you did and I am not changing my tale now.'

While I was at Cambridge, I followed with great interest and benefit the activities of the new society, P.E.P. (Political and Economic Planning), which Father had helped to found in 1931, and which today is part of P.S.I. (Policy Studies Institute). Greatly concerned with the then unprecedented level of unemployment − nearly three million − eminent men of all political views and parties and from various walks of life came together to organize and support an independent institution which would collect knowledge in the econ-omic, industrial and social fields, suggest remedies and make them available to policy makers in government and publicly, through reports and surveys under the P.E.P. imprint. The main idea was to try to influence politicians on a non-political basis to work for industrial development for social ends. Politicians like Harold Mac-millan and Hugh Gaitskell, economists of the calibre of Keynes and Beveridge, writers like Huxley, and trade union leaders like Walter Citrine, were all members and worked together. What I learned from practical business economics at Marks & Spencer (and I frequently visited the Marks & Spencer Cambridge store), from P.E.P. and from Father, who soon became one of the leading lights of P.E.P., was a valuable complement to the more theoretical knowledge I acquired at university. This combination stood me in good stead when, in my third year, I used to go to meetings of the Marshall Society, the university's premier club for the discussion of economic matters.

I used to attend Maynard Keynes's fascinating lectures. Keynes took an interest in the Marshall Society and, when on one occasion Sir William Beveridge was invited to talk to them, Keynes invited me to dine with him, his wife, the former ballet dancer Lydia Lopokova, and Sir William, before the meeting. At dinner Sir William asked me a number of questions, which I did my best to answer with more self-confidence than knowledge. As we were leaving for the meeting, he said to me, 'What books have you written?'

I replied, 'None, Sir William.'

'I am surprised,' he said.

'I am only a third-year undergraduate,' I replied.

He looked at me thoughtfully and said, 'I'm afraid I didn't catch your name when Maynard introduced us and Maynard calls you Marcus. What is your surname?'

I told him my name was Sieff.

'Ah,' he exclaimed, 'any relation of Israel Sieff?'

'Yes, he's my father.'

'That explains it all,' he concluded.

One of the best things that happened to me at Cambridge was meeting Victor (now Lord) Rothschild, who became a lifelong friend and today is the head of that remarkable family. He was a great all-rounder – brilliant academically, first class at games, especially cricket, a daredevil motor-car driver, widely admired, an intellectual, and very attractive. Our friendship has given me much pleasure and still does. We meet frequently and, while I was writing this book, I had a discussion with Victor about it. His letters to me normally are only three or four lines long, so I was surprised to receive, on 12 July 1985, the following letter. I quote it here as some explanation to my patient and long-suffering publishers and because I find it relevant:

10th July 1985

Dear Marcus,

You referred briefly last night to your autobiography. You may or may not know that I had a disgraceful academic career at Cambridge (at any rate at the beginning) and was awarded a Treble First Ordinary Degree in English, French and Physiology. Perhaps I should mention that it was the only Treble First ever awarded to someone taking an Ordinary Degree. As a result, I have taken some interest in the writing of English and, with a good deal of hesitation, put forward certain propositions in this letter, together with an outstanding short book on the subject. The propositions are:

1. When you have just about finished the book, do not send it to the publisher but put it away for a minimum of one month and then re-read it yourself. You will be astonished at what you will find. If, during that month, you think of something which you would like to include or exclude, write it on that notepad by the side of your bed, but do not get the typescript out of that drawer in your desk. Pay no attention whatever to any howls from the publisher.

2. Cross out almost all qualifying adverbs, e.g. 'obviously true', 'strongly object', 'fully aware' and so on. Qualifying adverbs are useful in some cases, such as 'not fully aware', but I think all the cases where they convey something are negative ones. 'But I want to emphasize the point,' I hear you saying. Nonsense. It does not add anything to the truth of some statement, nor to its perception by others, to put the word 'obviously' before it.

3. Whenever there is a short Anglo-Saxon word for the one you used, cross out the latter and put in the former.

4. Do not use cumbrous circumlocutions, e.g. 'succulent bivalve' for oyster.

5. Any sentences which begin 'It may, however, be of interest to know that,' or similar phrases should simply be crossed out.

6. Drastically reduce the frequency with which 'I' is used, but not at the expense of cumbrous circumlocutions.

7. If, as I hope, you are going to have an index, remember that there are professional indexers and that a good index is a pleasure to study. The author must co-operate in its preparation.

I think I can guess where you are going to put this letter.

V

Another valued friendship which formed at Cambridge was with Jack Heinz, later head of the family of '57 varieties', whom I first spotted because he always wore gym shoes. Interrupted only by the Second World War, our acquaintance of over fifty years has been celebrated most years by an annual lunch, just the two of us, one frequent topic of discussion being what can be done to help solve the problem of feeding the Third World.

After the end of the first term of my second year at Cambridge I was afflicted with a mysterious disease which for several months had me listed as a fascinating case. I was studied with great interest by a number of famous and highly expensive doctors, including the celebrated Lord Horder. The beginning of the illness was as mysterious as its end. Just after Christmas 1932, I was giving lunch to some friends at the Coq d'Or in London when, just before the coffee arrived, I developed an excruciating pain in my ear. It became so bad that I had to excuse myself and staggered home to Regent's Park, to where we had moved after the St John's Wood fire. I could not get hold of the family doctor, my parents were in Palestine, Michael was away on a business trip and the last thing I wanted to do was to bother Simon. But the agony was intense and I had to telephone him at his office, three-quarters of a mile away in Baker Street. He said, 'Your Aunt Miriam has just come into the office. Can you manage to get here? She'll look after you.' My Aunt Miriam, who seemed to know every medical man in London, phoned Douglas Harmer, one of the leading ENT surgeons of the day, who had me in a nursing home within an hour and performed an operation on my eardrum that evening. This greatly eased the pain in my ear, but pains then developed in my joints; Harmer was surprised at this and decided to call in an eminent general physician, John Ryle. By this time my joints were not only torturing me but swelling. 'Were you taking much exercise?' Ryle asked me.

'Yes,' I said, 'rugger, squash and fives, and I rode quite a bit.'

'Then I think this is a reaction to being forced to stay in bed,' he said. 'I think it will shortly go away.' 'It', whatever 'it' was, did not go away and a few days later, still in agony, I began to sweat. The sheets were drenched. Of course this was before the days of antibiotic medical drugs.

This time Lord Horder and Dr Gow, the Chief Physician of Bart's, were called in; frequently they visited me together. One, I forget which, believed in the patient's windows being open and the other believed in them being closed. So, while one was examining me, the other opened the windows and, when it was his colleague's turn to examine me, the other shut the windows. I continued to have pains everywhere. By this time my parents, who had been in Egypt and Palestine, were returning home by ship and Michael was sent to meet them at Marseilles and tell them what was happening. I sweated away several stones – in all I lost 70 lbs in four months.

It was now decided that, since this mysterious illness had begun in the ear, the ear or thereabouts must be the clue to my recovery, if recovery – and some doubted it – was on the cards. In Europe were two world-famous ENT doctors – Neuman in Vienna, and another in Berlin whose name I have forgotten. He specialized in treating ear complaints, including some kind of operation involving the jugular vein. Somebody resolved that the jugular vein man should get the job, but the day before he left Berlin my British doctors found a blood clot in the pulmonary vein, which went into the pericardiac. They presumed me as good as dead – in fact, one of them told my parents I *was* dead – and tried to prevent the jugular man from catching his train in Berlin on a fool's journey. But he had already left. I can remember lying in a daze and hearing five eminent British doctors and two Germans arguing – a curious exchange of views, because the British spoke virtually no German and the Germans virtually no English – whether the jugular vein should be tackled or not. Then they decided to take another look at me and found to their surprise that the blood clot was dispersing and had not passed from the pericardiac into the heart. The English majority then ruled against the Berlin doctor performing his celebrated operation but, as though it were a consolation prize, let him perform a mastoid operation. The mastoid was subsequently found to be perfectly healthy, possibly the only healthy part of my body.

After the German had gone back to Berlin, Lord Horder decided I should be leeched and cupped. I still remember the five or six leeches in a little circle around my heart sucking away at the blood until they were satiated and fell off. I was warned that on no account was I to try to pull them off because if I did they would leave their teeth in me.

Whether any of these treatments did the trick I do not know and I doubt if anybody else did – they certainly did not claim to – but I began to feel better. The improvement began at the time the clot dispersed and I begged my parents, if they wanted me to live, to get me out of the nursing home. My brother Daniel's tragic death, news of which had been kept from me, had just occurred in the house in Regent's Park and they did not wish me to go back there. So I said, 'Then let me go to Claridge's hotel.' We were good customers of Claridge's, who agreed to have me, but had no wish for an ambulance to arrive at the front door and a stretcher to be brought across the vestibule; so I was taken in through the service entrance and up in the service lift. After six weeks there and a short bout of pleurisy, though weak, I was able to walk a little, and the time came, seven months after I first entered hospital, when I could leave Claridge's and recuperate. I said I would like to go to the South of France, to which the doctor said: 'You're going in an ambulance to Bournemouth with a wheelchair and a nurse.' The weather was delightful. I began to feel better, but life was boring. One of the hotel guests was a young lady who owned a sports car and one sunny day I asked her to run me into Bournemouth to buy some gramophone records. 'Will it be all right with your nurse?' she asked. 'Of course,' I said. As we drove past the front of the hotel I saw my nurse standing on the steps with her fists clenched above her head, dancing with rage.

Fate avenged her; while I was in the basement of the store the lift went out of action and, still too weak to climb stairs, I had to be helped out to the car. I felt lousy, was ticked off by my nurse, put to bed, and the next day was ill. My doctor came down from London. He examined me and said, 'You have been very stupid; you have pneumonia.' Pneumonia was a serious illness in those days before antibiotics came to be used. He continued, 'If you don't lie quietly for seven days, Marcus, I can assure you you will die.' I lay absolutely quiet for twelve days. I had learned a lesson and was never so obedient before, or after, in my life.

One person in whose debt I shall always be was the famous Spanish mezzo-soprano, Conchita Supervia, a great star of Covent Garden, the New York Metropolitan and the world's other famous opera centres. I remember seeing her sing Carmen at Covent Garden, a magnificent performance. She was a lovely and beautiful woman with enormous vitality and a close family friend; during my illness she would, when in London, visit me in the nursing home two or three times a week. She had the ability to transfer her vitality to you as she talked and she helped me maintain the will to live. A few years later her young son, George, phoned me in the office; he was trying to get hold of Father or Simon, and told me that his mother had just died in childbirth at the age of only thirty-seven. I remember her so well.

The other result of my illness was that to a great degree it screened from me the tragedy of my brother Daniel's death. Daniel was eighteen months younger than I, not so extrovert as Michael, not so pushy as me, quiet, thoughtful and sensitive. That he was of high intelligence was evident from his early childhood. I remember his reading the *Manchester Guardian* at the age of five, talking at length about books to my father's friends before he was ten, and doing outstandingly well at school. His bent was scientific and his intention was to read science at Trinity College, Cambridge. Chaim Weizmann predicted a first-class scientific career for him.

One day, when I was still in pain, I read in the nursing home a sentence or two in *The Times* saying that Daniel was dead, that he had committed suicide. When next my parents came in to see me, I asked them about this, and they told me that he had died very suddenly and they had kept the news from me because of my condition. I had more than four months in which to get used to his absence before I resumed normal life and, by the time I did so, I had assimilated the shock of the bereavement. My father then told me his account, blurred with his own grief, sparing me most of the details since I had been so near death's door myself. What with my grief and shock at Daniel's death and my own state of health, I was in no mood to press for more information and did not wish to probe my parents' tragedy when I later resumed normal life. This seemed natural at the time and nobody knows to this day what really happened, although I discovered years later that the coroner's verdict was suicide while temporarily of unsound mind.

A little time after Daniel's death Mother and Father discussed with Dr Weizmann the setting up of some kind of memorial to him. Weizmann suggested that they establish an institute of scientific research in Palestine, where many Jews were going to live and where natural resources were few. Weizmann said it would be a fitting tribute to Daniel, and that is how the Daniel Sieff Research Institute, later to become the famous Weizmann Institute of Science, came into being on the edge of the desert at Rehovot in Palestine.

I worked hard in my final year at Cambridge, compressing almost two years' work into one, and managed to get a Second. It was during this time that I took part in my first Arab/Jewish debate with Sabah es Said, fellow undergraduate and the son of Nuri Pasha es Said, the Iraqi Prime Minister, who was later assassinated. He and I were friends and headed teams debating the rights and wrongs of Jewish immigration to Palestine; honours were evenly divided when votes were cast at the end of the debate. Sabah became a pilot and was, I think, killed in an inter-Arab fight. After I had passed my finals I had to spend a term in residence in Cambridge to qualify for my BA. This residence was nominal and with the aid of exeats I was virtually on a permanent late pass, spending most of that time either in London or driving to and from it. My father gave me a generous allowance and money went much further in those days than it does today. I had a Lagonda drop-head coupé, which I think cost about £700; today I suppose it would be at least fifty times as much. Out of term I visited the South of France, staying in Cannes, Monte Carlo and Nice, and once drove over the Pyrenees to Barcelona and Sitges in Spain, which was then a quiet and delightful little summer resort, very different, I am told, from the crowded place it is today.

In the early 1930s the 400 nightclub opened in Leicester Square. I went to the crowded opening night with two or three friends, but, when I asked for the bill, was told that I was the guest of the club and there was no charge; this made me feel I was under an obligation. The club was well run, the food and drink were excellent, and the music was good, beautifully played and quiet, especially when compared with the noise that one hears today in such places of entertainment; it was easy to hold a conversation. I returned subsequently to find the club almost empty. Despite the high standards, it lost money and after several months Jack Harris, a famous bandleader and the club's owner, offered me a quarter share for £500. This was in 1934 and, while I was prepared to continue to support the club, I said I did not want to buy a quarter share in it. This was a mistake. A few nights later when I went in I was asked if I would mind not having my usual table because a distinguished guest was coming. I agreed; a few minutes later the Duke of Kent arrived, and it was duly reported in the social press. He obviously liked the club and came again on a number of occasions. From that evening the club became more and more popular; it became the premier club of its type in London and internationally renowned as well as highly profitable.

The deputy head waiter, when the 400 opened, was a charming Italian called Rossi, with whom I got on well. It was run as a bottle club; that is, you ordered a bottle of whisky, gin or any other liquor, a label which you signed was put on the bottle and that bottle was brought out to you on any subsequent visits until it was finished. In my experience the club was always well and honestly run. I served abroad without home leave from December 1940 until July 1945. On my return I found the 400 club still going strong. When I went in, Mr Rossi, by this time in charge, said, 'Good evening, Colonel.' I had forgotten that it was a bottle club and I said to Rossi, 'Please can

I have some whisky and gin.'

'Of course,' he replied, and produced two half-filled bottles with my name and signature on the label, which I had last used in 1940. The 400 club eventually folded in the 1960s, but until its closure it continued to maintain high standards.

After the fire in 1929 had largely destroyed our St John's Wood house we moved, as I have said, to nearby Regent's Park, but after Daniel's death my parents did not want to stay there and so we moved again; this time to Brook House on Park Lane, then a fashionable part of London, where we had a large flat. It was located with about ten others on the site of the house that had formerly belonged to Lady Mountbatten's father, the millionaire Ernest Cassel. The original house had been pulled down and in the new one the penthouse was occupied by the Mountbattens; we occupied the floor below. There was a music room, a fifth-floor wine 'cellar', a gymnasium, five bathrooms and a library which could seat up to thirty people. It was the sort of place where, whenever we had guests, we dressed for dinner. We left soon after the war began and never lived in anything like that style again.

Brook House was the scene of many dinner parties which my parents gave for people in public life, in music and the arts, in Zionism, in business and industry, and particularly those who were involved, or interested, in P.E.P. Though my mother was mainly preoccupied with her women Zionists work and visited Palestine regularly, my father was most concerned about unemployment; he had written a book on the subject, which he never published, but which was summarized in a series of articles published in the *Morning Post*. Next to his concern about unemployment came his interest in planning, which brought some members of the government, several MPs of all parties, and many distinguished economists and civil servants around our table. There were spirited discussions, among those taking part being Sir Basil Blackett, Sir Arthur Salter, Noel Hall, who was then professor of economics at University College, London, and his protégé, Hugh Gaitskell; Leonard Elmhirst, the founder of Dartington Hall; Beveridge and G. D. H. Cole; Walter Elliot and Duff Cooper, then Tory MPs; with a liberal Conservative, Harold Macmillan, and industrialists like Lord Melchett; another member was Walter Citrine, the very able left-wing head of the TUC; there was Max Nicholson, who was to play a considerable role as a civil servant advising the post-war Labour government; and, nearly always present, the secretary and chief architect of P.E.P., Kenneth Lindsay, a right-wing Labour MP.

My family was friendly with Irene Ravensdale, Lord Curzon's eldest daughter, whose sister Cynthia was married to Sir Oswald Mosley. Irene asked Father one day if he would have a discussion with her brother-in-law, Mosley. At the meeting Mosley told Father that his New Party (later to become the British Union of Fascists) would sooner rather than later become the majority party, take over the government, and he would become Prime Minister. He asked Father whether P.E.P. would become an advisory group to the new party, what today we would call a think tank. Father said, 'No, its findings, publications and advice are available for all parties.' The group was anonymous and published its broadsheets under the name of P.E.P. Mosley said to Father, 'Well, Israel, you're making a mistake.' He then asked Father if he could meet some of the leading businessmen who formed the P.E.P. industrial group, of which Father was chairman. Father asked a dozen of them to dinner with their wives. After dinner, as was then customary, the men and women separated and Father then invited Mosley to tell his guests about the new party. He spoke most interestingly for about twenty minutes and then began to describe what a party must do to come to power: 'It must capitalize emotion and a political party in a hurry must have a hate plank in its platform. Today the best hate plank is the Jews.' This was just after Hitler had started to implement his viciously anti-Semitic policy. It was also the first time that Mosley had expressed anti-Semitic sentiments, and the effect on the group was electric. Mosley added: 'Of course it doesn't apply to Jews like you, Israel.'

I remember Father rang the bell and said to the butler, 'Sir Oswald is leaving.'

'I haven't finished my brandy,' said Mosley.

'Sir Oswald is leaving, Charles,' said Father, and threw him out. He never saw Mosley again. Mosley claimed until his dying day that he was never anti-Semitic.

I was twenty-one when I left Cambridge and my youth was coming to an end. For a few like me, who had money and easy access to most places, life was pretty good; a pint of beer, bread and cheese and pickles cost a modern 3p, a suit made in Savile Row some £15; you could buy a small Ford car for under £100. On the other hand, there were still more than two million unemployed, and a man out of work, with a wife and two children, drew a dole of thirty shillings a week and was often below the poverty line. I was very lucky to have so many good things served up to me on a plate, but I also appreciated the grounding I had in the harsh reality surrounding millions of my fellow men. This I had learned about from my family's philanthropic interests and activities, which, however limited, will always be much in my mind. My memories of the pleasures of the 1930s are agreeable, but of no great consequence, whereas the lessons I learned from Father and Simon, often not properly appreciated at the time, have been the base on which I have built some of the values and the objectives which have made and continue to make an adult life worth living.

CHAPTER THREE

SIMON'S first objective when he returned from the United States was to build bigger and better stores. To raise the capital for this he had, as I have said, to go public, meeting several reverses on the way until the Prudential Assurance Company decided to support him. The first new store was at Darlington, no wider in frontage than Brewer Street, Soho, but about 100 feet long, about four times Soho's size. The next new store, at Blackpool, had a 60-foot frontage, and that size became the new so-called 'big store'. It was now possible to display a wider variety of goods. Those were the days when Wool-worth's directors and executives made occasional, patronizing visits to our stores. They would pick up goods from the counters and put them back saying, 'It's a lemon' — which meant they were no good. They used to say M & S stood for 'Mud & Sand'.

The other major changes put in train in the late 1920s turned out well. The first was the introduction of the checking list, which helped to control better the stocks of goods we were selling. Instead of waiting for quarterly or bi-quarterly reports on what was selling and what was not, the checking lists enabled Simon to call for fortnightly reports. Anything that was selling could be quickly re-ordered, and what was sticking reduced and cleared. Turnover became faster and profits rose. Simon's policy of selling at a maximum of five shillings eliminated the cheap 'jumble' of which he had complained. Clothing became the leading section of our business — three times larger than any other, and this changed the public's image of Marks & Spencer. Our growth reflected the increase in the demand for clothes, especially women's; fewer women wanted to make their own clothes at home; they wanted variety and colour, and lighter clothing for leisure. To a lesser degree this applied for men too.

There was another important development during this period: new materials and new techniques for handling them had come into the world of textiles and, influenced by Dr Weizmann, who was a considerable industrial chemist, Simon was determined to exploit them on Marks & Spencer's counters. As Father put it, 'We came to regard ourselves as a kind of technical laboratory. We felt we should provide our suppliers with good technical information about the new materials and processes which the advance of technology was making available. We saw ourselves, in a limited way, as production engineers, industrial chemists, laboratory technicians.'

Simon and Father agreed that not only should Marks & Spencer supply information, but we should try to persuade manufacturers to use it to make goods to specifications agreed with us. We began to exercise an active influence on improving the quality of goods produced for us and on the textile and clothing industry in particular. There were no middle men or wholesalers now between Marks & Spencer and the manufacturers, a relationship almost revolutionary in those days and one which led both to improved quality and to better values. Marks & Spencer enjoyed the benefits of stable supplies of goods which they knew would sell at relatively low prices because of the size of the order; the manufacturer got the benefit of large guaranteed orders for goods produced on the basis of specialized information which he would not normally have. This was the real revolution − to get the manufacturer to make goods, if not all his output then at least part of it, not for the general wholesale market but specially for us. This co-operative relationship between Marks & Spencer, its manufacturers and the raw material suppliers has been one of the main contributions to our progress and our ability to satisfy the customer. That relationship is still strong and important.

Simon preferred to visit stores rather than manufacturers, so visits to manufacturers became one of Father's main jobs. He travelled widely after he joined the firm full time, trying to persuade manufacturers to work closely with us. Some were inhibited because they were involved with, or at the least had friends in, the textile wholesalers' associations; others were hostile on other grounds. Some did not like the idea of outsiders advising them on what to produce, let alone on how to produce it; others felt it beneath them to co-operate so intimately with a chain of what until recently had been penny bazaars.

An important incident in the development of our textile business occurred in 1926, when Father visited Corah of Leicester, who had been in the textile business for well over one hundred years. He saw Jack and Reggie Corah, the heads of the firm, but they politely threw him out, saying that not only did they not do business with shops of the type of Marks & Spencer but also that they did business only through wholesalers. When he called in the second time, he told the taxi driver to keep his engine running as he expected to be thrown out again — which he was, again politely. He was accompanied on his way out by Cecil Coleman, who was in charge of Corah's production. On his way through the men's sock department Father saw many machines idle. He said to Cecil, 'You have idle machines and I could give you an order for five hundred dozen socks a week in three colours.'

Cecil replied, 'Do you really mean it?' — to which Father said, 'Yes.'

'Well, Mr Sieff,' said Cecil, 'I am going to do business with you on my own responsibility. Will you give me an order now?' Father did so, and, when he got back to London, he said to Simon, 'I think we made a breakthrough.'

Corah's business was done with Marks & Spencer under a code number. Some months later one of their customers in Tunbridge Wells received by mistake goods intended for Marks & Spencer, Tunbridge Wells. They complained to the Corahs, who sent for Cecil and wanted to know what it was all about. Cecil then confessed that he had been doing business surreptitiously with Marks & Spencer for several months and had not informed the chairman and managing director. He was sacked. But at the same time Jack or Reggie checked the amount of business Corah had done with Marks & Spencer's Tunbridge Wells branch in the few months they had traded together and compared it with their other Tunbridge Wells customers who bought Corah's branded St Margaret goods. The Corahs discovered that they were doing more business with Marks & Spencer than with all their other customers together. Cecil Coleman was reinstated and eventually became the managing director of Corah and, during World War II, the government's hosiery controller. Even after this Corah tried, for a period, to keep it secret that they did business with Marks & Spencer. On one occasion, when a wholesaler was going round, he saw parcels addressed to M & S, Oxford Street and he asked who this customer was. 'Marshall & Snelgrove!' said Reggie quickly. Starting business with Corah was indeed a breakthrough; our turnover with them in 1985 was £56 million. Over the next few years many firms of repute followed suit and dealt direct with Marks & Spencer.

Corah sold their goods under the St Margaret label. It was in the 1930s that the idea of a brand name for Marks & Spencer goods started and finally it was decided to call them St Michael, 'canonizing' my grandfather, Michael Marks, who started the firm. Everything produced for Marks & Spencer for many years has been made to specifications agreed between Marks & Spencer and the manufacturers and bears the St Michael label. Both sides have benefited from the exchange of information, agreed specifications, long-term developments and, in most cases, a growing business. Usually we are our suppliers' largest customer; we have been doing business continuously with one hundred and twenty-five of them for over twenty-five years, forty-one for more than forty years, and with Dewhirst we have done uninterrupted business for more than a century. These companies are the backbone of our business and are our friends.

There was another important innovation in our relations with suppliers. The credit for this goes to Simon, and it is a perfect example of how quick and bold he was to see possibilities, harness and exploit them. In the early 1930s Simon lived in Grosvenor Square, London. He often used to take a stroll in the garden of the square and frequently encountered another man who also lived in the square, who turned out to be Henry Dreyfus, the founder of the firm which later developed into British Celanese. Simon was curious about other people's business, especially if it had the remotest connection with his own, and as their acquaintance ripened he asked Dreyfus many questions. By now those concerned at Marks & Spencer knew a good deal about the merchandise they bought and the materials used in making them; it occurred to Simon that British Celanese might make materials to specifications agreed with Marks & Spencer. He mentioned this to Dreyfus, who at once said he was interested. Out of these peripatetic conversations came the development of a rayon (artificial silk), which was called V-30. This was sent from the factory direct to our manufacturers, to be made up mainly into St Michael ladies' underwear.

Simon, as I have said, was obsessed with quality and was never satisfied. Whatever we had, however good, there must, he thought, be something better being developed somewhere, and Marks & Spencer had to look for it. The V-30 was followed by V-31, V-32 and V-33, each supposed to be better quality than the previous fabric. One day when I went into his office Simon was looking at the four fabrics, holding each in turn between thumb and forefinger. He had a remarkable feel for quality, a good judge of surface and texture — but on this occasion he couldn't tell or feel the supposed differences between these fabrics. 'The question is,' he said, admitting defeat, and indulging a little boy's humour, as he did engagingly from time to time, 'do we really know that V-33 is better than V-32, V-31 and V-30? "Vee" don't know and "vee" are bloody well going to find out.' And that was when our merchandise development department was born, soon to be put under a gifted industrial scientist, Eric Kann, who came from Germany. Eric Kann, unknown in Britain at the time, later became a member of the board of Marks & Spencer and a famous figure in the British textile industry. He died in 1983 and his achievements were recognised in a remarkable obituary in *The Times*.

The effect of Simon's practical development of this idea not only led to the production for Marks & Spencer's customers of goods of better quality and value, but also stimulated our manufacturers into making better use themselves of technological developments and new raw materials. The constant efforts to upgrade and the resulting increase in sales led to further quality improvements and better value.

I joined the firm officially in September 1935, just after it had celebrated its golden jubilee. My first posting was to our Hammersmith Broadway store. 'You start at the bottom,' said Simon, and I certainly did; Frank Ross, a senior member of our personnel department, started me on a wage of £2.10s a week which was 10/- below the minimum then for management trainees. I think this was to compensate for the fact that I drove to the store each morning in a large Packard Roadster, the first of its type in the United Kingdom. Hammersmith was a medium-sized store with a fairly wide range of goods — toiletries, glassware, crockery, haberdashery, gramophone records, an increasing amount of clothing, and some simple foods like packets of biscuits and loose sweets. About fifty people worked in the store, of whom about forty were women. The men were the manager, his deputy, an assistant and three or four warehousemen. When I joined the staff at Hammersmith in 1935 most parents did not consider Marks & Spencer an attractive prospective employer for their children as they did Harrods, Selfridges, John Lewis, and the other department stores. In fact, with few exceptions, retailing in general was looked down upon as a fourth-rate career.

Even in my grandfather's early days our employees were treated well by the standards of the day, limited, of course, by the resources available. Simon and Father substantially improved conditions. When I joined Hammersmith amenities included a good dining-room and well-cooked meals for the staff at a low price. I worked at Hammersmith branch for about a year, starting work at 8.15 am and going on until closing time at 7.00 pm, except on Fridays and Saturdays, when it was 8.00 pm. Sunday was a day off, and in addition everybody got a half-day off each week. My first six weeks were spent in the basement stockroom, where I received and opened packages of goods, checked them against the delivery notes, put them into the proper stock bins and then, in response to requisitions from the sales personnel, heaved them upstairs to the counters. There were no lifts then.

One of the most important parts of a salesperson's equipment is knowledge of each of his or her products, and for the manager it is very important to know what is selling and what is not. You can find out quite a lot in the stockroom. I also served in most of the departments and learned something about the likes and dislikes of our customers. One of the most difficult departments was toys. When parents, often accompanied by their children, wanted to buy them something, the children were frequently very pushy, nearly always wanting something costing more than the parents wished to spend, with the result that the parents then became difficult. I can remember winding up tiny firemen that climbed ladders on fire engines, to the point where I began to feel very wound up myself. In those days it was all counter or rack service and you were stationed inside the island counters or behind the side counters. You learned a good deal from contact with customers, some of whom wanted detailed advice and aid, others to be left alone to make their choice. It is different today in Marks & Spencer stores: they are mostly self-service, with sales staff around to advise and help, and in the food department there is complete self-service.

I got a good grounding in the business at Hammersmith, where I learned that the most important person was the customer. In general I worked with and served people who came from the low income groups; spending the day with people from different backgrounds to my own was an eye-opener. However, it was clear that all of us — well, nearly all of us — are capable of kindness, appreciate good advice and help, and generally respect good manners. It was encouraging to learn from direct experience that Father's philosophy of the importance of good human relations at work not only sounded good but actually worked: this philosophy is still far from universal, even today, in many business organizations. The one person who troubled me at Hammersmith was the store manager, who did not agree with the way in which top management's attitudes to staff were developing. He considered the staff were being spoiled by Simon's and Father's policy. I didn't like the manager, but I think I managed to conceal it from him. 'He's a bastard,' I said one day to Father, who typically replied, 'Oh, you mean he's one of the old school.' This manager did not typify what I had heard Father and Simon talk about so many times at home. He didn't ask, he gave orders; in dealing with his staff there was never a 'please' or 'thank you'. If something was badly done he was critical; there was no praise if something was well done; there was no warmth between him and his staff. He thought that was the way to manage; he did not have the training of today. Nowadays we might have trained him to be a good manager. From what I know now a potentially bad manager, if caught in time, is sometimes redeemable. Some years ago, when I was personnel director, I found the manager of a store I was visiting in many ways very competent but his relations with his staff were poor. For example, when his assistants gave information on weekly sales to me in front of him, saying, perhaps, that they had sold about eight dozen of this or that, he would interject, 'No, we didn't: it was eight dozen and four.' There was friction between him and his staff, and staff turnover was high. I decided to move him from that store, which was of medium size, and put him as deputy to a very good manager of a well-run big store. He is now a most successful manager of one of our biggest stores and his staff think well of him – a brand from the burning.

In fact the practical, caring attitude which Marks & Spencer developed so impressively in the 1930s was an inheritance from my grandfathers, Michael Marks and Ephraim Sieff. The origin of this philosophy was more definite and datable in Michael's case; when he came to build his own premises for the first time – his headquarters in Derby Street, Manchester, at the turn of the century – though he employed only a dozen or so people at the headquarters, he provided a staff dining-room and a kitchen where they could cook their own food. But I can go even further back than that. In the summer of 1984 I went with my wife Lily to Leeds to open a block of flats for the elderly which Marks & Spencer had financed as one of our centenary community projects. There we retraced the steps my grandfather took one hundred years earlier — first to Dewhirst's warehouse, then to the site of the open market stall, and then to the much larger stalls in the closed market which my grandfather started renting in the 1890s. Incidentally, the market manager showed me the rent book signed by my grandfather; he paid 5/- a week rent; the rent today for the same stall is £115. That day I was introduced, in the lounge of our Leeds store, to Mrs Elsie Stoker, who had lunched in the store's rather fine dining-room. Elsie was eighty-nine and told me she had worked in our original penny bazaar for five years from 1908, when she was thirteen years of age, to 1913, when she left. I said, 'Why did you leave?' She said, 'Well, I really wanted to make a career with Marks & Spencer but I was last in, first out, and we were cutting back on staff.' She went on: 'You know, we didn't have anything like this,' referring to the lounge and dining-room where we were sitting, 'but even in those days we had a little place over the stall where we could make hot drinks and have our sandwiches.'

One of the spurs to improving facilities for the staff resulted from a single incident in the early 1930s. Unemployment in Britain, following the great economic crisis of the western world which started with the Wall Street crash of 1929, was very high. When Father and Simon were visiting a store, they thought a salesgirl behind a counter did not look well. They asked her how she felt and, though she said she was quite all right, Father went back and made enquiries. He found that the girl's father and brothers were unemployed and she shared her wage with her mother in order to feed the family. Unemployment benefits were small in those days, not enough to keep people above the poverty line, and members of a family like our salesgirl's did not have enough to eat. Simon and Father agreed that no one who worked for us must go hungry and they installed kitchens and rest-rooms in every store where a midday three-course meal cost 6d; even today it is only 20p, with morning and afternoon refreshment breaks costing 10p; so that everybody who worked for us could — and still can — eat well. The provision of such facilities would today be regarded as normal practice by many employers, but in the 1930s it was revolutionary.

The development of these staff restaurants was followed in the next twenty-five years by the introduction of medical, dental and hairdressing facilities, chiropody, of which many people make use —

it's tiring standing on your feet for several hours a day – and a range of other benefits much appreciated by the staff. A good deal of this work was carried out by the remarkable Flora Solomon, whom Simon had recruited for the purpose. In her memoirs she writes that it was she who started our welfare department. This is not accurate. Her great contribution over twenty-five years was to extend, expand and improve what was already under way, and she did it outstandingly well. Eventually the great majority of the people in top management throughout the company learned the value of treating people well.

In the early 1930s we developed another practice that applies to this day: management recruits who hope eventually to come into a head-office department must spend at least two years in the stores. The exceptions are specialists like technologists and engineers, and even they are supposed to spend two or three months familiarizing themselves in stores before they take up their head-office jobs. I went from Hammersmith to Bristol and then to Market Street, Manchester, both much larger stores than Hammersmith. By the time I went to Manchester all stores – other people's as well as ours – were much busier than they had been two years before, as a result of the rise in employment and the increase in purchasing power brought about by rearmament. Nowhere could this be more clearly seen than in Marks & Spencer, Market Street. Fridays were busy, but Saturdays were a rat race. This was largely because the average working man's hours were so long on the other weekdays that he and his wife did much of their shopping on Saturdays. As many people worked on Saturday mornings, the afternoons were even busier, and in stores in industrial areas 35–40% of the whole week's trading was done on a Saturday, a large part in the afternoon.

My recollection of those Saturdays is of a milling throng of customers and sales assistants under pressure; in particular I remember the pile of cardboard shoe boxes. We had not been selling shoes for long, but the new department had caught on and was expanding fast. In Market Street shoes were located in a large alcove on the lower sales floor. In accordance with the Marks & Spencer principle of seeing and feeling the goods, the shoes were taken out of their boxes and arranged along the counter, being (at least in theory) replaced with pairs of the same type and size as soon as a sale was made. As the pace of the shopping speeded up on a Saturday there was no time to take discarded boxes back to the rubbish area and they were supposed to be stacked in neat rows in the back of the alcove. When the pace became really hot, there was no time even to stack them; the boxes were thrown on to the pile. By closing time there was a huge mountain of empties, in spite of the efforts of three warehousemen to get them and the tissue paper taken away.

I learned a good deal in the two years I spent in the stores, and in 1937 I moved into head office, where I was assigned to the then disappearing departments of gramophone records and toiletries, though toiletries have enjoyed a great renaissance in recent years. The food departments were beginning to make progress and, as I was interested in their development, I was also assigned to the food group. In the early 1930s we sold only a few food items – packets of sweets, packets of biscuits, biscuits from tins, broken biscuits, a few cakes. One of the broken biscuits we sold in substantial quantities was Kit Kat. I had become friendly during my early days in the business with George Harris, a noted chairman and chief executive of Rowntrees, who manufactured Kit Kat. One day, when visiting Rowntrees, I said to George Harris, looking at the production of Kit Kat, which was largely mechanized and seemed pretty efficient, 'I'm surprised that you have so much broken Kit Kat available for us.'

'We don't really have all that much available,' he replied, 'but come with me and I will show you.' He took me to a place where, to my surprise, they were breaking up into smaller pieces perfectly good whole pieces of Kit Kat. 'This,' he said, 'is for you; your demand for broken Kit Kat is greater than our supply, and as it's profitable to sell to you direct without going through sales representatives we do a little special production.'

The latest development, when I joined the food group, was that of the fruit department, especially for the sale of oranges and grapefruit. Citrus fruit was selling well and the fact that they were Jaffa from Palestine encouraged us to promote them. We pioneered the grapefruit, which at that time was relatively unknown in Britain. In the early days many customers took grapefruit for a kind of orange and tried to peel them. We had to issue a leaflet with each purchase on how best to eat them. After a while I concentrated largely on the fruit department. We did not have the direct contacts we now have with growers and farmers but had to buy in the market, mainly the old Covent Garden. The fruit department was headed by the brothers Webb. Four mornings a week or so I got up at 4.30 am to be in

Covent Garden by 5.00 to 5.30 am. I went around the market visiting the various wholesalers, buying on the basis of the sample boxes on display. These were supposed to represent the general quality standards of the purchase; but often the sample boxes had been specially prepared and the bulk could be of a much lower quality. Yet, even in those early days, we were tough about quality standards and the wholesalers learned it did not pay to take us for a ride. We were greatly helped by the close association we developed with a large wholesaler, Lehman & Candia, who became important suppliers; eventually John Candia worked full time for Marks & Spencer, while, I think, retaining an interest in his family firm, not something we normally permit.

John Candia in his life story writes about our first meeting:

I remember having driven up from Great Oaks, being on parade at four o'clock in the morning in our large and quite dingy warehouse in Long Acre and seeing three gentlemen suddenly arrive. One was the then Mr Marcus Sieff, eventually to become the Chairman of Marks and Spencer, followed by Bruce Goodman, who was then the head of accountancy research and became a very great friend of mine, and Mr J. R. Clarke, a gentleman who had formerly been in the Merchant Navy, then became manager of Marks and Spencer's Swansea office. They walked in. I said, 'Good morning. My name is Candia.'

'Good morning, Mr Candia,' they introduced themselves. I thought, oh dear, something has gone wrong.

'Could we have a look at the fruit?' I said, 'Certainly,' so with my big hammer I opened boxes of oranges, boxes of apples. We looked at the fruit and I said, 'Well, gentlemen, my office is extremely dingy.' They said, 'That's not important.' So I said, 'Please come up.' They asked me whether I did in fact honour the debit notes sent to me by the stores. I was extremely irritated. I said, 'Of course I do. If there is one thing you cannot accuse me of, gentlemen, it is dishonesty – ineptitude, perhaps.' A big roar of laughter – everybody smiled at me and they said, 'Neither dishonesty nor ineptitude, in our opinion.' Then Goodman said, 'You are the only one who pays the debit notes, Mr Candia.' I swallowed hard, gave a sickly grin, and we went round to the Nag's Head to celebrate this meeting at 4.45 in the morning, by drinking tea and eating toast. I had the honour of entertaining a delegation from Marks and Spencer, I think at the cost of somewhere approaching half-a-crown. I was relieved that nothing had gone wrong and then I had a call from Mr Marcus Sieff. Mr Webb was to be engaged in other activities and was leaving them for another section of the fruit trade.

He would like me to meet his father, Mr Israel Sieff. The call was at seven o'clock in the morning, inviting me to breakfast with him at Arlington House [into which Marcus Sieff had moved after his marriage] at eight o'clock. I asked if it could be 8.30, the reason being that I could get a shave at Horne Bros. in Leicester Square at eight o'clock and also buy clean shirt. I had breakfast with Mr Marcus Sieff at Arlington House. We then proceeded to Michael House in Baker Street, where he introduced me to his father, Israel Sieff.

Israel Sieff was a man whom I respected for the rest of my life. Not only was he extremely efficient, but he was also kind. He had a fundamental knowledge of business and merchandizing, but, perhaps equal in importance, a fundamental understanding of people. Mr Sieff said to me, 'Mr Candia, Mr Webb is leaving us and we are seriously considering the elimination of the fruit department from our stores – something which we could regret, but I am asking you whether you would be willing to act in a consultant capacity for the possible restructuring of the department.' I gasped and I suddenly thought this is something which could never happen to me again, the possibility of going into the retail side of our industry. I looked around the big office. I looked at the kind, smiling face of Israel Sieff. I said, 'Mr Sieff, this is a great honour. I know nothing of the retail side of the business – I would love to learn.' He said, 'That is a very good turn of phrase, Mr Candia. Now if you would like to follow on this discussion with my son, Marcus, I would be delighted.' We did not prostitute this meeting with any mention of finance. He rang the internal telephone and said, 'Let me take you down.' He did not send me down to my assignment with Marcus. We went down and I was handed over to Marcus Sieff.

I sat down and a piece of paper was passed over to me. As usual, as with anything to do with Marks and Spencer, a generous financial offer was made with pleasant dignity. Marcus said to me, 'Is that satisfactory?'

'Oh, certainly, Mr Sieff.'

'Right now', he said, 'you are in complete charge of the fruit and vegetable department in every one of two hundred and thirty stores which are merchandizing that department. You have a completely free hand, Mr Candia, and we hope that within a year we shall have re-established the department at a viable and commercial level.' To me it was quite a fantastic feeling, having always been rather on the fringe, that I should suddenly have the opportunity of facing this challenge as departmental chief, backed by vast resources, not only financially, but administratively.

And that was how John Candia became the head of our fruit department from 1937 to 1947. He, more than anyone, worked during this period to develop our fruit and produce department and put it on a sound basis. Today it is one of the biggest departments in our food group. John was a man of quality with whom it was a pleasure to work.

In the two years before the war we introduced cooked meats, pies, sausages and similar food lines, which had considerable success. However, it was to the home-grown British tomato, and an inferior one at that, that I partly owed my promotion and my professional entry into Simon's good graces. Most of us used to visit the stores regularly and I found that the quality of our tomatoes was poor. I said so to Alec Saxe-Cohen, Simon's cousin and the executive in charge of food buying. I was outspoken, perhaps even more in those days than I am today; I was reasonably polite, but reacted strongly when he told me that the tomatoes he bought for Marks & Spencer were good. I remember saying, 'They're bloody awful – soft, bladdery and without flavour.'

'This time of the year', he retorted, 'they're the best we can get.'

'Well,' I said, 'in that case we should not be selling them. If we can't find better, we shouldn't be in the business and anyway I'm sure we can find better tomatoes.' I suppose this was the red rag to an already irate bull.

'If you're going to make a nuisance of yourself in my group, I'll put you in your place right now,' my boss said. 'You'll come with me to see the chairman.' I hadn't bargained for this and certainly hadn't intended it, but there was no backing out of the situation even if I had wanted to. So there and then we marched along the corridor to Simon's office.

'Well?' asked Simon, staring at us with some surprise.

'It's Marcus,' said his cousin. 'He's making a nuisance of himself.'

Simon leaned back in his chair. 'What's he doing?' he asked.

'He's complaining about our tomatoes.'

Simon turned to me. 'What's wrong with our tomatoes?'

I remember my exact words. 'They're awful: soft and bladdery and flavourless,' I said. 'He says they are the best we can get, so I told him that if that was the case we ought not to be selling them because the quality is not good enough.'

As the reader will have realized the word 'quality' was like a war trumpet to Simon's ears. 'Anyway,' I said, 'I'm sure we can get better.'

'How do *you* know about the tomatoes anyway?' asked Simon.

'I checked them in a store,' I replied, 'and I thought they were so much below our standards I checked in other stores to see if they were as bad. And they were.'

Simon took a puff of his cigar. 'If Marcus doesn't like our tomatoes,' he said, 'if Marcus thinks he can buy better, perhaps he'd better take over the department and buy *all* our fruit.' He pretended to be thoughtful for a moment and added, 'No, not yet. Perhaps, Marcus, you've struck unlucky in your samples. Let's see how the tomatoes look a little later on' – whereupon he turned in his chair and resumed his work. But when, later on, he inspected the tomatoes himself he also found their quality was poor. He gave me credit for having discovered this and for having stuck to my guns, and as a result I was given greater authority.

Some years after the Saxe-Cohen episode I was showing the senior executives of a great American food chain around Marks & Spencer. In Kingston we visited a number of food shops and our own store. We were still buying tomatoes from the market, not yet having direct contacts with growers, and market quality that week was poor, so we had none for sale. The American executive asked why we had no tomatoes on our produce counter while all the other shops did. I explained the problem of poor quality, to which he replied, 'Well, if you don't have tomatoes for sale when your competitors do, your customers will cease buying tomatoes from you.' I said I didn't agree. 'You'll see,' he said. We did. I was right and he was wrong. A fortnight later good tomatoes became available and, after being without tomatoes for nearly two weeks, in the third week we had the highest sales ever recorded until then in the business.

As well as tomatoes, tennis became a link between Simon and me. He enjoyed playing and was quite good; I was average to poor. However, we used to play with some of the world's leading players; one was Tilden, the greatest player of his time, who won Wimbledon twice; another was Danny Prenn, the former German Davis Cup number one. Prenn was born a Russian Jew, but as a youth emigrated to Germany. I don't think he was ever beaten at the Rot-Weiss tennis club in Berlin; in one famous Davis Cup tie he beat Fred Perry, the Wimbledon champion, and Bunny Austin. He left Germany in the early days when Hitler started to persecute the Jews, came to this country as a refugee and, beginning as a sweet salesman, sold sweets to Marks & Spencer. He was very able, and had taken an engineering degree at Berlin University. In Britain he developed a major business in various fields, including electronics and clothing. He never forgot people who had helped him in the past and, when he became wealthy, was immensely charitable, often anonymously. We have been friends for over fifty years.

On one occasion Simon suggested I partner Tilden, while he played with Prenn. I said, 'No, playing with Tilden makes me nervous.'

'O.K.,' he replied, 'you play with Prenn.'

Tilden had a favourite shot. He loved to run round his backhand and then hit the ball low, hard and sharply angled across the court — a devastating shot which only a great player could perform well. Tilden and Simon won the first set easily. Prenn played well, but I was appalling. In the second set Tilden opened the serving. I played in the left-hand court. His first was out, his second was not lethal and I drove it to his backhand. I had set him up for one of his blistering cross-court forehands, and sure enough he ran round his backhand and hit a forehand drive across the net like a shot from a gun. I was completely beaten, had no clue, shut my eyes, put my racket down to my feet and feebly moved it forward; it connected with the ball, which whizzed back across the net, a perfect half volley, and took Tilden by surprise. He only had time to make a simple return and Prenn was able to smash it back past him. From then on Prenn played beautifully and I could do no wrong; we won the next two sets. Tilden did not like to lose, however unimportant the game; Simon did not care whether he won or lost. He said to me, 'I had no idea you had it in you to play a shot like that.'

'I did it with my eyes shut,' I said.

'Well,' he said, 'I won't say you made it seem as easy as that but it was certainly a hell of a confident shot.'

I explained that literally I had had my eyes shut when I hit the ball, but he didn't believe me — or pretended not to.

I worked hard, but it wasn't all work and no play. I had met Rosalie Fromson in 1935; she had been born in Britain but, when she was still a baby, her parents emigrated to the United States. Rosalie retained her British citizenship. She was a most attractive girl, very likeable and with great charm. She decided to become a dancer, a profession she took seriously. Soon after her twenty-first birthday she came from New York to London in a show which ran for many months at the Dorchester Hotel, just a few doors up Park Lane from my home. I took her out a great deal during her stay in London. I must have seen the show in which she performed twenty times. My parents also grew fond of her. In the end we were going everywhere together, but I didn't want to get married at the time; I enjoyed the company of other girls as well, and so, when the show ended, she returned to New York to continue her career.

About that time I also became friendly with Mary Brian, a star of the silent film days, who was playing the lead in a London show; one day she said to me, 'Why don't you visit Hollywood some time?' I promised I would. 'I'll be in Hollywood one year from today, but only if you agree to come out with me.'

She said, 'Well, if you come and I am there, whatever I am doing you can take me out.' I was cheating slightly because I had already booked on the maiden voyage of the *Queen Mary*, which was to sail fifty weeks later. So I knew I would be in the United States at the time.

The *Queen Mary* sailed on 27 May 1936. The five-day voyage, a record at the time, was one long party. In New York I saw a great deal of Rosalie before going on to stay in Chicago with Jules and Doris Stein, longtime friends of the family. It was at the time when Jules was founding what is today the famous Music Corporation of America, one of the world's greatest entertainment complexes. I decided to go back to New York, partly to see Rosalie but mainly to see the return heavyweight championship fight between Joe Louis and Max Schmeling, but suddenly I saw 'Mary Brian' written down in my diary and telephoned the number she had given me. She answered and asked who it was. I said, 'Marcus.'

'Marcus who?' she replied, which slightly set me back. At first she hadn't a clue who I was. I told her I was on my way to Hollywood to take her out, and at last the penny dropped.

She arranged to meet me at the airport. The plane was an early type DC3, which flew at about one hundred and fifty miles an hour and had a pretty limited range, necessitating many stops. The journey took about thirty hours and I arrived a semi-wreck.

When Mary met me, she asked, 'Do you have a dinner jacket? We're going out tonight, if you would like it, to the one place in Hollywood where one has to have a dinner jacket.'

We were taken out by Paul Lucas and Mary Astor, leading film stars of those days, and delightful people. Suddenly in the middle of dinner in a rather smart restaurant I saw a man approaching the table dressed in a turtleneck sweater and a pair of slacks; it was Cary Grant, whom I had known back home. He greeted us all warmly and said, 'I don't understand, Marcus, why you didn't let me know you were coming here and why you are not staying with me.' I couldn't understand how he knew about my coming and why he was there until I saw that he was very friendly with Mary. He explained that he would have been with us that evening but he was on location making a film somewhere outside Hollywood and had come in just to say hallo. He again repeated his invitation to stay with him at his house in Santa Monica. I said I couldn't impose, but he insisted. 'Anyway, I'll be back after the weekend. Come and lunch with me on Monday and see whether you like it.'

After he left Mary said, 'Now I hope you're not going to stay with Cary; if you do, I have a feeling I shall see nothing of either of you.'

On Monday morning Cary sent a car to take me down to the house at Santa Monica, which was literally on the beach, with a swimming-pool and the sea a hundred yards away. I took one look at it and said to Cary, 'You can send for my luggage.' I had a marvellous two weeks there being royally entertained by many of the leading celebrities of Hollywood, such as Norma and Constance Talmadge. On one occasion Louis B. Mayer, one of the great movie moguls, gave a dinner which he said was for me; in fact he was launching Sonja Henie, a beautiful girl who had been world ice-skating champion and became a famous film star.

In those days Hollywood considered itself the centre of the world. This was before the age of television; the cinema was at its peak. I was having a marvellous time when I received a telegram from Simon Marks enquiring when I was coming back or had I resigned? I cancelled all my engagements and took the first plane back to New York, from where, after a brief reunion with Rosalie, I sailed back on the *Ile de France*.

By the time I got home I found myself missing Rosalie more and more and so we decided to get married. We had a traditional Jewish wedding followed by a lunch and a wonderful party at the Savoy Hotel. Freddie Brisson was our best man. We had a marvellous honeymoon in the South of France; life was most enjoyable.

CHAPTER FOUR

LIKE other young people, when I came down from Cambridge I was becoming more politically minded and uneasy with the policies of the government of the day, formed by the Conservatives under Neville Chamberlain. I did not join any political party, but I suppose my approach was a little left of centre because of my concern for the nearly three million unemployed, some of whom I met when I served in the stores. Father and Simon talked a good deal about unemployment and did what they could to help those without jobs.

I was moved by the episode of the shirts for the men of Mountain Ash. In that Welsh mining village of about four thousand, thirty per cent were unemployed. The minister of the local Baptist church wrote to Marks & Spencer saying that hardly a man in Mountain Ash possessed more than one shirt and that was generally pretty ragged. Some of his congregation had donated some money; he had worked out what the men on the dole could afford. Was it possible for Marks & Spencer to provide some shirts at something like that price? He had heard of the firm's desire to be helpful; perhaps we might give his request favourable consideration. He said nobody in Mountain Ash wanted charity, only a chance to buy a clean new shirt. Father and Simon decided to send six thousand shirts as a gift but, due to the haste with which the shirts were sent, there was a misunderstanding and an invoice accompanied the shirts at the price of 2/11d each (15p today). By return Father received a letter from the minister enclosing a cheque and saying he would never have believed a shirt could be bought so cheaply. 'Thank God,' he wrote, 'for men who understand what self-respect means to an out-of-work miner.' He was thanked for his thanks, and his cheque was returned to him with an explanation.

By 1938 the mass unemployment of the early 1930s had fallen, largely due to the rearmament programme and the Chamberlain government's policy of initiating industrial development in the 'depressed areas'; but now the government's foreign policy was much criticized, because it had let our defences run down and was slow to build them up again. There was widespread resentment against an attitude to Hitler and Mussolini described as appeasement. We Jews didn't know everything about the character and objectives of Hitler's regime, but we knew more than most because of our contacts with fellow Jews in Europe and with Jewish emigrants who were leaving Germany to settle here, in the United States and in Palestine. Many influential people in the country did not know, or did not wish to know, of the persecutions, almost amounting to pogroms, and of the concentration camps already being set up. In fact, some important people used their influence to discourage the dissemination of such information; they thought that Germany had been unjustly treated after World War I, or they saw Germany as the bulwark of a capitalist, Christian Western Europe against the hostility of godless Communism.

Again, some did not believe there could be another war so soon after World War I; others of us believed that war was coming. I, like thousands, joined the Territorial Army in 1938. Mainly because it was geographically convenient and I would be able to carry on my work at Marks & Spencer, I joined the local regiment of the Royal Engineers; our task, in the event of war, was to operate searchlights for our anti-aircraft guns and also to use Lewis guns against low-flying attacks and parachutists. We trained in a drill hall once a week near the Houses of Parliament. I went to the annual Territorial camp. We had few searchlights and even fewer Lewis guns. I had been a volunteer for nearly a year when it looked as though war would break out because Germany demanded the return of the Sudetenland from Czechoslovakia. Chamberlain flew to Munich to meet Hitler and returned waving the famous piece of paper signed by both of them which, he claimed, guaranteed 'peace in our time'. I had been called up a few days previously and had spent the time with the rest of my company digging trenches in Hyde Park. I returned home that night feeling relieved and hoping that Chamberlain's predictions were right.

Jan Masaryk, son of Tomáš Masaryk, the founder and first president of Czechoslovakia, was the Czech minister in London. He and Father were good friends. He was coming to dinner that night; he arrived late, fuming with rage and deeply upset. We asked what was wrong. He said, 'It's that so-and-so Joe Kennedy.' Kennedy was the United States ambassador in London and known for his then relatively good opinion of Hitler and his low opinion of Britain's will and capacity to defend herself. Both Kennedy and Masaryk had been in the Commons to hear Chamberlain report on his 'peace in our time' visit.

'As I listened to Chamberlain,' he said, 'I knew that my country's existence was at risk and I couldn't take it. So I left Parliament and thought I would walk here to try to cool off. In Park Lane a car pulled alongside me and Joe Kennedy leaned out and said, "Isn't it fabulous news, Jan? What a marvellous job Chamberlain has done. Terrific, isn't it? Can I give you a lift?"' Jan went on, 'I blew my top and said to him, "You bastard, that's what you think of the news, but I have just heard the death knell of my country." And I hurried away from him.'

I thought Jan was exaggerating, but of course he was right. By spring Hitler had occupied Czechoslovakia and it was only a question of where he would go next.

I continued working in the business, but there was also more army training. After we had married, Rosalie and I had bought a modest flat in Arlington House, a new block next door to the Ritz Hotel. We were the first tenants. Rosalie and I were very happy; we had a delightful circle of friends and, although I worked hard, we also played hard. We had made friends before we were married with a charming girl from Germany called Anna-Marie Soerensen; she left her country because she was partly Jewish and was entirely opposed to Hitler's views. She was maid of honour to Rosalie at our wedding and was a regular visitor to Arlington House. Another close friend of mine was Johnny Henderson, a tall, good-looking man who was wealthy but lost a major part of his wealth through gambling. He was able and intelligent, and he joined Marks & Spencer. Somehow or other Anna-Marie and Johnny had never met, despite Rosalie's and my attempts to bring them together. One Saturday, however, she came to lunch when he was due to come out with us in the evening and they met as she was leaving; they hit it off immediately and he persuaded her to join us. The following day Rosalie and I went to Le Touquet, where I was to play in the tennis tournament, partnered by Billie Yorke, who had been Wimbledon doubles champion. Even she couldn't carry me beyond the third round and we were beaten. Rosalie was expecting our first child and we had therefore just bought a house in St John's Wood, for which we paid a good deal of money. She had made me promise not to combine gambling at the casino with tennis. I rarely gambled but, having been knocked out of the tennis half-way through the week, I became bored. On the Saturday morning, a week after we had introduced Anna-Marie and Johnny to each other, they appeared in Le Touquet together. They told us they had been married that morning, but we didn't believe them until they produced their marriage lines. They said they had come to Le Touquet to tell us first, as without us they wouldn't have met. Of course we had a terrific party and then went to the casino; Rosalie said to me, 'Now remember, darling, you are not to gamble.' I asked Johnny how much loose change he had in his pocket. He had a few francs, which I put on number 13 on the routlette table. 13 came up; I won quite a sum. I left the maximum amount on 13 and it came up again; I was now winning a lot of money. I then moved it to 33–36 and 33 came up. By this time the table was crowded with sightseers. After each win, Rosalie collected a quarter of the winnings, but after a couple more bets I lost a little and stopped playing. I remember going to change the chips into cash and the cashier saying he didn't think I should walk back to the hotel with such a large sum of money. This was one of only two occasions in my life when I won a really substantial amount by gambling. In fact the celebration of Anna-Marie's and Johnny's wedding paid for about a quarter of the house I bought. I never saw Johnny after the war started. He joined the Welsh Guards and, tragically, was killed just before the war ended.

Our son, David, was born in March 1939. In July, prior to my going to Territorial Army camp, Rosalie and I went for a holiday to Cannes in the South of France. When we got back in August, I went straight to the annual camp and while I was there war broke out. The regiment was divided into four companies and each company into four troops. Each troop manned six searchlight and Lewis gun sites and was commanded by a second lieutenant. I had been commissioned as a second lieutenant in April 1939 and was in charge of a troop. The overall area covered by the regiment was many square miles; it formed part of the anti-aircraft defences of Hendon, which was one of London's major aerodromes in those days, and we stretched as far north as Colney Hatch, not far from Stevenage, famous then for its lunatic asylum.

During the nine months before Dunkirk, the period of the so-called

'Phoney War', there was little to do but drill and pass the rest of the time largely with spit and polish and having kit inspections; but we did some training. We expected parachute attacks and there were mock exercises to prepare for them. I distinguished myself when, in one such exercise, we captured the umpires but the parachutists got through. We were on duty twenty-four hours a day for six days a week and we had the seventh day off.

In October 1940 I was appointed regimental adjutant, a job for which I was unsuited. I had to move to regimental headquarters and was promoted to captain. I think my commanding officer, Lieutenant-Colonel Wilson, liked the wine, some of Father's, which I kept at my troop headquarters and thought I would bring it to regimental headquarters. An adjutant's job is largely administrative and requires considerable knowledge of military matters, especially of the *Manual of Military Law*. I knew little about such things; the colonel and I did not get on well; I didn't like him or my job and he did not like me either. I don't know how long he would have stood me, but it was never put to the test. We received orders to go overseas and joined our convoy in December 1940. We set sail for the Middle East on the SS *Tamaroa*, flagship of Rear Admiral Reyne, the convoy's commodore. He was a charming man and an able sailor; we got on well. I was appointed ship's adjutant, which meant I liaised with the *Tamaroa*'s captain in matters concerning the troops on board. Our voyage to the Middle East took seven weeks because we had to go round the Cape. The Mediterranean had been closed to us by the Axis powers. There were about twenty troop ships and cargo vessels in the convoy, with an escort consisting of the cruiser HMS *Ajax*, an aircraft carrier and two destroyers.

Prior to my going overseas there had been a personal attack on my family by the traitor Lord Haw-Haw, broadcasting from Germany. He announced that the family would be dealt with appropriately when Germany conquered Britain. The reader may wonder why a relatively obscure family like the Sieffs should have been included in the same category as those great British leaders, like Churchill, whom the Nazis said they would hang. The reasons were, perhaps, my family's public and outspoken criticism of the Nazi regime and the fact that Marks & Spencer, who prior to the Nazis coming to power had bought goods from Germany, ceased buying and said so publicly. Possibly the most important factor was my mother's visit to Germany on behalf of the Women's Zionist Organization in 1936. With the agreement of the German authorities she visited a number of the still existing Women's Zionist groups in various German towns to discuss how Jewish children could be brought out of Germany. She discovered as she left the towns that a number of the people whom she had met were being arrested. She was a woman of considerable moral and physical courage; she cancelled the rest of her tour and went to Berlin, where she sought an interview with Goebbels. She actually met his deputy and told him what she thought of the Germans and their behaviour − she spoke pretty good German. She then left Germany. The following week the leading Nazi newspaper, *Der Sturmer*, published a huge, grotesque caricature of Mother, who was a very good-looking woman. So, when I was ordered overseas, I arranged for Rosalie and David, who was nearly two years old, to go to the United States, where Rosalie's family lived.

The highlight of our voyage was the attack made on us by the heavily armed German battlecruiser, the *Admiral Hipper*, on Christmas Day 1940. The *Hipper* had been able to get into the Atlantic earlier in the month and had started to raid British shipping on the route to Sierra Leone. We were caught napping when she came for us out of the sun. I received instructions to order the troops below but, as ship's adjutant, was allowed to be on the bridge. We were lucky on the *Tamaroa*; the *Hipper*'s first salvo hit the ships each side of us and the second hit one of our escorts, the cruiser *Ajax*, knocking out a large part of her armaments and killing some twenty officers and men. The *Hipper* continued to attack but, instead of coming straight at us, turned to starboard and steamed parallel, firing at the convoy and escorting ships.

Later Rear Admiral Reyne explained to me that if the *Hipper* had continued on her course towards us she would have got among the convoy and probably, with her heavy armaments, have destroyed half of it because our own escort vessels would have been reluctant to fire into the middle of the convoy. As a result of keeping out of the convoy, she was effectively counter-attacked and eventually driven off.

The convoy had scattered, but later re-formed at Freetown. After six weeks at sea we spent three days at Durban, where we had a wonderful party, being entertained by a number of young ladies who were on or associated with the reception committee. Most of their husbands had joined the army and were already somewhere in the Middle East. I gave a dinner party with Rear Admiral Reyne as guest of honour.

We disembarked at Suez in February 1941. Two of our companies were stationed on the Suez Canal, one in Haifa and the other at Tobruk. I was stuck in the regimental headquarters in the desert about ten miles outside Cairo, while the CO was out for days at a time visiting the various units. I became little more than a post office and was bored stiff. One day a telephone call was put through to me; the telephonist explained that a Brigadier Hewer of GHQ Middle East had asked for the CO and, on being told he was away, asked to be put through to the adjutant.

The brigadier, who was in charge of Middle East movements, without preliminaries said, 'You have an officer called Sieff; I would like to see him at GHQ. I have a job I think he could do.'

'I think,' I replied, 'you should speak to my CO first, sir. He will be back in two days.'

'Why?' asked Brigadier Hewer. 'You're the adjutant, aren't you?'

'Yes, sir, but I am also Sieff.'

'Well,' said the brigadier, 'I am ordering you, as adjutant, to instruct Captain Sieff to report to me personally at GHQ in Cairo tomorrow morning' – and that was that.

When we met, he explained that there was a job available in movement control which he thought I would find interesting. It would entail a good deal of responsibility for the organization and supervision of transport in the western desert and liaising with other units and services, particularly the Navy. I wanted to get out of the adjutant's job and Rex Hewer made movement control sound so interesting that I accepted. I asked how he knew about me and he replied, 'You made a good impression on Rear Admiral Reyne and he put in a very favourable report on you when he got to Suez.' 'Oh,' I said, 'it must have been that party I gave for him in Durban.'

My commanding officer was furious on his return and accused me before other officers of going behind his back to get a job at GHQ. I said it wasn't true but, as he had accused me, he could verify it with a telephone call. He was silent. In view of the fact that he had made the accusation in front of other officers I asked him to retract it, which he did. I can't say that we parted the best of friends.

In Cairo periods of exciting activity were mixed with periods of boredom. However, the boredom was relieved by the Cicurel family, who owned the great department store in Cairo and the Oreco chain store group. Clemy, whom I first met in Paris before the war, gave me the freedom of their flat and introduced me to several Egyptians, a number of whom became good friends and taught me much about their country and culture.

General Wavell might well have won the North African campaign and driven the Italians out of Africa in 1941 had he not received instructions to divert a substantial number of troops and considerable armaments to Greece, which the Italians had invaded. The Germans joined the Italians, who were not making progress, then attacked and defeated our troops first in Greece and then in Crete. They cleared all Allied troops from Greece, Crete and the Aegean Islands, and increased their stranglehold on the Mediterranean. Meanwhile Rommel had arrived in North Africa and, with two German mechanized divisions, drove the weakened British troops back into Egypt. He reached the Egyptian frontier and all Wavell's gains were lost. In fact we were back where we started.

One night, when I was duty officer, a signal came in which read more or less like this:

From Prime Minister to Commander in Chief, Middle East: I pour gold in the form of men, arms and vehicles into the never satisfied maw of the Middle East.... There seem to be far too many men behind the lines for each fighting soldier. Please investigate and explain.

As a result of the Prime Minister's request a committee of investigation was set up, consisting of Major-General Abraham, Brigadier Kisch and Major Sieff (I had been promoted to major in September 1941). It turned out to be a fairly active committee; instead of sitting around, we went into the field and investigated the bureaucratic structure that had built up over previous years at brigade, divisional, corps headquarters and GHQ. We worked hard for three months and came to the conclusion that much work behind the lines was unnecessary. We recommended the elimination of a great deal of paper and administrative work and other activities which had little relevance to the military situation, so that many men became available for more important work, particularly in the field.

In June 1941 the newly created British 9th Army and the Free

French invaded Syria and the Lebanon, driving out the Vichy French. It was in this campaign that Moshe Dayan, later to become Israel's commander-in-chief and Defence Minister, acting as an advance scout for the British forces, lost his eye. I had been for a short time at British headquarters in Jerusalem, but was then transferred to the headquarters established in late 1941 in the Lebanon at Brouhmana, a beautiful little town in the mountains above Beirut.

Churchill had been trying hard to persuade the Turks, who were neutral at the time, to let him send them British troops and, more important, modern British equipment, since he was concerned that Turkey could well be invaded by the Germans and that the Axis powers would then squeeze us between the Germans in the north attacking our rear and the German/Italian armies in Africa attacking from the west. The Turks refused, politely saying that they would rely on their own forces. Churchill considered that the Turks were unlikely to side with the Russians, but would fight the Germans, if attacked. He also considered that, despite their fighting prowess, because of their poverty of modern arms they were likely to be defeated. It was then proposed that, if the Germans attacked, we should try to hold a line on the Bosphorus. I was told that I would have certain work to do in connection with the movement of men, weapons, ammunition and all other paraphernalia of war needed in such an operation, and would probably be based in Istanbul. By now it was early 1942. In order to make an estimate of what we might be able to do I needed information about the facilities which existed in the port area. This was not available locally and I was told that the best thing I could do was to go and see for myself. So I bought a blazer and some grey flannel trousers at Cicurels' store in Cairo and went as a tourist to Turkey. I spent a week in Ankara, where our main embassy was, and picked up what little information there was. I did, however, dine at the Karpiç, a restaurant where the Allies sat on one side of the room, the Turks in the middle, and the Axis powers on the other. I then made my way to Istanbul, where we had a sub-embassy. There I talked to the naval attaché, Lieutenant-Commander Wolfson. He couldn't give me the information I wanted about the port area, so I said I would go to look for myself. He advised me, 'You will be going into a prohibited area. If you're caught, there's nothing we can do for you.' 'Well,' I replied, 'I'm just a tourist having a look around.' To establish my *bona fides* as a tourist

I went to Santa Sophia, the famous cathedral of Crusader days, where I listened to a lecture on the Crusades being given by the eminent historian, Steven Runciman. He spoke in English and it was translated into Turkish. His lecture was magnificent: I was spellbound. (He told me years later at a party given by George Weidenfeld that he was then the professor of Byzantine art and history at Istanbul University.) After Santa Sophia I attempted to visit the prohibited area, but was caught by a policeman just as I was entering it. I tried to explain in English that I was a tourist; I don't know whether or not he believed me, but he let me go and went away. I set out in the opposite direction and entered another gate, apparently unguarded, and walked straight into the arms of the same policeman, who promptly – and understandably – arrested me. I was put in gaol that night near the docks. It was a frightening experience because there were rats in the cell. Earlier in the day I had seen the carcass of a horse half eaten by rats and, when I saw them scurrying around the cell, I decided that, however tired I was, I would not allow myself to fall asleep. The night proved to be one of the most exhausting I have ever experienced; I dozed off and woke to find the rats scurrying away from me when I moved. I was exhausted when, the following morning, I was hauled up before some form of magistrates' court. I was in civilian clothes, and I spoke no Turkish. I said I spoke no French either, and insisted on an interpreter. I explained that I was a tourist and had wandered into the port area out of curiosity. When they asked me what proof I had that I was a tourist, I proceeded to quote from Steven Runciman's brilliant talk at Santa Sophia. The result was that I was given twenty-four hours to get out of Turkey; if I did not I would risk imprisonment.

I don't know whether or not those concerned believed my story, but I had a feeling they really didn't want to press charges. Having experienced one night with rats in gaol, I determined to get out within the stipulated twenty-four hours. There was only one way for me – through the Turkish/Syrian border at the far south-eastern end of the country; the other way would take me into the hands of the Germans. So I boarded a crowded train and stood in the corridor for some twelve hours, arriving at the Syrian border with two hours to spare before my deadline expired. I was lucky.

By now Rommel had defeated us in North Africa and driven the British forces out of Cyrenaica back into Egypt. However, a decision was taken by Mr Churchill and the war cabinet greatly to reinforce the Middle East; throughout the summer our strength in North Africa was built up in preparation for 'Operation Crusader'. General Auchinleck had replaced General Wavell as Commander-in-Chief, Middle East, the latter becoming Commander-in-Chief, India; General Cunningham was put in command of the 8th Army. There was a British offensive in November, which made some progress, but was eventually stopped by Rommel. Generals Auchinleck and Cunningham decided they would resume the offensive in 1942, but before it could be put into operation Rommel attacked and pushed us back nearly to the Egyptian frontier again. Once more Rommel attacked when we were about to launch an offensive; again we were defeated, and retired three hundred miles east to El Alamein. But Rommel himself was by this time overstretched. His troops were exhausted, he was short of supplies, and he could not pursue us further into Egypt to inflict the final defeat.

Every now and then during this toing and froing I used to go up from Cairo to inspect the ports and various movement facilities recovered during an advance, though we never got much further than Benghazi in that period. David Curtis was port commandant at Benghazi; I first met him in Cairo after he had been driven out of Greece and Crete in 1941. He has been a close friend of mine ever since; he was an excellent officer and a good companion. On one occasion I remember spending the night with him in Benghazi. It was at a time when the Germans had air supremacy and, since ports were always one of the main targets, that night Benghazi was attacked. We walked outside the hut which served as the dock office. Planes were coming in low and we watched one caught in the searchlight. I said to David, 'Put your tin hat on. You may not think it necessary, but it's a good example to your men.' I certainly had mine on. So he followed suit; at that moment a bomb fell through the roof of the hut we had just vacated and blew it to pieces. Some fragments flew above our heads, wounding people a few yards away, but we escaped unscathed. I was lucky again. David Curtis and I were to have a long wartime association, leapfrogging each other across North Africa, in Sicily and then in Italy, during the period when I was concerned with ports and, on some occasions, beaches.

Some time before the battle of El Alamein I was a member of a party sent to investigate the possibility of building a road from West

Africa through Central Africa to the Sudan. The Mediterranean was closed to Allied shipping and virtually all reinforcements, stores and ammunition for the 8th Army and Middle East theatre had to go round the Cape. This meant risking submarine attacks and a very lengthy voyage, which tied up a huge tonnage of shipping. At that time the United States was sending by sea fighter planes broken down into parts. They went first to Takoradi in West Africa; the planes were then assembled and flown across Central Africa to the Sudan, to reinforce the Allies in the Middle East. Because the range of these fighter planes was limited, airfields had been hacked out of the jungle at regular distances to provide refuelling facilities on their flight through Central Africa. Roosevelt and his advisers now conceived the idea of building a road, with the intention that cargo and troop ships would discharge at West African ports and that men, ammunition and stores would proceed through Central Africa to the Middle Eastern theatre. This would save much shipping for use in other war zones and should save time. It was decided that a reconnaissance party should examine this project. About six of us, under the command of Group Captain Whitney-Straight, were to fly in a Hudson fitted with long-range fuel tanks from the battle area in Egypt to Lagos in Nigeria. We had a magnificent pilot, but he had never flown this particular route before — in fact I'm not sure whether anybody had — and when we ran into head winds we didn't have enough fuel to reach Lagos. When the fuel was running very low the pilot flew along a single-track railway line and eventually we were lucky to find and land at a modest airfield at Kano, six hundred miles from our destination. We then refuelled and flew on to Lagos, where we discussed the proposal for the road with the military and civilian authorities there; we then flew back over the route the fighter planes used from West Africa to the Middle Eastern theatre. Whenever we landed in those primitive airfields in the middle of the jungle a native fire brigade appeared, dressed only in loin cloths and magnificent plumed helmets. We came to the conclusion that the scheme was not worthwhile because of the amount of fuel required, just to transport men and stores through Central Africa to the Middle Eastern theatre and then to return the trucks for further loads. I don't know whether we reached the right conclusion, but a few months later, after the Axis powers were driven from North Africa, the Mediterranean was open to our shipping.

The Middle East was now commanded by Alexander, the 8th Army by Montgomery. At the end of October Montgomery successfully counter-attacked Rommel and defeated him in the famous battle of El Alamein. This was the beginning of the end. It had been agreed that I should go forward with the 8th Army to open the port of Tripoli in Libya if and when we captured it. I took with me a reconnaissance party of about twelve people, following just behind the attacking troops; we were ordered to keep out of the battle itself. We set out with a car and two 30-cwt trucks, but eventually in the many weeks' campaign one truck became unserviceable and we had to crowd into the other. I used to post sentries at night in case of attack or sudden redeployment. One night the sentry on duty fell asleep; in the morning the battle had moved away and we didn't know whether our troops had advanced or fallen back. We saw a small convoy a mile or two off across the desert. We did not know whether it was ours or the enemy's but decided, as we were running out of petrol, to get near it in our one truck. It turned out to be an RASC unit taking supplies to the New Zealand Division and, to my surprise and pleasure, it was commanded by my cousin, Gabriel Sacher, the first member of my family I had seen for nearly three years. He gave us petrol and we gave him some stale loaves of bread, about fifteen days old.

Army rations in the desert were generally poor and I didn't have available any of what I called morale boosters. I had by then learned that the best boosters for people, particularly after a hard day's work or a night of heavy bombing, were a scotch whisky for those who drank and Cadbury's milk chocolate for those who didn't. I had made an arrangement with some friends back at GHQ Cairo that whenever a North Africa supply convoy sailed to a port I was in it would bring with it a case half full of scotch, half of chocolate, the case being labelled 'Medical Stores for Major Sieff' and entered on the ship's manifest as such. So often did this happen that somebody drew it to the attention of Brigadier Richards, the director of ordnance services in Cairo, whose only comment was: 'That fellow Sieff must be the sickest man the British army has ever had on active service.'

After a number of vicissitudes, Tripoli was captured by the Allies on 23 January 1943. The main body of troops of the companies to work the docks came twenty-four hours behind, commanded by Major George Palmer, an officer of much ability, who was invaluable to me in working the port over the next few weeks. Initially the 51st Highland Division helped to work and clear the port, followed by the New Zealand Division; both were great fighting divisions, though the New Zealanders didn't think that work on the quays should be taken too seriously and I had quite a few problems with them. We were subject to nightly air attacks, but did our best to work the port twenty-four hours a day. Among the stores that we unloaded were bombs, various types of ammunition, and drums of high-octane aviation fuel. A number of the New Zealanders would insist on smoking while working at night, though this was forbidden, and they would do this even when handling the high-octane fuel. I put a number of the men on charges but these were subsequently withdrawn on the request (instruction really) of General Freyberg, the famous fighting commander of the New Zealand Division.

It was at Tripoli that I learned how important it was for morale and for good human relations for those in charge to be seen around at all hours of the day and night, particularly at night, encouraging those who were doing the physical, repetitive and often dangerous jobs. It was never more important than when the troops working in the harbour were under air attack. Our ack-ack defences were good, but the enemy airforce attacked Tripoli harbour almost every night. This didn't improve its condition, which was bad enough when we captured it, so bad in fact that it took at least six weeks to get it into full working order. Winston Churchill was to visit Tripoli to review the victorious 8th Army and tour the city and port on 3 and 4 February. General Robertson had been appointed general officer commanding Tripoli after its capture. Before Churchill's visit he came to see me and said, 'The Prime Minister might like to go around the port and see something of the nearby city area and you, Marcus, will accompany him.' He then asked if I was confident that security was total.

'No,' I said, 'it's not. There are tens of thousands of Italians wandering around and so far as the Prime Minister personally is concerned he is not safe.'

'Well, the Prime Minister likes to wander around. If he wants to see places where you are not certain about the security, stop him.'

'Sir,' I replied, 'I am a major, you are a general — you should stop him.'

Subsequently Mr Churchill took the victory parade and then inspected the port. A few minutes before he was due to arrive, one of my officers informed me, 'There are three gentlemen in civilian clothes who wish to see the Prime Minister.' 'Who are they?' I asked. He didn't know. As the Prime Minister was just arriving I said, 'I can't deal with them now; to be on the safe side lock them up.' I went to meet the Prime Minister, who was in a good mood after his review of the victorious 8th Army. He was complimentary about the speed with which the port was being put into working condition, despite the aerial bombardments. While I was flattered and delighted with what he said, I pointed out we had a lot to do to get the port working to anything like one hundred per cent and my people were weary. He said, 'Sieff, tell your men they are not unloading stores, they are unloading history.' I did so and the speed of unloading increased by 20%.

After he had gone, the officer who had come to me just before his visit asked what he should do with the men he had locked up.

'What men?' I asked.

'The ones you told me to lock up,' he replied, 'just before the Prime Minister arrived.'

I said, 'Find out who they are and come and tell me.' He returned in a few minutes to say that they were the leaders of the Moslem, Christian and Jewish communities of Tripoli who had come to pay their respect to the great Prime Minister. 'Bring them here,' I responded, 'and react sensibly to whatever I say.' When the three civilians were brought in, I made fulsome apologies through an interpreter and pointed in assumed fury at my subaltern, saying, 'That man is an idiot and he will be severely punished.' I assured them that their messages of goodwill would be passed to the Prime Minister in the immediate future. I don't think they were satisfied, but they went away somewhat mollified.

I had established my headquarters in the palatial residence of the late Air Marshal Balbo, who was the last Italian Governor of Libya. The bathroom had magnificent marble floors, a huge and splendid bath with gold or gold-plated taps – in fact, it had everything except water. We didn't get the water running while I was there. My boss, Brigadier Bagnall-Wild, was at rear 8th Army headquarters about six miles from Tripoli. I used to hold nightly meetings in my port headquarters; among those regularly present were the naval officer-in-charge, who was a captain, Major George Palmer, the officer in charge of the dock workers, a transportation officer, the ordnance officer and my assistant. These meetings were to review our performance of the previous twenty-four hours and see if it was necessary to make any changes in the plan for the following twenty-four hours.

Frequently Brigadier Bagnall-Wild and David Curtis attended these meetings, since it was intended that David should go forward to open the ports of Gabes and Sfax in Tunisia when they were captured. When Gabes was on the point of capture, I remember Bagnall-Wild warning David, who was leaving at first light the following morning, 'There will be many hazards. It will be dangerous, but I can rely on you – yours is the glory, yours is the honour. I shall follow after.' This sounded like leading from the rear, but the brigadier could not understand why we laughed. In fact Brigadier Bagnall-Wild was a courageous man who did not have a reputation for following!

General Sir Brian Robertson was now in overall command of the military administration in Libya and the 8th Army was facing the Germans in Tunisia, who had established their position on the Mareth line. Either he or another senior officer informed me that it was Montgomery's belief that, if Rommel attacked before the end of February, we should have to fall back. This would mean not only giving up Tripoli but also possibly Benghazi as well and going right back to the Egyptian frontier. If, however, Rommel didn't attack until the end of the first week in March, we could probably hold our own. An attack after 12 March meant that we should probably win. Montgomery and his planners based their assumption on the then order of battle, that is the estimated number of men, guns, armour and ammunition he would have available at the Mareth line in Tunisia on the respective dates. Like everybody else, I was concerned with what had become the pattern of the desert war: advance soon to be followed by retreat; a thrust forward only to be followed by being pushed right back. It seemed to me essential that this pattern be terminated, that this time we should not have to retreat but should instead continue our advance until final victory in Africa was achieved. The problem generally was that, when we had made an advance in the past, we had not been able quickly to bring up enough men and materials to the new forward positions to repel an enemy counter-attack. The solution, I decided, was to devise a means of getting far greater deliveries of men and equipment to the new front, and getting them there faster. To do so at this point in the campaign would be demanding, since the line of communication to Mareth from Tripoli was largely along a single road through the desert with soft sand on either side. I decided to go and see for myself what could be done. On my journey to the front in Tunisia I took an anti-aircraft gunner, a signals officer and an engineer. We found along the desert road three places of hardstanding where vehicles could be parked to one side, but apart from these it was a sea of sand. I was beginning to work out a method by which we could accomplish our objective. I wondered whether we could send the many thin-skinned (non-armoured) vehicles through at full speed during the day and the fewer heavy-armoured vehicles at night with headlights on to make as good speed as possible. We had air superiority.

The engineering officer assured me that the hardstanding would take quite a large number of vehicles if, for one reason or another, they broke down or were going too slowly. The signals officer told me he could easily fix up a field telephone line from Tripoli to the front with instruments at each of the hardstanding places. The gunner officer said we could warn vehicles at night to switch off their lights before an imminent air attack by stationing at intervals ack-ack guns that would fire a shell with a coloured light. I suggested subsequently to those concerned that any vehicle which broke down on the road and could not make it to the hardstandings should be pushed into the sand and recovered later if possible; this was agreed.

On my return, I decided to put my plan into operation, thus speeding up the order of battle so that Montgomery would have his troops and armaments earlier than previously envisaged. I went to rear 8th Army to see Brigadier Bagnall-Wild, who approved my plan. However, when I got back to my headquarters at Tripoli, he sent for me again and told me he had been considering it with a senior colleague, who was also a movements officer and who thought my plan was impracticable. 'But that officer,' I said, 'hasn't been up to the Mareth line. How can he advise without going to see?' To which the brigadier replied, 'I have listened to both your arguments. Both of you have made good points and when I'm not sure I take the advice of the more senior of my officers. He is senior to you, so we go back to the old order of battle.' At this I made out, quite untruthfully, that I had given the orders for the movement to start and couldn't stop it. I left his caravan in a temper and he called me back. 'When my officers leave me they salute,' he said, and I took the hint. Back in

Tripoli once more I made sure the movement of troops got under way and confirmed to Brigadier Bagnall-Wild it couldn't be stopped.

I then started off at the crack of dawn for Mareth. The first unit we moved up was the New Zealand Division. When I got to the first hardstanding, there were four Sherman tanks and a New Zealand major; my subaltern – I had stationed a subaltern on each hardstanding along the road – heaved a sigh of relief.

'What's the trouble?' I asked.

The New Zealand major, very angry, said, 'These are General Freyberg's battle tanks and they have been stopped.'

'Quite rightly,' I replied. 'The thin-skinned vehicles of your division go through first and the armoured vehicles tonight.'

'Yes,' he retorted, 'I understand, but you don't seem to. These are General Freyberg's battle tanks and they must go up now. He has gone on ahead and his battle tanks always go with him.'

'They can't, they will delay the other vehicles.'

He repeated, 'You don't understand. These are the general's battle tanks.'

'If you wish to make use of this telephone,' I said, 'you may do so and speak to whom you like but these are my orders and I command movement on this road. I shall say that you are attempting to disobey my orders.'

With bad grace the major gave up his attempt. After going up to the line I returned and realized the movement was very successful, far faster than I had anticipated. What I had thought would take at least thirty hours had been achieved in only eighteen.

However, I found that in an enemy air attack the quarters of one of my dock companies had received a direct hit. The company had just returned from work and gone to sleep. A large number of men were killed and wounded, including most of the officers and senior NCOs; they had been blown to pieces. In the next twenty-four hours I had the dreadful experience of attending a mass burial, because the victims had been so horribly mutilated that most could not be identified; it was heartbreaking.

Over the next few days the speed of movement of troops, guns, vehicles and stores of all kinds exceeded our most optimistic expectations. Shortly before Rommel attacked at Medinine on 6 March we were able to send up two regiments of field guns which had not been scheduled to move until days later, and then for good measure, because Montgomery liked to have as much stores and equipment of all kinds as possible when launching an attack, some hundreds of heavy trucks loaded with additional stores. The result was that, when the Germans attacked, the 8th Army was far better prepared to stand up to the onslaught than Rommel had anticipated and the Germans were heavily defeated; they suffered several thousand casualties and lost one hundred tanks. Our casualties were minimal; in fact, Montgomery cabled Sir Alan Brooke, chief of the general staff, the day after the battle: 'I LOST NO TANKS AND MY CASUALTIES IN KILLED AND WOUNDED WERE ONLY 130.'

This defeat of Rommel was the beginning of the final phase of the destruction and capture of the German forces in North Africa. However, Brigadier Bagnall-Wild had not been too happy a few days before the Medinine battle with my changing the order of battle, despite his original agreement. He rightly harboured the suspicion that I could have gone back to the first plan and had misled him in saying I could not. He had me before him and started a kind of semi-official enquiry into my activities. He implied that I had disobeyed orders and some form of disciplinary action would follow. This 'enquiry' started just as Rommel attacked. After our victory General Robertson forwarded me a signal from General Montgomery which read as follows:

TO: COMMAND TRIPBASE FOR MOVEMENTS (R) REAR ARMY
FROM: MAIN H.Q. EIGHTH ARMY

PLEASE CONVEY TO MOVEMENT STAFF AND PERSONNEL MY SINCERE THANKS FOR THEIR GREAT EFFORTS IN DEALING WITH THE VARIOUS FORMATIONS WHICH HAVE BEEN MOVED UP DURING THE LAST FEW DAYS. THEY CAN WELL FEEL THAT THEY HAVE CONTRIBUTED IN NO SMALL WAY TO ROMMEL'S LATEST DEFEAT.

GENERAL MONTGOMERY.

I was in command of the movement group concerned. It was for these 'efforts' that the court of enquiry had been established. I gave the signal to Bagnall-Wild, who read it and remarked, 'Does change things a bit, doesn't it?' The enquiry was adjourned; I am still waiting for it.

CHAPTER FIVE

THE war in Africa ended on 12 May 1943 with the surrender of the Germans in Tunisia. I was recalled to GHQ Cairo and promoted to Lieutenant-Colonel. There a senior officer told me that the British 8th Army under General Montgomery and the American 7th Army under General Patton would invade Sicily. I was appointed AQMG (M) 8th Army with increased responsibilities. It was at this time that I first met David Belchem, the youngest general in the British army, Montgomery's chief of operations. We got on well, but it surprised me to read in his book about both the desert campaign and the Sicily invasion, *All in the Day's March*, published thirty-four years later, that I was considered to be responsible for developing the new system of what was called 'build-up control', to be used both in the Mediterranean and later in Europe, which he claimed was an improved system of movements in both static and mobile battle conditions.

After a week's leave I was told the invasion was to be launched in fourteen days' time by a combined British-American group under the command of General Alexander. My first role would be to open the port of Syracuse, but in the event of Syracuse holding out I would be expected to start operating from the beach.

In the week before the 8th Army set sail for the Sicily invasion a full-scale rehearsal was to be carried out in the Gulf of Aqaba, the long, narrow stretch of water leading off the north-west corner of the Red Sea. The order that I was to be the chief shore umpire came as a surprise; I knew a little about assault by land, but nothing of assault from the sea and of the key craft to be used in it, such as the DUKWs, which would carry troops from the ships to the shore and then run on to the beach, and the LSTs (tank landing ships), common enough nowadays but novel then, which could move armour, guns, stores and troops on to the shore.

I embarked for the rehearsal at Suez on the *Duchess of Richmond*, a liner converted into a troop ship but retaining some limited elements of her former luxurious accommodation. I was quartered with about twenty junior officers in a cramped space crowded with hammocks. However, I learned that Brigadier Hewer was not coming aboard until the next morning and that he had a suite on the ship, so I helped myself to a bed in his cabin for the night. When I reported to him the next day, he inquired, 'Is your accommodation all right, Marcus?'

I said, 'No, sir, it's terribly crowded, with twenty junior officers sleeping in hammocks.'

'Well,' he said, 'why didn't you use my cabin last night?'

I replied, 'Well, actually, sir, I did.'

'Yes,' he said, 'I know. You left your pyjamas behind. All right, you'd better move back in.'

Twenty large ships now moved up the Gulf of Aqaba; the 4th Indian Division represented the enemy and was stationed between Aqaba and what is now the town of Eilat in Israel, which did not then exist. As soon as the ships were in position the assault was launched. It went well; the enemy, the 4th Indian Division, was soon overwhelmed, so speedily that though the assault was a success, the rehearsal was a failure, partly due to me. Since I was the chief umpire I had a charmed life, and could pass through the fields of dummy mines unscathed when they exploded. A number of attacking troops noted this and followed me through, taking a sector of the defences by surprise. The 4th Indian Division was not pleased. The convoy then returned to the Suez Canal; the great majority of the troops were not allowed to disembark in case they leaked anything about the rehearsal, while a few of us went back to GHQ for further briefing, prior to embarking for the Sicily attack.

Participation in the Sicily invasion was a new experience for me in two respects: first, it was an assault on a large and concentrated scale; second, it was by sea. It was essential to get the port of Syracuse operating as soon as possible and I had to decide whether to accept an invitation to go in on a cruiser or on one of the troop ships. As the captain of the cruiser, who thought he would be there first, said he could only find accommodation on the voyage from Egypt for me and three others, instead of the fifteen I had in my advance reconnaissance party, I decided to go in on one of the troop ships. I was able to land with the men of the 5th Division a few miles south of Syracuse. My experience of getting from the troop ship to the beach was not a pleasant one. The Sicily invasion was the first, so far as I know, in which we used substantial numbers of planes towing gliders full of assault troops. Due to lack of experience, the pilots of the planes in some cases cast off the troop-filled gliders too far away from the beach (gliding was not such a well-practised sport then as it is today) and they crashed into the sea, with many casualties. As we went from the ship to the assault on the beach there was nothing we could do for the unfortunate troops and crews from the crashed gliders, some of whom were badly injured and struggling in the water. The beach was being subjected to enemy fire but we crossed it quickly; my reconnaissance party was soon taking shelter in a vineyard.

Lucky that we were: within a few minutes the beaches were attacked by German dive-bombers, a few bombs landing in the vineyard. I had just decided that I would get my men to better cover when a stick of bombs exploded near us. We all flung ourselves to the ground and I suppose at such a moment one's hands clench as they touch the soil. I had put my hand on something that was moving and sinuous; it was a snake, which was as frightened as I. I took my hand away and it slithered off. I am frightened of bombs, but not so frightened as I am of snakes, so I rushed forward through the vineyard on to a ridge of higher ground; by now the bombers had gone. We pushed on another couple of hundred yards, our own troops dealing with the Italians who had been firing at us. Suddenly I realized that in throwing myself to the ground, then jumping up after my meeting with the snake, I had dropped a bottle of Scotch. I had no intention of going back anywhere near the snake, but one of my men, hearing about the Scotch, went back to recover it — for which his colleagues blessed him heartily that night.

Meanwhile our assault gathered momentum, the Italians retreated and we were in Syracuse the evening of D-Day. When the cruiser which had offered me a lift came into the port the next morning I was standing on the quay to greet its captain. The 8th Army landed just south of Syracuse in the south-eastern part of Sicily; the American 7th Army, under General Patton, some thirty miles away at Gela on the south-western coast. The success and speed of the first stage of the invasion resulted in Syracuse port being in fairly good shape. We got it into working condition quickly and started to unload ships. Though we were subject to regular air attacks, our defences were adequate.

The 8th Army under Montgomery began to advance towards Catania. At this time Brigadier Miles Graham came to see me and said, 'Marcus, the army commander wants you to know the plan. He will advance up the east coast, capturing Catania, Messina and Milazzo, and then turn westwards, eventually taking Palermo on the north-west point.'

'Sir,' I asked, 'can you please tell me what General Patton and the American 7th Army will be doing?'

He replied, 'They will hold our left flank while we advance.'

Somehow or other I don't think Patton's temperament and capabilities were fully appreciated at that time by the 8th Army Commander.

The 8th Army's initial and fairly rapid advance up the east coast was halted outside Taormina, where German batteries of 88 mm guns commanded the road and we became bogged down. If we couldn't dislodge the Germans, the 8th Army might have to work their way around the enemy by going inland, a much more difficult task.

Miles Graham came to see me and said, 'We have got to destroy those German batteries. Marcus, can you dig out all the 25-pounder ammunition in the convoy you are now unloading?'

'I can get you the 25-pounder shells out, sir', I replied, 'but you must realize that, if I do this, it can have a serious effect on the other aspects of your plan. If we have to go from ship to ship digging out odd lots of 25-pounder shells and not fully unloading one ship at a time, the rate at which we shall discharge stores of all types could fall by fifty per cent, and ships will be held here much longer, at the risk of being hit by bombs. So, if I dig out the 25-pounder shells, when you have blasted out the German gun positions you will have far fewer stores with which to continue the assault up north and, therefore, will have to do so with many fewer men.'

'Very well,' he said, 'I shall discuss it at army HQ and let you know our decision. Carry on as you are for the time being.'

Knowing that General Patton was by now advancing with dramatic speed up the west coast, I asked innocently, 'By the way, sir, what's happening now to General Patton? Is he still holding our left flank?' To which Graham replied, 'We don't discuss General Patton and his movements at army headquarters these days if we can avoid it.'

Eventually we drove back the Germans outside Taormina and began to advance up to Messina, while General Patton continued with ever-increasing speed up the west coast, captured Palermo and swung eastwards towards Milazzo. The Germans, recognizing the risk of being trapped between the two armies, began to evacuate

Sicily. On 25 July Mussolini was overthrown, and the Allies completed the occupation of Sicily on 17 August; we began the invasion of the Italian mainland on 3 September.

The port of Syracuse was still in relatively good condition. However, before evacuating the town, the Germans had emptied the aviation fuel tanks into the harbour. The walls of the rather primitive quays were porous and the petrol, pushed about by the tides and winds, soaked into them. From time to time there would be an outburst of fire from the surface of the quay, into which the petrol had soaked, but fortunately there were few casualties. However, there was one lively moment when I was carrying out one of my normal port inspections. I had just come on to a quay alongside which there was a ship from which we were unloading ammunition. There was a lot of ammunition on the quay. Suddenly, near where I was standing, there was a burst of flames; they spread pretty quickly over a wide area. The fire wasn't continuous; it would suddenly go out and then burst through again in the same area. The ship from which the shells were being unloaded also contained bombs and aviation fuel; it was clear that, if the ship caught fire, there would be an explosion which would cause much damage and probably many casualties. The lieutenant in charge of the port ordnance section, John Search, a Lancashire man, was on the quay with his men. He and I started to set an example by picking up the shells and heaving them into the sea. The shells became hotter and hotter. Search's men followed his example and worked exceedingly well, but I think the skin on my hands was thinner than that of Search's and his team and, as the shells got hotter, I decided to stand around to give moral encouragement while the others continued the work. It was amazing that none of the shells exploded before, eventually, the flames died down.

Search had set a marvellous example and he and his men had performed outstandingly well; if things had gone wrong, it could have been a severe setback affecting the forward movement of the 8th Army, so I decided to recommend Lieutenant Search for an immediate award. The person making such a recommendation has to state how he knows about the action he is describing. I wrote, 'Throughout the entire action Lieutenant Search never left my side.' I phrased this carefully, reflecting that possibly I might, as well as getting an award for Lieutenant Search, get something for myself. He got an immediate award of the George Medal; I got my just deserts – nothing. However, I was subsequently awarded the military OBE for my performance in Syracuse, with a flattering citation.

Discussions were going on at the top level among the Allies about what should be their next move. The American chief of staff didn't think that an assault on Italy would put direct pressure on the Germans; he urged an assault across the English Channel. But the situation changed when, on 25 July, news came that Mussolini had been captured, his regime had been brought down, and the King of Italy, with the support of the majority of the Grand Council and the leaders of the Fascist party, had charged Marshal Badoglio with the duty of forming a new cabinet of service chiefs and civil servants. One British and one American staff officer met the Italian General Castellano in Lisbon to make preparations for drawing up an armistice agreement, but it was clear that the Italians would not have the nerve to sign unless we agreed to make landings on the mainland. The armistice was signed on 3 September in an olive grove near Syracuse.

Meanwhile I had been in charge of Messina with instructions, when we crossed the Straits, to take over Reggio di Calabria. Montgomery assembled some hundreds of heavy and medium guns in the hills above Messina, from where Reggio di Calabria was heavily shelled. I had been ordered to wait for thirty-six hours before crossing, so I stood around on the quays at Messina while the shells whistled by overhead as though the heavens were full of express trains. Montgomery, if he had known, could have saved his fire because there was little or no resistance on the mainland; the Germans had already left. When we crossed we were greeted by the local town band. Five days later the American 5th Army, under General Mark Clark, landed at Salerno just south of Naples. My orders were somewhat confused; there were no enemy troops in Reggio, in fact there was no enemy within a considerable distance, as they had retreated up the heel of Italy. At the same time General Alexander was convinced that the Italian port of Taranto could be captured if he landed the British 1st Airborne Division there. Since there was no normal transport available either by sea or air, six thousand troops were put on British warships and, on the day of the Salerno landing, the Royal Navy steamed into the harbour. They put them ashore unopposed, although one of our cruisers struck a mine and was lost.

I was ordered to go to Taranto as quickly as possible to open the port. One of our main strategic objectives was the capture of the Foggia airfields, some one hundred and twenty miles up the east coast of Italy, and two hundred miles north of Reggio. The plan was to mount from there vast air raids (I heard mention of a thousand-bomber force) on the Rumanian oil wells, including the great oil centre of Ploesti, which was a major source of German fuel. Our planes would then fly on to land in Russian-occupied territory. These oil wells were out of range of bombers based in Britain. I was given a jeep and a batman and started the journey to Taranto. We really didn't know where the Germans were and proceeded cautiously. I remember when we got to the town of Crotone, a third of the way there, the German garrison had fled but had left behind all their drink and a large number of young ladies. We had a few drinks but left the girls alone — time was too short — and continued our drive northwards. On the second night we had to sleep in a field; there were no signs of human beings or habitation. I awoke with a start, not sure whether it was a German or Italian who had woken me and was standing over me. I was frightened and jumped up, whereupon the Italian cow that had started to lick my face became even more startled and ran off.

We reached Taranto on the third night. I received orders to go on to Brindisi, across the heel of Italy, and open up that port. The Italian capitulation had not been announced; that was to come later, on 8 September. One of the peace terms stated that how the Italians were to be treated would depend to some degree on what assistance they gave the Allies in the war against their former partner. This condition much affected my activities in Brindisi.

On arrival there I found the King, the court, the government and many Italian military leaders, together with thousands of Italian sailors and other troops. Meanwhile the Germans had captured Rome and Mussolini had been freed. My job was to get Brindisi operating as a supply port for the 8th Army, which was working its way up the centre of Italy. The Italian sailors who were to assist me belonged to the Ionian fleet, commanded by Admiral Rubartelli. I dealt with his commodore, whose appearance was unforgettable; he looked like a particularly malevolent Charles Laughton in his Quasimodo role. In order to communicate with my labour force of Italian sailors I had acquired as interpreter a dynamic merchant captain from Trieste who, despite the fact that he had been sunk twice by the British, admired us and disliked both the Italians and the Germans. I think he was a member of the Croatian element in Trieste, but his Italian was perfect and his English excellent. I am sure he took considerable licence in translating my English to the Italians and much exaggerated my authority.

We had no forces in Brindisi; initially, in fact, I was one of the most senior Allied officers there apart from General Mason-MacFarlane, who was working on the terms of the co-belligerency treaty with the Italians. It was clear to the Italians that, while there were tens of thousands of their own people there—not to mention the German units some thirty miles to the north—the active Anglo-American force at that moment in Brindisi consisted largely of my batman-driver, my Croatian interpreter and myself. (There were in fact a few others, including the crews of the merchant vessels from which we began to unload stores for the Foggia airfields build-up.) When they realized this the Italians consistently failed to carry out my orders. The number of men I had asked for didn't arrive or arrived at the wrong place; the air-raid alarm was set off frequently, stopping all work, though there was no enemy plane in sight. After several days of this I became convinced that it was deliberate sabotage and made an appointment for the following day to see Admiral Rubartelli.

That evening at about eight o'clock the air-raid warning sounded; there was no sign or sound of an aircraft, no anti-aircraft fire, all was quiet. It was a hot night and I had been working hard all day; I was dirty, sweaty, wearing just shorts, a shirt and shoes. I lost my temper, jumped in the jeep and told my driver to drive to Admiral Rubartelli's headquarters near the King's residence and the government offices in a hilltop castle. We drove to the outskirts of the town; when we reached the main gate to the headquarters area we were stopped by a sentry, who ordered us to dim our lights. 'Tell him to go to hell,' I told my interpreter, 'I'm in charge in this town. He's to take me to wherever Admiral Rubartelli is.' My co-operative Croat interpreter translated this with much delight. We were escorted to the Admiral's office, where there was only a sentry. He informed us that the Admiral was in the air-raid shelter, which was situated below ground. I was growing increasingly annoyed, and with my Croat I went down to the shelter.

It was well furnished, a kind of underground luxury hotel. The Admiral and his staff, some twelve of them, were dressed in white uniforms with small silver daggers at their belts; they were having a drink. Conversation ceased on my entry as all heads turned to gaze at this apparition in dirty khaki shorts. The Admiral inquired, rather curtly, 'What can I do for you, Colonel?' I told him that the urgent work of the Allies, with whom he was now co-belligerent and therefore supposed to be co-operating, was being held up so drastically that I suspected sabotage. I gave him my reasons and told him he was failing to implement the terms of the armistice. The Admiral's attitude changed; he said those responsible would be brought to justice; I think my interpreter said he would have them shot or severely punished. I said to the interpreter, 'Tell him I don't want anybody punished. All I want is the men at the right place at the right time. Tell the Admiral also that I am taking over control of the air-raid warning system.' In fact I wouldn't have had any idea how to deal with it. At that moment the Charles Laughton-like Commodore made a loud remark. I said to the Croat, 'Translate that, please.' He interpreted: 'The Commodore says it is not right for Italian sailors to work on the quays; they are sailors and should be at sea and that is why they don't carry out orders and work properly on land.' I lost my temper and said, 'Tell the Commodore that the Italians are no good at sea, so if they can't work on land they're going to have a hell of a time trying to earn a living.' I wasn't proud of that remark afterwards; it was a result of my temper and was, to put it mildly, lacking in tact.

The reaction was instant. They were sailors; black looks crossed their faces and a number of them put their hands on their little daggers. 'I have said what I want to say,' I told the interpreter, 'and we are now going to leave.' I hesitated for a few seconds, turned round and, presenting my back to the Italians, wondered whether it would not be safer, though less dignified, to back out. The interpreter said something and we walked out quickly side by side.

That night I sent a signal to 15th Army Group back at Algiers saying that I suspected sabotage and was making little progress. The next day General Robertson flew in; I gave a resumé of the situation. Brian Robertson said, 'Arrest the Commodore.'

'How do I arrest the Commodore, sir, when there are about thirty thousand Italian troops in this town and I've got one British other rank and an Italian interpreter?'

Brian Robertson replied, 'Don't do anything. Leave it to us.'

They immediately arranged for the town to be garrisoned by a battalion of crack Indian troops, and later the Commodore was indeed arrested. By this time I had left Brindisi for Bari, a much larger port, fifty miles to the north and half-way to Foggia. Our progress to Bari meant that from there we would be better able to supply the 8th Army, who were continuing their advance up the centre of Italy; meanwhile the Germans still in the Naples area considered the 8th Army advance a potential threat to their rear and retreated to the north.

Bari was a large port in fairly good condition. I found David Curtis waiting there to take over Barletta, a smaller port some miles to the north. I was given plenty of support and we soon had Bari working well. As well as being the supply base for the army's advance it was also to be the main port of entry for the Foggia build-up and the attack on the Rumanian oilfields. There were some enemy air-raids, but they were few and not very effective. I think their main effort was devoted to attacking the American 5th and the British 8th Armies. Meanwhile GHQ was anxious that we should press on with our unloading of stores in order that we could capture Foggia as soon as possible. Convoys came in thick and fast and the port became congested. I was in charge of port security, but the safety of the ships once there was the responsibility of the naval officer-in-charge, a naval captain. He was a brave man, highly decorated, but because he was fixed in his views it was not easy to have a discussion with him. I asked him if he could do something to ease the pressure on Bari by dispersing the ships to some of the smaller ports like Barletta, which was capable of taking several ships. He said, 'No.' I knew what I was talking about because I had visited Barletta, which was to be used for an end-on run. This meant embarking troops there who would be landed behind enemy lines further up the coast to attack them in the rear. These smaller ports were also used for supplying our special forces and the guerrillas in Yugoslavia.

There were at this period twenty-six large cargo ships in Bari and we could unload only about six or seven at a time. Once again I asked the naval officer-in-charge whether we couldn't ease the congestion by dispersing some of the waiting ships, but again he refused.

I went once more to Barletta because General Alexander, commander-in-chief of 15th Army Group, wanted to visit it. He arrived with a driver, an ADC and another obviously very senior officer. I took them around the port and I remember the other senior officer saying, 'Looks like a remarkable place for a rat hunt.' He was quite right; Barletta was overrun with rats. I still didn't know who this senior officer was, nor did I know his rank because I failed to recognize his badges. It was only when we were half-way round the port that General Alexander turned to me and said, 'Have you met Field-Marshal Gort?' I said, 'No, sir, I've never met a field-marshal before and never seen a field-marshal's badges of rank.'

A few days later I was ordered to Cairo. The reason was that the Sextant Conference, between Churchill, Roosevelt and Chiang Kai-shek, was to open there on 23 November. Its purpose was to outline to the generalissimo the programme of operations proposed for South East Asia, but Churchill and Roosevelt held other meetings on the side to discuss operations in Europe and the Mediterranean. The Americans were pressing for all available shipping, especially landing craft, to be sent to British waters in preparation for the cross-channel invasion, which at this time was thought to be more imminent than it turned out to be. Churchill was urging that shipping in the Mediterranean should not be depleted until the whole of the Mediterranean area was under our control.

I spent about a week in Cairo. My main job was to be in attendance at certain meetings. I was at one when Lord Leathers, Minister of War Transport in the war cabinet, was present. He was particularly interested in my views about the use of shipping. I described the way in which it was frequently wasted in the Mediterranean owing to poor planning. When Lord Leathers encouraged me to be more frank I let myself go and obviously upset a number of my seniors. On the evening of the second day of that particular meeting I was sent for by the 8th Army director of movements, Brigadier Rhe-Philippe, with whom I had got on well in North Africa and Italy. He said to me, 'How did you come to be attending this particular conference?'

'Well, sir,' I said, 'it seems to me I'm sitting in almost by accident.'

He replied, 'You know what top priority movement is, don't you?'

'Yes, sir, the fastest possible transport movements for prime ministers, commanders-in-chief, army commanders, and so on.'

'It's top priority for you', he said, 'to be out of Cairo tomorrow morning and back to Bari, where you ought to be anyhow.'

It was clear that my too frank speaking at the Lord Leathers meeting hadn't gone down well with all my superiors.

I left the next day and arrived that evening in Bari. I went to report and have a drink with my brigadier, Tom McCarthy, at his headquarters in town. There had been little German air activity for some days before I left for Cairo and evidently none while I was there, but while I was telling Brigadier McCarthy about the Cairo Conference we heard a plane approaching. The Brigadier's headquarters were in a substantial building which was Bari's municipal offices. In a few seconds a bomb came through the roof at the other end; we were shaken but not hurt. Almost at once there was a shattering explosion when a second bomb scored a direct hit on a naval ammunition ship in the harbour. There were still twenty-six ships either alongside the quays or anchored alongside the break-water; those along the quays were full of high octane fuel and bombs for Foggia. The others had various kinds of ammunition and stores. Ships began to catch fire and some to explode. We had one piece of luck: the wind that night was blowing offshore so that the ships on the quayside were saved.

I rushed to the nearby headquarters of the naval officer-in-charge and urged him to order every possible ship to sail out of what was now becoming a holocaust. Most of the front of his building had been blown in and I remember him standing there, arms folded like Napoleon, telling me (incorrectly) that it was impossible for any ship to get out to sea because the mouth of the harbour was blocked by one which had just sunk. I then ordered all the ship's manifests showing what is loaded in each ship to be brought to me immediately. To my horror I saw that one of the American ships along the breakwater, the ss *John Harvey*, carried mustard gas shells. I told the naval officer-in-charge, 'If you can't get that ship out, sink it, because, if we don't and the wind changes, God knows what will happen to this town tonight.' He said he would have the ship sunk at once, and disappeared; indeed he reported to me that it had been sunk. In fact, he did not manage to sink it, because the ship received a direct hit from exploding ammunition; it split in two, one half sinking and the other staying tied to the breakwater. (It has recently transpired that, amongst those who suffered ill-effects from the gas, there may be as many as 600 British servicemen and merchant seamen. Only now, after forty-three years, is the matter being fully investigated.)

My mother, Rebecca.

My father, Israel, and (*left*) my uncle Simon Marks.

With my brothers Michael (*left*) and Daniel (*right*).

Dr Chaim Weizmann, my mentor.

Playing tennis with the champions: (*left to right*) Danny Prenn, Edmond Burke and Simon Marks.

'To Marcus Sieff in friendship and appreciation' – David Ben-Gurion, 1952.

In Italy during the Second World War.

Lily and I were married on 3 January 1963.

Golda Meir with Lily, Daniela and me.

Flanked by Lady Elliot and Lord Byers on my introduction to the House of Lords.

Struggling with a trout.

With James Callaghan and Harold Wilson.

In front of the Capitol, Washington, with Senator 'Scoop' Jackson.

Sharing a joke with Henry Kissinger and his wife Nancy.

Escorting H.M. The Queen round the Marks & Spencer stand at the Royal Agricultural Show, 1981.
A meeting in Cairo with President Sadat and David Frost, 1981.

With Teddy Kollek, the mayor of Jerusalem.

Relaxing on Barbados with Victor Rothschild.

Six generation of Sieffs: my great-grandfather, my grandfather Ephraim, my father, me, my son David and grandson Simon.

With Shimon Peres (*centre left*) and Mrs Thatcher at the Weizmann Institute, Rehovoth, in May 1986.

Me and my family.

By now some sixteen or seventeen ships were ablaze. It is estimated that during the night 100,000 people fled the town. The explosions could be heard twenty miles away. When some of the ships exploded and sank, they created small tidal waves which poured over the anti-aircraft guns, turning them over on top of the gun crews. There were hundreds of casualties – people around me were blasted out of my sight or terribly maimed by flying debris. Hundreds of sailors were flung into the water as their ships exploded; some were rescued and taken to hospital half drowned. A number had swallowed mustard gas, and the following morning their cheeks became very pink; I think about 150 died, their lungs having been burned by the gas-infected water.

In the end, despite what the naval officer-in-charge had said earlier, nine ships got up steam and reached the open sea. I believe many more of them, including the one loaded with mustard gas, could have sailed out, thus saving hundreds of lives.

The port, however, was left in a terrible state; a train could have passed through one of the holes blown through the massive main breakwater. Fires raged for nearly three days before we got them under control with equipment brought in from all over southern Italy. I lived on pills for those three days and did without sleep.

We learned afterwards that the bombing was a most unfortunate freak. The pilot of a German plane which had been bombing Tito's partisans in Yugoslavia discovered on his way home that he still had two bombs aboard, so, he dropped them on Bari and rendered the port unserviceable for quite a while. There was an enquiry at the time into the disaster; the naval officer-in-charge blamed us for having too many ships in the port. I replied that I had on two occasions asked him to disperse them as I also considered there were too many in the port. A number of witnesses were heard. I was exonerated, but the naval officer was severely criticized – no reference whatsoever was made to the mustard gas at the enquiry. Nor did I hear any references to the gas casualties until forty-three years later.

In March 1986 Norman Fowler, the Secretary of State for Social Services announced that one man's war pension was being back-dated because of the injuries he suffered as a result of the great Bari mustard gas explosion, and that 600 other cases were being investigated. I can bear witness to their suffering at that time; it was a most terrible sight.

The combination of three days without sleep, my hectic week in Cairo and the struggle to get the port back into working order at least ensured that I was given a fortnight's leave. I had become friendly in the previous three or four months with a most attractive girl named Phyllis Rasmussen, personal assistant to the commander of the Balkan air forces. She was one of the few people who were permitted, for some strange reason, to wear civilian clothes. She was also free to come on leave, so we decided to spend the time in Positano just south of Naples. David Curtis came with us. Among the people there was Diana Gould, later the wife of Yehudi Menuhin. She was touring in an army ENSA show, starring with Madge Elliott and Cyril Ritchard. Naples was by then an area of comparative peace. Positano in those days was a large village, not the built-up holiday resort it is today. We had a most enjoyable and relaxed few days at a charming little hotel called the Buca di Bacco.

In the first weeks of 1944 our situation in Italy didn't look too good. Our armies' advance up the Italian peninsula to Rome was still blocked by Kesselring's Gustav line, of which the hinge was Monte Cassino, where the Allies suffered huge casualties. The chief of staff decided to bypass it. 50,000 seaborne troops and 5,000 vehicles were landed at Anzio, thirty-three miles south of Rome, on 22 January. The landings were successful, almost unopposed, but the Germans soon hit back with tremendous force. Hope of a swift advance from Anzio to Rome began to fade. To try to force the way through it was decided that the 8th Army should move to its west, redeploy and break through Cassino, while on its left the 5th Army would burst out of Anzio. My ports were extremely busy sending up supplies to the 8th Army. The first five months of 1944 in Italy were a hard slog. After many checks and considerable losses, the Allies – with the Americans the first in – took Rome on 4 June.

Two days later attention swung to France when the Allies launched their invasion across the Channel. Fateful decisions were being made. The Americans had their hearts set on what was first called 'Operation Anvil', later 'Operation Dragoon', a massive landing in the South of France. Churchill was opposed to it, arguing that it would take much of our strength away and that the Italian campaign would be emasculated. He, on the contrary, wanted the Italian campaign to be developed into a great Anglo-American thrust to liberate Austria and Hungary and thus create a balance of power *vis-à-vis* the Russians in the Balkans. This, he was also sure, would avoid huge casualties in Normandy. He was, however, overruled and on 15 August 'Operation Dragoon' was launched. The American 7th Army under General Patch and the French 1st Army under General de Lattre de Tassigny landed on the French Riviera, but it was a great disappointment to Churchill and a sad day for the free population of south-east Europe.

The build-up for 'Operation Dragoon' meant for us in Italy that our military strength was substantially reduced. There was virtually no opposition to our entry into Rome, but within two weeks Kesselring, who commanded the German armies in Italy, had stabilized his forces on a line south of the Arno, eighty miles north of Rome. If forced to retreat, he would have strong defensive positions on the Rivers Arno and Po. The Germans fought bravely and the months of July to September were frustrating. The combined chiefs of staff decided to withdraw more troops from Italy for the western front and the 8th Army became exhausted and short of ammunition.

Our original aim had been to finish the Italian campaign by Christmas, but this was not to be. In August, when Churchill visited Rome, General Alexander told him the 15th Army Group had been starved and our targets must now be abandoned. Churchill commiserated with the senior staff since he would have preferred to continue a massive campaign to drive the Germans out of Italy.

At this stage I was posted to 15th Army Group headquarters, first in Algiers and then at Caserta in Italy. In Algiers I met Robin (Bob) Fox, one of my oldest friends. I had known Bob since we were boys. Most of his family was involved in the theatre; Bob himself was not an actor, but became the representative in the UK of the Music Corporation of America. In the early days it was my brother Michael, I think, who introduced Bob to the attractive Angela, an excellent actress, whom he married. They had three sons: two of whom are well-known and successful actors, Edward Fox, my godson, and James; the youngest, Robert, is a successful producer. It was with great pleasure that I met Bob in Algiers. He had been wounded in Tunisia and awarded the MC; now he was convalescing. We had a good time together, starting a party which continued at various times over the next few months until we were both in Rome. Our long party came to an end at a club in Rome where Bob, David Curtis and I drank deeply and decided to perform an improvised ballet. I remember Bob climbing on to the back of a couch and diving into my outstretched arms, which failed to hold him. He crashed to the floor. Some American officers were present and justifiably criticized our poor behaviour, but because I was the senior officer did nothing about it. Sadly Bob died of cancer in 1963; but our families have remained fond friends.

It was while I was in Algiers that I learned that Rosalie had been seriously ill in New York, but was now recovering. I was sent on a 'mission' to Washington, though part of it was really compassionate leave. I travelled in battle-stained battledress via Rabat and the Azores to the States and at Rabat my suitcase, including my one decent uniform, was stolen from the plane. I arrived in Washington looking scruffy. There the British army staff quartered me in an hotel which I found dowdy. Having discovered that one of the best hotels at that time in Washington was the Mayflower, I went there and asked the clerk at the reception desk for a room. He, taking one look at the state of my uniform and my minimal hand luggage, said the hotel was full. At that moment a short man turned round, looked at me in surprise and said, 'It's Marcus Sieff, isn't it?' 'Yes,' I replied, wondering frantically who he was. He turned out to be Isadore Lubin, a senior member of Roosevelt's White House staff and an old friend of Father's. Turning to the desk clerk, he said, 'You're looking after Colonel Sieff properly, aren't you? Make sure he gets what he wants.'

The clerk immediately said, 'Of course, Mr Lubin,' and I was shown up shortly to an excellent double room.

I then went to a tailor to try to buy a uniform. He said he would be happy to make a British uniform, but it would take about three months. I threw up my hands in despair, explained that I had just arrived from Italy and that my uniform had been stolen en route. I implied, without actually lying, that I was attending a meeting with someone very high up, and looked in the direction of the White House. The tailor then said that he understood and would fit me up with an American uniform, which he did, on to which he sewed British titles, buttons and badges of rank – quite a combination. Subsequently, when I was wearing this hybrid uniform, General Eisenhower rather tartly remarked, 'You really do represent Allied co-operation, don't you, Sieff?'

In Washington an American Brigadier-General was appointed to look after me and took me to a meeting, for which I wasn't properly briefed; there was an Admiral in charge whose name I didn't know. During the course of the meeting, when he asked me whether I thought that shipping was being used efficiently in the Mediterranean, I replied, 'No, a great deal of shipping has been and still is being wasted,' and gave my reasons why. The Admiral pursued the matter tenaciously. As I left, the Brigadier-General said he thought Admiral King — it was he who had been chairing the meeting: he was naval commander-in-chief of the US Navy and a member of the joint chiefs of staff — had been pleased to hear my views. This was not surprising. Admiral King, I discovered later, was at this time doing his best to get as much Allied shipping as possible transferred from Europe to the Far East. He thought Japan was the immediate enemy.

My wife Rosalie, now much better, joined me in Washington. That evening we went to the theatre. When we returned to the hotel, the Brigadier-General was waiting to show me a top-secret signal to the combined chiefs of staff in London. Points 1, 2 and 3 dealt with operational matters; point 4 said: 'Colonel Sieff has just come from 15th Army group headquarters with considerable experience of all movements in the Mediterranean and considers that much shipping is being wasted. Action must be taken.'

I said to the Brigadier-General, 'You can't send that message off with my name — you'll get me sacked.'

He muttered, 'I'm very sorry. We couldn't wait — it's gone.'

I thought there was nothing to do but enjoy myself until the chop came. However, within forty-eight hours he brought me the reply, the only part of which really interested me being: 'Reference your point 4, action is being taken.' That established my reputation in Washington.

After spending another few days in Washington I flew back to North Africa in a Liberator via Toronto and Newfoundland. 15th Army group headquarters had meanwhile been established at Caserta and I was posted there as AQMG (M) at the end of 1944.

My job now was concerned with the general movement of military personnel and stores throughout the area of Italy which was under Allied control. Responsibility for the civilian population in the area, and contact with the Italian government, was exercised by the Allied Control Commission (ACC), located in Rome. This was composed partly of military personnel, partly of Allied civilians. I remember one charming and able man, Merrit H. Taylor, from Philadelphia, but in general the calibre of the people was not high. General Rhe-

Philippe, the director of movements, who was my boss, ordered me to represent him at one meeting of the ACC's transportation sub-commission. I found that the population of Rome was swollen by a million refugees and that there was food and fuel for only a few days. In general the more I probed the more inefficient the sub-commission's operation seemed to me to be and the more irritated most of its members became. I didn't pull any punches and told them that if they went on like this most of the Allied army's capacity for movement would largely cease and all stores would have to be diverted to deal with civilian problems; the army would become immobile and they would be largely responsible.

Two days later General Robertson sent for me; he was now in charge of all administrative matters. He said, 'I hear you were rather outspoken, Marcus, at the ACC sub-commission meeting and you ruffled a few feathers. Would you like to go to Rome and take charge of the sub-commission?'

'No thank you, sir,' I replied.

'I'm not inviting you, I'm ordering you,' he insisted; and that was that. However, he agreed that certain officers whom I considered were incompetent should be transferred and I was allowed to take a couple of my own people with me.

I was supposed to be quartered in army accommodation, but instead managed to acquire a floor for myself in a house in the Via Gregoriana, a beautiful place just near the Spanish Steps. It belonged to the Duchess di Cesari, who was the wife of a former Italian Foreign Secretary and a niece or grand-niece of the last Czar. As I didn't smoke in those days I paid the rent with my cigarette ration. She used to tell me stories of her past life, the grand never-to-come-again past. She had two beautiful daughters; while I was her lodger one of them married a scion of a famous Milan family. I was invited to the wedding in the Vatican Chapel. I couldn't go, but went to the party later in the day. There the array of good things to eat and drink surprised even me, though I had learned much through my work in civilian and military transport about the black market and the widespread bribery and corruption. Indeed, on one occasion, if I had turned my back and agreed to a few trucks making a journey from Rome through occupied lines, I could have made a small fortune – but I resisted the temptation.

It had been the Allied plan in the early winter to launch an offensive to drive the Germans out of Italy in the hope that the Italian war could be quickly finished; but Naples was still the only major port for both civilian and military supplies on the west coast. Because of the huge civilian demands for stores of all types, particularly for Rome, the rate of unloading military stores was below target. I came to the conclusion that it was essential to have the use of an additional port in the west. I was told that in pre-war days a large proportion of goods destined for Rome came through Civitavecchia, which I knew had been damaged, but it seemed to me sensible to re-open it.

When I visited the port, I found that the enemy had made it apparently unusable by sinking ships in the berths alongside the quays. I asked an engineering colonel how he could make the place serviceable. After examining it, he said it could be done by cutting the superstructures off the sunken ships and building out platforms as quays across their hulls, which would provide the foundations. When I asked him if he could start immediately he said, 'I can only do it if I get permission from my bosses and if I can have a minimum of two engineering battalions. In that case the port could be workable within a month and would have eighty per cent of its former capacity.'

I said, 'I don't think there will be any problem in getting agreement from your superiors or getting the engineering battalions.' I couldn't have been more wrong.

I went to his boss, a major-general, and asked for what was needed. I don't think he cared much either for me or for the Allied Control Commission and he flatly refused, saying he didn't approve of the idea and thought it would be a waste of manpower and equipment. I went to more senior officers and still got nowhere. It was now the beginning of 1945. I had been promoted full colonel, but had been overseas for over four years and, I suppose like millions of others, was getting war weary. I was depressed and fed up. I then decided I would ask for a meeting with Harold Macmillan, at that time minister-resident in the Mediterranean. He saw me immediately and the first question he asked was if I was any relation of Israel Sieff's. When I replied that Israel was my father, Macmillan was most complimentary about him. When I told him my tale and asked for his help, he said he thought my idea was a good one. I became optimistic, but then he said that getting troops for the work I wanted was outside his jurisdiction and he was sorry there was nothing he could do. I went away depressed.

A few days later the first engineering battalion which I had requested appeared out of the blue, followed shortly by the second, and the port reconstruction began; we handed it back to the Italian authorities within a few weeks. In March I went with Mr Macmillan to visit Civitavecchia, though at that time he was not prepared to acknowledge his part in the affair.

Some eight years later in 1953, when I was walking through the little hallway of a block of flats, Macmillan, then Minister of Housing, was walking towards me. He had only seen me a couple of times in uniform and I didn't think he would recognize me, so I said nothing. As we passed, however, he turned and said to me, 'It's Sieff, isn't it?' 'Yes, Mr Macmillan,' I replied, and he went on, 'We didn't do a bad job at Civitavecchia, did we?' Nearly thirty years later, at a dinner celebrating the fiftieth anniversary of the founding of P.E.P., I was sitting next to Harold Macmillan and he told me the tale of how he got the port opened. 'I didn't think that I would be any more successful with the generals than you were,' he said, 'so I went to see my friend the commander-in-chief, General Alexander, and told him that I thought your idea of opening Civitavecchia was a good one, that it had been turned down by your superiors and that if I were to suggest it it would be equally turned down. But, I suggested that, if it came as an order from him, as his idea, they would have to carry it out. And that's how you got the engineering people who rebuilt the port of Civitavecchia.'

We were able to launch our offensive, but it was not successful; we were held up on both the Rivers Arno and Po, and the war dragged on until 7 May, when Germany finally surrendered. I returned home in July 1945, posted to the Royal Artillery depot. I'd had enough of war, particularly in peacetime, and went round to the War Office to see Colonel Bobbie Lawrence, an old acquaintance of mine, who was concerned with demobilization. I had met him in the desert in 1943, when he had to return home at short notice. There had been difficulty in getting him transport and I had intervened to arrange this, a service he much appreciated. He greeted me with, 'Hallo, Marcus, what can I do for you?'

I thought this was a good start and said boldly, 'You can authorize my immediate demobilization.'

'I thought you might have that in mind,' he said. 'I've got your papers here. You have been given fourteen days' leave, promoted to brigadier and, when you return from leave, you go to Burma.'

That was my welcome after more than four-and-a-half years overseas. Of course, I knew nothing then about the existence of the atom bomb and the possibility of it being used. People believed that the war in the Far East might go on for a long time. 'You must be out of your mind,' I declared. 'I'm not going to Burma. Why should I?' He said, 'It seems that you did a paper on how to organize a "build-up control system" and you drew up a corresponding order of battle for use on a single road in the 8th Army campaign at the time of the Battle of Medenine and the Mareth line. It went to the War Office, who were impressed and sent it out for information to all commands. In Burma they're going to have a big offensive on a single road and they would like to have you there. That's why you are a brigadier with fourteen days leave.'

'Bobbie,' I said, 'I don't want to be unpatriotic but I have been overseas for more than four-and-a-half years. There are plenty of people who can go to Burma, many of whom would like to be brigadier. Anyway, they've got my "build-up system" – all they have to do is apply it to their road. As for me, I have my rights as a Territorial Army volunteer and under existing regulations I am entitled to be demobilized.'

'You are quite right, in theory, but you haven't read the small print,' retorted Bobbie. 'Officers of the rank of full colonel and above have no such rights. So, provided you are fit, you go to Burma. I'm sorry, but that's how it is.'

I left the War Office fed up, wondering what I could do, and then remembered Bobbie's remark, 'provided you are fit'. I had contracted some disease in my left eye in the last desert campaign and from time to time the eye played up; in fact I became partially blind, partly perhaps because in Rome I had done a good deal of work in a semi-darkened room lit only by a small electric light. Actually the eye was now much better, but still not perfect. The chief ophthalmologist to the army was Brigadier Duke-Elder, the famous eye surgeon, whom I had known in pre-war days. I telephoned him and asked to see him immediately; he saw me the same morning. I told him, 'I've been offered a good job in India. Would you please examine my eye and tell me candidly if it's all right for me to go?' After examining the eye he decided, 'You can go if you are willing to risk losing the sight of your left eye.' 'Please,' I asked, 'put that in writing for me right now.'

'I think you must have an ulterior motive, Marcus,' he said, 'but it's the truth.'

In the afternoon I went back to see Bobbie Lawrence, who read Duke-Elder's note and said, 'That makes things a bit different, doesn't it?'

I said, 'Yes,' shook him warmly by the hand, went back to my parent's flat, took off my uniform and put on a suit — which was no longer the right size for me.

As I imagine most people did, I learned a good deal from the war. I had been very fortunate; although a number of the people with whom I had worked closely were killed or wounded, I was never hit. In fact, apart from one attack of malaria and the eye infection, my health was excellent. I had served in many countries; much of my work had been interesting; whether that work was successful or not had depended to a considerable extent on my own initiative. Before the war I had led a rather sheltered and relatively easy life. Although I had worked hard in Marks & Spencer for a couple of years, I could always turn to someone for advice; in fact, I was always working under super-vision. In the war, though always subject ultimately to somebody's orders, I had much time on my own and (like many others, of course), had to make decisions affecting the lives of my fellow soldiers, and the progress of the battle, without being able to consult anybody else. I learned something of personal initiative and I suppose I acquired more self-confidence. I am immodest enough to say that I discovered that I had some leadership ability and could take responsibility; I learned also that, providing you treat people decently and are pre-pared to share the risks, the response of the vast majority of people is first class; in fact, I learned a lot about good human relations, in which I had had a grounding at Marks & Spencer but about which I learned much more during the war. I learned how important it was in times of pressure for those in charge to be seen among their people, encouraging them; I learned the value of teamwork. I learned something about that pre-eminent tradition in the British fighting forces which says that an officer's first responsibility is to look after his men. At the same time I learned that, wasteful bureaucratic habits tend to become permanent and it needs quite an effort to break away from them.

CHAPTER SIX

I RETURNED to Marks & Spencer in the summer of 1945. Though the principles of the business had not changed during the war, the physical structure had. Over 1500 men and many women had served in the forces; sixteen stores had been destroyed by enemy air attacks and many others damaged. During the war the government had requisitioned 1,500,000 sq. ft of the company's space for storage of foodstuffs, and the two top floors of our Baker Street head office as the headquarters of one of the special operations groups. Because of the space taken by the government at Baker Street, and for security reasons, head office had been split, and while the main policy section, merchandise control, food buying and personnel were still at Michael House, Baker Street, the textile buying departments had been moved to Leicester, the finance department to Bath and the administration to Blackpool. In 1946 all head office activities were brought back to London but, because space in Baker Street was insufficient, some departments were still accommodated elsewhere: two sections were in Oxford Street and administration was at Mile End. All head office departments were only brought together into one building when the new Michael House, at 47 Baker Street, was completed in 1958.

During the war and in the seven years following it, the supply of goods, particularly clothing, was limited; there were not enough goods to cover the counters. With so many people in the services or at war work, and because of food rationing, public demand for eating out grew, so we had installed cafeterias in a number of stores; by the end of the war we had seventy. Catering became a profitable department. As the supply of goods continued to be restricted for several more years, we expanded our catering division and by the end of 1947 had 107 cafeterias.

Simon Marks, by then Sir Simon Marks, the chairman, in his annual reviews for 1945, 1946, 1947 and 1948, emphasized that the principles of the business had not changed; that we still sought goods of high quality and good value; that we continued to co-operate closely with our suppliers, and that we and they, in partnership, were looking for improved methods, using the latest developments in science and technology, to upgrade goods. But progress, reported Simon, was held up by the continuing clothing utility scheme and by food rationing (which did not end until 1954). He stressed our commitment to having goods produced in the United Kingdom wherever possible. He also emphasized our continued concern for the welfare of our staff, and the steps we were taking to implement this policy. He pointed out that in general incomes were rising and, as supplies were inadequate, too much money was chasing too few goods: inflation had increased.

He and Father were joint managing directors; Father's younger brother, my uncle, Teddy Sieff, had been appointed assistant managing director; my brother Michael headed textile buying under the overall control of Teddy; I started to learn something more about the food departments and played an increasing role in their development.

Of course compared with our operation today, where annual sales are approaching £4 billion, sales then were modest, even after allowing for inflation between the late 1940s and today:

Year ending	March 1947	March 1986
	(£ million)	
General Sales	18·3	2324.8
Food Sales	8·0	1410·0
Total Sales	26.3	3734·8

By the standards of those days, however, and in the circumstances in which we operated, the 1948 figures represented considerable progress. We employed 15,000 people; today we employ more than 50,000 in the United Kingdom alone.

The Labour Party had come to power in the 1945 general election. Its plans for increasing nationalization caused many who believed in the value of free enterprise to feel uncertain about the future. They began to look outside Britain with a view to increasing their business through the development of export markets and interests abroad. Simon decided in 1947 to enter into an agreement with the founder of Woolworths, South Africa, Max Sonnenberg, who was a member of parliament under Smuts. Simon had met Max, who was highly regarded at home and abroad, and thought him a desirable trading partner. Marks & Spencer acquired a shareholding in Woolworths and Woolworths a shareholding in Marks and Spencer. (I should make it clear that the only thing that Woolworths, South Africa has in common with the great American Woolworth firm is the name.)

In December 1947 I went with Simon and his wife Miriam, my business colleague and cousin Michael Sacher, and my cousin Ann Laski to South Africa to look at the firm with whom we had entered into partnership. We had made our decision to acquire our share in Woolworths without having seen the operation and stores on the ground; we had seen only photographs and the reports of the business. The turnover at the time was about £3 million. We sailed on the *Athlone Castle* and had a most enjoyable voyage. Bruce Goodman and Wilfred Norris, two of the firm's directors, followed a few days later.

In South Africa we met Elie Susman, Max Sonnenberg's partner, who in his early life had been a trader in Rhodesia at the time of Cecil Rhodes. His twenty-three-year-old son David was asked by his father to help look after the younger members of our party. David became my lifelong friend and also a non-executive director of Marks & Spencer, where I found his views helpful and constructive. It was not his original intention to join his family firm or go into retailing at all, but our visit changed his mind and, after leaving university and having a spell in Israel, he took up what was to become a highly successful retailing career. David met my cousin Ann Laski, Elaine's lovely daughter; they fell in love and two years later were married. I was flattered when their son Simon, now thirty-four years old, named his firstborn after me.

On this visit to South Africa Simon Marks was appalled by the quality and standard of the goods that he found in the first store we visited. Max Sonnenberg, as the chairman, was with us, and Simon, who was nothing if not frank, said to Max, 'You really can't offer these goods for sale; they should be given to the bishop for his charity garden party.' After we arrived at the second store and Simon had a further chance to examine the merchandise he said to Max, 'You can't even give this stuff to the bishop for his garden party - you must burn it.' That was the unlikely beginning of a long and fruitful co-operation with Woolworths South Africa.

This was at the time when Smuts was Prime Minister and before the formal proclamation of apartheid. We divested ourselves of our shareholding in Woolworths in 1971, but we have kept close contact and still co-operate. Woolworths have become one of the leading stores groups in South Africa; their business is based on excellence; they have developed and implemented a policy of good human relations at work and have done much to eliminate the divisions set up under South Africa's apartheid laws; they operate a system which enables white, coloured and black to work together.

I had a fascinating time in South Africa, visited many Woolworths stores and increased my shopkeeping experience, particularly learning what type of merchandise not to have on one's counters. I also had an enjoyable time away from the business, including an exciting visit to the Veld and to the Victoria Falls in southern Rhodesia.

My journey to South Africa had been made on my own. Rosalie and I had tried to get back together after five years' wartime separation, but the break had been too long; we had grown apart and we finally agreed to separate. She divorced me in 1947 and was given custody of our son David, of whom I had seen all too little. The war had started a few months after he was born and he was in America with his mother from 1940 to 1945. He went to school at Repton, where he did quite well. Before he was accepted, Rosalie and I went for an interview with Mr Lynam Thomas, the headmaster. We took the train to Derby; I suggested to Rosalie that to make a good impression on the headmaster she should remove most of her make-up, which she did somewhat reluctantly in the ladies' washroom at Derby station. We arrived at Repton, saw Mr Thomas and then joined him and his wife for tea. Peggy Thomas was a most attractive lady, beautifully made-up, more or less as Rosalie had been prior to my asking her to remove her make-up; I was not popular.

David was, I think, at the time he joined Repton the only Jew in the school. He pointed out to the understanding Mr Thomas that being Jewish, he must observe the Sabbath and could not work on Saturday mornings. Mr Thomas said he fully understood and that on Saturday mornings he would arrange for David either to attend synagogue in nearby Derby or to have some form of rabbinical tuition - whereupon David decided that perhaps it would be better after all to attend school on Saturdays.

Rosalie and I remained good friends until she died of cancer in 1964.

*   *   *

On my return from South Africa I settled down to work. I was appointed a member of the merchandise organization committee, with a senior position in the modest but developing food group. It was during 1948 that Nate Goldenberg joined the firm as senior food technologist. He was a food chemist of great ability and where quality was concerned the word compromise did not come into his vocabulary; he insisted on high standards of hygiene, both in the factories that produced foodstuffs for us and in our stores, and played an important role in establishing the standards which have made our food business what it is today; I learned much from his approach.

Following my return to the business I had become close to Simon, with whom I frequently spent weekends in his country house at Sunningdale; en route to Sunningdale we used to visit stores on what became known as the 'Royal Route', such as Hammersmith, Staines, or those which required only a short detour like Windsor or Ealing. When I was not weekending with Simon I generally spent my free time with Father, who had a fourteenth-century thatched cottage at Brimpton in Berkshire. I also occasionally stayed with other members of the family like my mother's youngest sister Elaine, who had a lovely home in the East Grinstead area. Elaine died in November 1985 aged eighty-three-years old, as active and dynamic as ever, and a very good-looking woman until her dying day.

Some time in 1947, after Rosalie and I had divorced, I went for the first time since the war for a holiday to the South of France with my brother Michael, his wife Daphne, and Bob and Angela Fox. At the time you were only allowed to take out of the country £75 of foreign exchange per person, which went a lot further in those days than it does now, but not all that far. The six of us drove to the South of France and stayed at a modest but pleasant hotel some forty miles west of Cannes, where in pre-war days I used to stay at the Carlton Hotel. I was depressed and irritable and not a very congenial companion, so after two or three days I left and went to the Carlton in Cannes. I remember having drinks and lunch with Nada Milford Haven and Marie Burke, sister of the tennis player, after which I was on my own. About nine o'clock I was in the foyer of the hotel when I met Julian, who was the famous head night porter, whom I had known well in the 1930s. He was talking to a lady but turned to greet me warmly. I smiled at the lady, whereupon Julian said, 'Mr Sieff, you know Miss Gosen, don't you?' We both said, 'No,' shook hands and chatted for a few minutes. She was charming and attractive, and I asked her to have dinner with me. She refused because she was leaving for Italy early the following morning. I said she should take pity on a lonely man and eventually persuaded her. We hit it off well and had a pleasant evening. She said she would be in Italy for a week. I replied that I would be at the Carlton for several days and hoped that she would return from Italy before I left: I looked forward to our getting together again. I was flattered when she came back earlier than she had planned and we spent a few days together.

Elsa Gosen was an executive in a major American firm called Seligman & Latz, which controlled one of the world's largest hairdressing businesses. She was going to see some of the members of her family in London before returning to New York, so she agreed to drive back with me.

I had bought Elsa an expensive handbag in Cannes and, when we arrived at Lympne (having flown the car over from Le Touquet) the customs officer asked whether I had anything to declare; I produced the handbag. This was the one and only time in my life I did not declare the full price I paid for an article; I gave a figure substantially less than the purchase price. The customs officer said, 'Are you sure this is the price you paid?' Rather foolishly I stuck to my original figure. He said again, 'Are you quite sure?'

'Yes,' I maintained, my heart sinking.

He asked me for my passport and once more asked me the price. Once more I told him the same amount. He said, 'Well, Mr Sieff, in that case' - I wondered nervously what would follow – 'you've been taken for such a ride I can't charge you any duty.' I heaved a sigh of relief and made a vow that I would never be so silly again. It was a good lesson.

But my life was now to change. Britain had given up the Palestine mandate, which we had held for over twenty-five years, and the United Nations had decided by a majority that Palestine should be divided into two states, one Arab, one Jewish, in the hope that they would work together in peace. The refusal of the neighbouring Arab states to accept the UN decision, their declaration of war on the new state, and their threat to wipe out the Jews created an upheaval in my life, as well as in the lives of hundreds of thousands of others.

CHAPTER SEVEN

AS a youth I was perhaps more conscious of being a Zionist than a Jew; I was an early disciple of Weizmann. Though Simon followed with enthusiasm and commitment, it was Father who in 1913 led the two families into Weizmann's camp. Weizmann, then a lecturer in chemistry at Manchester University and president of the English Zionist Federation, was virtually, though not officially, the leader of world Zionism. Father had become a Zionist seven years before he set eyes on Weizmann; he had joined the Zionist Organization at the age of seventeen but, as he recorded, 'The moment I met him he became my master. I listened to him rapt.' The following week Father introduced Simon to him. He said, 'Simon too immediately fell under his spell.' From his first meeting with Weizmann, at supper with some friends, Father began to raise funds for him on a scale he had not attempted before, and with considerable success. He became Weizmann's part-time, unpaid private secretary. Harry Sacher, Father's brother-in-law, Herbert Sidebotham, the famous leader writer of the renowned *Manchester Guardian*, Simon and Father together established the magazine *Palestine*, the organ of the British Palestine Committee, to bring the views of British Zionists to the government's attention.

Early in the First World War Weizmann, who had met Mr Balfour in Manchester some years previously, went to see him in London; he was then Foreign Secretary. Father went with him; in fact he paid for his train ticket. On 2 November 1917 the British Government published the Balfour Declaration, which promised 'the establishment of a national home for the Jewish people in Palestine.' When the Zionist Commission was appointed to go to Palestine and make recommendations on how the Declaration was to be implemented, Father went as Weizmann's personal assistant. He accompanied him to the Versailles peace conference of 1919, at which the British Government was given the Palestine mandate, and to the San Remo Conference of April 1920, which confirmed the Declaration and the mandate.

King Feisal, then King of Syria, had welcomed the Balfour Declaration. He and Dr Weizmann had a number of conversations at the Paris peace conference. During one of their talks Feisal said to Weizmann, 'Are you going to send a representative to me in Damascus so that we can work together on the implementation of the Declaration?' Weizmann replied, 'Yes, I'm going to send Dr Eder.' Though he was an able man, Eder was getting on in years, and the King knew it. So he said, 'Well, that's very nice but I would prefer that you send young Sieff.' Father was attractive, able and spoke well; however, it was unlikely, because of his many commitments, that he would have gone. In any case France threw Feisal out of Syria within a few months and Britain appointed him King of Iraq a year later.

For the next ten years or so Father went frequently to Palestine as Weizmann's man in Israel. Mother was also involved. In 1920, with five other enterprising women, including Weizmann's wife Vera, she co-founded WIZO, the Women's International Zionist Organization, which led to her spending several months of most years in Palestine, and afterwards Israel, until her death in 1966. Her ambition was to improve the lot of children and women of all ages, religions and races through day-care centres, youth clubs, schools, women's centres and advisory bureaux. It was she who did most to develop the Women's Organization into a worldwide movement, herself travelling to every continent, setting up branches in many countries and speaking about the purpose, aims and achievements of the Organization.

There is no need for me to say much about the unhappy history of the policy of various British governments towards Palestine and Israel in the thirty years which followed the Balfour Declaration, or to describe the distress it caused to those of us who were both British patriots and devoted Zionists. There were always leaders such as Churchill, Lloyd George, Leo Amery, Walter Elliot, and others who consistently supported the implementation of the Balfour Declaration and gave cause for hope that Britain would fulfil its promise. But they were in the minority. All I shall do is relate briefly what had taken place in the six months before I decided to take leave of absence from Marks & Spencer and go to Israel in May 1948.

Britain's problems *vis-à-vis* Palestine came to a climax in February 1947. The government threw in its hand and Ernest Bevin, the Foreign Secretary, announced in the House of Commons that the mandate would come to an end in May 1948, when Britain would withdraw; in the meantime the Palestine problem would be handed over to the United Nations. This announcement led to much trouble in Palestine, the Arabs trying to throw out the Jews before a possible Jewish state could be established, the Jews, fearful, defending their tenuous positions. The UN set up the United Nations Special Committee on Palestine, UNSCOP, to hear from Jews and Arabs their case for control of the whole or parts of Palestine. This committee produced its report in September 1947; it advocated the partition of Palestine into Jewish and Arab states, with Jerusalem as a *corpus separatum*. The UNSCOP report was accepted by a majority vote in November 1947. There was of course no Israeli government then, as the state did not yet exist. Though the Jewish leaders were disappointed with the small area they had been allocated they accepted it and proposed to the Arab leaders that Jews and Arabs should work together for their mutual benefit. Tragically the Arab leaders both in Palestine and in the countries surrounding Palestine voted against the UN decision and rejected Jewish overtures for peaceful co-operation.

There followed six months of unofficial war in Palestine. The British Mandatory Government in Palestine, still responsible for law and order there, behaved in a way which Abba Eban described as 'sympathetic neutrality, which enabled the Arabs to operate with ease, bringing in arms and men from neighbouring countries, while it hindered the Jews in every possible way'. Casualties on both sides were considerable. The Jews defended themselves tenaciously but the Arabs had overwhelming superiority in arms and numbers and, seeking to wipe out the Jews before the new state was born, attacked relentlessly. There was as yet no Jewish fully uniformed defence force; on 9 April 1948 the Irgun, then a terrorist group, attacked the Arab village of Deir Yassin, killing a number of women and children as well as men.

On the day after the end of the mandate, 14 May 1948, Ben Gurion, now Prime Minister, proclaimed the new State of Israel. Fifteen minutes later President Truman recognized the new state on behalf of the United States, and immediately afterwards, incredible as it may sound today, Russia recognized Israel; more than thirty other members of the United Nations, a majority in those days, followed, but Britain did not recognize the new state. On 15 May Egyptian planes bombed Tel Aviv and, soon after, the armies of

Lebanon, Syria, Jordan, Iraq and Egypt crossed Israel's borders. Some British Foreign Office officials had predicted that, if a war broke out, the Arabs, with their great superiority in arms and numbers, would drive the Jews into the sea; I don't think they would have been much concerned if that had happened. They thought that the new State of Israel would be a nuisance and a cause of unrest in the Middle East, which from their point of view turned out to be true, but they ignored Jewish rights, the UN decision, and the fact that the major causes of unrest in the area were, and still are, the mutual hostility and internecine fighting between the Arab/Moslem states and sects in that region.

A few days before fighting began I received a message from Ben Gurion. He anticipated that the proclamation of the State of Israel would be followed by war. Would I come out to Israel and help? I wanted to, but there were problems. What would Simon and Father think of my leaving the company, even if only temporarily, and how would I, a colonel on the British Army reserve, explain myself as a participant in a war in which a country whose existence Britain did not recognize was fighting against Transjordan, a British ally? The first problem was resolved in a matter of minutes; Father and Simon thought I should answer Ben Gurion's call. As for the other problem, I decided to consign it to the category of bridges to be crossed when you come to them. After all, British officers were fighting in the forces of some of the Arab countries. Within a few days of receiving Ben Gurion's invitation I had left London for Israel.

On 18 May a plane was to fly from Blackbushe airfield, southwest of London, to land in Haifa. I had just enough time to board it. It was a very battered looking DC3. I did not know at the time that it was partly held together by wire. It was brilliantly piloted by a German who had been a member of the famous Baron Richtofen squadron of World War I. I remember that the marks left by sabre cuts from a duel still lay across his cheek. It was a bumpy, noisy journey. We stopped to refuel in Rome and then made Haifa, the only airfield open on Israeli territory. The war had officially begun: once near the eastern shore of the Mediterranean we had to keep an eye open for Arab planes. On the small Haifa airfield I bumped into some officers who were waiting to go back to Britain following the end of the mandate. Among them were a couple with whom I had served during World War II. 'What the hell are you doing here?' they asked. I said I had come to see what was happening to our farm at Tel Mond, where Mother lived when she was in Palestine. The farm had its origin in the middle 1930s, when my family had bought some land about fifteen miles north of Tel Aviv near a village called Tel Mond; I had first seen it in 1935. It was largely sand; I couldn't understand why Father had bought it for what in those days seemed a high price. But my parents wanted a place in Palestine; having found water, they transformed sand into first-class soil and developed citrus and avocado plantations. These were well looked after for many years and lovingly developed by Yechiel Paldi, who, with his wife Lilly, became family friends. Subsequently, Yechiel was in charge for many years of the Marks & Spencer office in Israel, and has now been succeeded by his son Eilon. The Paldi family has now been working with us, first with the Sieff family and then with Marks & Spencer, for over fifty years. In 1938 Mother and Father built a house adjoining the citrus farm and developed a lovely garden: you might have been in a most fertile part of Sussex, even though, in those days, the desert sand was just a few hundred yards away.

To return to my arrival at Haifa airport: my friends said, 'You can't go there. The road's being shelled. You'd better get out, old boy. The Jews are finished.' This wasn't said in any anti-Semitic way but as advice to a friend. 'I'm sorry to hear that,' I said, 'but now I've come I must look around.'

'You know Jerusalem has fallen today?' they added. In fact it was the old city of Jerusalem which had fallen: the Jordanians had captured it that morning.

I was shocked, but wasted no time in looking for some means of getting to Tel Aviv, sixty miles to the south. I was able to hire a car. There was no coast road in those days and I had to take the internal road, parts of which were being shelled. The fire, however, was desultory, coming from the Iraqi forces around Ras-el-Ain, about ten miles from Tel Aviv. I arrived in Tel Aviv in the early evening and was met by Reuven Sazlani, who later changed his name to Shiloah. He was responsible then for both military and political intelligence. His appearance was that of a super-spy in a James Bond film, with strong features which had been damaged in an explosion at the headquarters of the Jewish Agency. The impression he created at first sight belied his intellectual calibre, now celebrated by a renowned institute for political studies which bears his name. Reuven briefed me on the state of the war. 'Of where the Iraqis are,' he said drily, 'you have personal knowledge. The Arab Legion, under the British Brigadier Glubb, is at Latrun, twenty miles east of here on the road to Jerusalem, and the Egyptian army is in the Negev, some twenty-two miles to the south; the so-called Arab Liberation Army is a few miles from Haifa; Jerusalem is surrounded and besieged. Now I must take you to Ben Gurion.'

That night I met Ben Gurion. He was Prime Minister of this five-day-old state, its Minister of Defence and Commander-in-Chief, thus combining three roles. Considering the intensity with which the Arabs had attacked a few days earlier, and that the old city of Jerusalem had fallen that morning, he was remarkably calm. He thanked me in a few words for coming to the help of Israel; he was not in the habit of thanking people very much, assuming they had the same sense of duty as himself. Then he told me why he had asked me to come. In general he hoped that as many Jews as could would come to Israel in her time of crisis and show their faith in her statehood by actually being there. (There were about 600,000 Jews there at the time, with millions of hostile Arabs in the surrounding countries.) In particular he thought my experience in the Second World War could be of considerable use in the defence of Israel against the Arabs. He knew that I had served in operations and on the staff in a number of countries and considered me an experienced soldier. He had an exaggerated view of my achievements during the war, but of course this was all relative to the limited experience of most Israeli officers, many of whom were fine and courageous fighters, but their experience was mainly in guerrilla operations; they had limited knowledge of large-scale military operations. Some later proved to be great generals, like Yigael Yadin, Moshe Dayan, Yigal Allon and Yitzhak Rabin.

When I arrived, the chief of staff was General Dori, previously president of the Haifa Technion, Israel's university of high technology, but he was taken ill and replaced by Yigael Yadin, chief of operations. Yadin was undoubtedly one of the main military architects of Israel's victory. He was a world renowned archaeologist. Nobody looked less like a military man than Yigael.

Many Palestinian Jews volunteered in World War II to serve in the British forces. It is recorded that approximately 100,000 men and women came forward, but initially the British Government, largely under the influence of the Foreign Office, discouraged the acceptance of Palestinian Jewish volunteers in the British armed services. Originally it had been decided that Jewish volunteers should only be accepted in the same number as Arabs, but few Arabs volunteered and many of them deserted. Finally, when we were hard pressed on the Egyptian front at the end of 1941, and largely because of Churchill's insistence, we took more Jewish volunteers. Eventually 30,000 Palestinian Jews served; in 1944 the Jewish Brigade, 5000 strong, was formed. It fought in Italy, but only after constant requests from the Jewish leaders for a Jewish fighting unit; this again was largely a result of Churchill's intervention. There were many well-known men who fought in the Jewish Brigade. They were a good fighting unit, but again few of the officers had been given the opportunities I had to operate in so many areas. But there were one or two; for example, President Herzog had been an officer in the Guards Armoured Division, part of 30 Corps, commanded by the famous Lieutenant-General Horrocks.

Several thousand Jewish volunteers (called Mahal) from many countries came to Israel during the first few weeks, many with war experience, but again in most cases it was limited; there were, however, one or two outstanding soldiers like the American Colonel Mickey Marcus, who had been one of General Clay's senior officers in the Normandy landings. He was tragically killed a few days after I arrived, shot by a Jewish sentry when he did not answer the Jewish sentry's Hebrew challenge – Colonel Marcus did not speak or understand Hebrew.

David Susman, whom I had met in South Africa following the Marks & Spencer/Woolworth South Africa link, arrived in June as a Mahal volunteer; he was a lieutenant commanding a company in an infantry battalion. We would meet from time to time and he would tell me what had been happening in the field. One episode in the field nearly proved fatal to him. His unit was involved in battle with the Syrians not far from the Lebanese border when he was shot in the neck and left on the field for dead. The Syrians were advancing when his friend Geoff Pearlman, who commanded the adjoining troop, saw what was happening, ordered his men to fix bayonets and charged the advancing Syrians, who were driven off; David was rescued, unconscious but alive. That must have been one of the last bayonet charges in modern warfare.

Ben Gurion had experience of guerrilla warfare on a small scale and of underground operations, but his experience of large-scale war had been limited to that of a sergeant in the British army's Jewish battalion in the First World War. It is an ironic commentary on Israel's military situation at the beginning of the War of Independence that Ben Gurion regarded me as a very experienced soldier. He was wrong, but I suppose at this time anybody with my record – a member of a well-known Zionist family who had reached the rank of colonel in the British army – looked much more qualified to help than in fact he was. So Ben Gurion notified the Israeli staff and recorded in his diary:

Marcus Sieff is hereby appointed adviser for transportation and supplies to the Minister of Defence. He is authorized to examine the situation of supplies and transportation at the centre and in the branches and in all army services (land, sea, air), to advise the above mentioned services, and to present a report from time to time to the Minister of Defence.

I felt bound to point out to Ben Gurion, in his capacity as Minister of Defence, that I could not, as an officer of the British Army Reserve, take the oath of allegiance to the State. of Israel, and that if he employed me he would have to take me on trust. He brushed this aside and said, 'Tomorrow you had better go out and take a look at the battle fronts and come back and tell me what you think.'

The territory held by the State of Israel at that time was geographically so small that to carry out his first instruction was not a time-consuming task. The furthest point I needed to reach was only twenty-two miles away. As I went from one part of the front to another my spirits sank lower and lower. Most of the Israeli troops I visited had spirit, but few had much training. Many of them were former inmates of concentration and refugee camps in Europe; many had been captured by the British en route to Palestine in the post-war period and interned in camps in Cyprus, from which they had just been released. Most did not have enough command of the Hebrew language to understand the simple orders they were given. In addition to the Jewish Brigade there were a number of native-born Israelis or early immigrants to Palestine who had excellent fighting experience as guerrillas. Some had been trained by the late Brigadier Orde Wingate of Burma fame, a remarkable British officer who in the pre-World War II period had taught the Jews in Palestine how to ambush the ambushers — the Arabs who were continually ambushing Jews and attacking the Jewish agricultural settlements in the days when Britain held the mandate. Wingate trained them well, but he did more than that: he advocated their cause. He believed that the Jews should have a country of their own and never hesitated to say so no matter who was present. Israel remains in Wingate's debt.

Among the Israeli units was the famous Palmach, a type of commando force except that its weapons were elementary. Overall there were not enough rifles to go round — and I am not talking about automatic weapons but of old-fashioned five-rounds-to-a-magazine rifles; there was no artillery, and not a single tank. The Israelis had some home-made mortars, which they called 'davidkas', which had a limited range. The shell they fired was modest, but they did make a loud and frightening noise. I think their largest and best anti-aircraft guns were 20 mm machine-guns, which could fire effectively only up to 12,000 feet. They had no war planes; there were two old DC3s, two Ansons, a de Havilland Rapide used for transport and a de Havilland Rapide originally made to carry a dozen passengers which was the main bombing plane. In addition the Israelis had about twelve Austers, whose range was 300 miles and speed ninety miles an hour. Their main use during World War II had been for artillery spotting; they had been made serviceable for their present use by cannibalizing parts from the twenty or so such planes owned by Jewish flying clubs. They were initially the main 'bombing fleet', the bomb load of 300 lb being thrown out of the cockpit by hand. The Arabs — as I knew from first-hand observation in the Middle East during World War II — had plenty of weapons and a number of bombers and fighters, sufficient tanks and armoured vehicles, and could put many men in the field. I returned to Ben Gurion's headquarters depressed, fearing the worst.

I had not, however, taken into account the guts and determination of the Israelis. Before the fighting ceased they would sustain casualties among men, women and children which, proportionate to the British population, would be the equivalent of some 2,000,000 killed and seriously wounded in the United Kingdom. And yet they won.

Reporting back to Ben Gurion presented me with a problem. For instance, though it was true that there were not enough rifles to go round, there was not much point harping on such a well-known fact and about which everything possible was being done. What would be useful would be to report on matters which could be remedied within the State of Israel's existing resources. I decided, therefore, that my first major submission would be on the state of the so-called Israeli air force — the Israelis were now beginning to buy and bring in a few secondhand war planes from Europe. Ben Gurion made notes on my report in his diary; what he wrote might interest those who would like to understand what the Israeli Government had to contend with at the time. I went to see Ben Gurion with Cecil Margo, a fine fighter pilot of World War II, who had been a squadron leader in the South African air force.

Thursday 22.7.48

On the 11th Margo and Sieff came to see me. Margo was accompanied by Trevor Siskin, his aide from South Africa.

Sieff reported on the results of his investigation into the air force.

The air force lacks co-ordinated representation with the authorities — the government and the army. The government does not understand the needs of the air force. They allocate funds for the acquisition of aircraft, but not for arrangements at the airfields, training, maintenance, tools, communications or vehicles.

The air force commander has not had air force training. There is no planning in the air force. Although good work is being done 'down below', the arrangements 'up above' are no good, although there has been an improvement lately. A shortage of hand tools is holding up repairs. The air force commander should be at headquarters. The general quartermaster branch should be concerned only with accommodation and personal equipment. Technical equipment should be the concern of the air force's own quartermaster branch. Liaison between the air force and its agencies overseas is not good. A weekly courier service is needed. Air force administration and supply are bad. Morale is good in combat units, but not so good in the others. The leaders should visit airfields and workshops. The pilots have not had enough experience with these aircraft. Tyres burst on landing, and the parts are old. Performance in the air is good, but the difficulty is in getting into the air.

There is no co-operation between the army, the air force and the navy. There have been occasions when naval vessels have fired on Israeli planes. Ground staff and aircrew must be trained during the period of the truce. Airfields and communications must be improved, and bombs and weapons planned.

The translation of Ben Gurion's diary is not very precise, but it shows how elementary and limited Israel's equipment was. I have no record of my report, but I well remember saying that the then air force commander was unsuitable; he was dismissed from his post within forty-eight hours. It was at this time that Israel acquired one or two real but old secondhand fighting planes.

At first Israel's GHQ was accommodated in a modest building in central Tel Aviv known as 'the Red House', but not long after I arrived it was moved out into Ramat Gan, where the premises were spacious enough to house a number of government departments, including the Ministry of Defence. Ben Gurion spent much of his time there. My office was near his; later I had offices near Dizengoff Street in central Tel Aviv, which I shared with two of Ben Gurion's top aides concerned with defence, Shkolnik and Koslowski. Some years later I bumped into an old friend in London whom I hadn't seen for a long time. He said in the course of conversation, 'By the way, Marcus, what became of those two chaps who were in your office when the war was on in 1948 – they seemed interesting?'

I said, 'They changed their names and did very well.'

He said, 'Do you mean they did well because they changed their names?'

'No,' I replied. 'Shkolnik changed his name to Eshkol and became Israel's third Prime Minister, and Koslowski changed his name to Sapir and became one of the leaders of the largest party in the country, Mapai, Minister of Finance and the main architect of Israel's economic development.'

Sapir came from Poland in 1929 and worked as a labourer in the orange groves of Kfar Saba by day and as an accountant's clerk at night. Large, broad, with a big, balding head and a high forehead, he was built like a huge tank and talked like a machine-gun. Even as a young man he exuded that physical and mental strength which was later to make him Israel's undisputed paymaster for more than a decade. He was a formidable figure, all the more intimidating for his ability to work sixteen hours a day with no sign of fatigue; as for his probity, he lived in almost puritanical simplicity to his dying day. At the time we worked together he was quartermaster to the Haganah (Israeli Defence Force), but he soon succeeded Eshkol as Director-General of the Ministry and later became Finance Minister.

When we were working together in 1948, Eshkol was the Director-General of the Ministry of Defence. He had come to Palestine from the Ukraine at the age of nineteen. Even in those days he showed those fundamental qualities – a sense of humour and a congenial spirit, a gift for compromise – which led to much of his success and also, I suppose, to the criticisms later made of him. I remember well one particular incident with Eshkol forty-eight hours before the end of the first ceasefire. The date was 8 July; in the afternoon Eshkol said, 'Let's go to one of the kibbutzim in the north.' It wasn't far from Degania, which was under siege. We arrived there in the late afternoon. The settlers were delighted to see us and morale seemed high. About midnight the Jordanians or Syrians broke the ceasefire and began shelling the settlement. We got into trenches, where we spent the next three or four hours while the desultory shelling continued. Before dawn broke, those in charge of the kibbutz said we had better leave, otherwise we would make a good target, spotlit by the rising sun as we climbed the hill from the settlement towards the road that would take us south. On the way up the car stalled; the only man, I imagine, who knew less about the mechanics of a car than I did was Eshkol. I lifted the bonnet, but hadn't a clue what to do or to look for. Suddenly the enemy opened fire and the shells began to come uncomfortably close. We couldn't think how they could fire at us relatively accurately while it was still dark until I went round the back of the car and found that Eshkol still had his foot on the brake pedal and two big red brake lights were glowing in the dark, making us an excellent target. Hastily he released the pedal, put on the handbrake, and the lights went out. I suggested that we made another attempt to start the car; both of us were highly relieved to hear the engine splutter into life. We drove back to Tel Aviv none the worse, though somewhat frightened by our experience. I remained friendly with Eshkol and Sapir until their deaths.

Because of my responsibilities, Ben Gurion often invited me to take part in the evening discussions he held during the War of Independence; generally there were four or five present – Ben Gurion, Sharrett, the Foreign Minister, Kaplan, Finance, Yadin, Chief of Staff; sometimes one or two others joined in. Occasionally we discussed economic matters, but usually we would talk about the military events and problems of the day and about plans for future action. At this time all imports of military and civilian stores, limited as they were, came through Haifa in the north, the only port operational in the new state. It had four quays where ships could come alongside for unloading; there was a limited amount of discharge to lighters, but generally there were several ships waiting to unload.

The width of Israel at the narrow point of the coastal plain from the sea to the West Bank, then held by the Arabs, was about eleven miles; the main fighting fronts and the bulk of the population were in the south, and stores of every kind had to pass along this narrow corridor. It worried me that the Arabs, if they made a determined attack, might cut Israel in two; then no supplies could be delivered either to the major fronts or to the majority of the Jewish population. I said to Ben Gurion, 'It is essential that we get some of the ships waiting to unload at Haifa brought down to Tel Aviv/Jaffa, then unloaded to lighter, so that we establish a supply line direct to the major fronts and are not dependent upon Haifa alone.' Sharrett, who was always a stickler for what could be done legally, said, 'The problem is that under our law we have no means of ordering ships that are supplying us to come down from the comparative security of Haifa to the more risky waters of Tel Aviv/Jaffa. There's nothing we can do.' Tel Aviv was being bombed by Arab planes. Some discussion took place; we didn't get anywhere. Ben Gurion had a great admiration for Churchill, not just because of Churchill's great and constant support for Zionism over many years, but also because of his courage, determination and refusal to accept defeat, and above all for his readiness to take decisive action when those around were hesitant. I found during the War of Independence that on the rare occasions when Ben Gurion hesitated to make a decision he would respond to a remark such as, 'Well, you know what Mr Churchill would have done.' On this occasion I said, 'Mr Ben Gurion, you know what Mr Churchill would have done in such circumstances; he would have given the order and somehow or other it would have been carried out even if there appeared to be no so-called legal means of doing so.'

Ben Gurion picked up the telephone and, though it was late at night, got through to Amos Landman, a man of enormous girth and much ability, who was in charge of Haifa port. He asked Landman about the position in Haifa. 'There are four ships unloading,' he answered, and I think he said six waiting to unload. Ben Gurion said, 'I want four ships to sail south within twenty-four hours to unload in the Jaffa/Tel Aviv area.' When Landman said he had no means of ordering them to do this Ben Gurion replied, 'Promise whatever is necessary, but get four of them there.'

Within thirty-six hours two ships were anchored off Jaffa; one was bombed by Egyptian aircraft, but not hit. The unloading was successful and there was a bonus. As a result of this incident certain western governments warned the Arabs that if ships going about their lawful business were bombed they would regard it, if not as a *casus belli*, at least as a serious affront about which action would be taken. The precedent of unloading at Jaffa/Tel Aviv had now been established. Fortunately Israel was not cut in two.

Fundamentally Ben Gurion was a man of peace, but he had an instinct for leadership in war as well as peace. During the first truce in June/July the Israelis smuggled in four modest field guns of ancient vintage. They were small enough to go in the trailer of a jeep and were fired over open sights, but these four guns were a real addition to the strength of the then virtually non-existent Israeli artillery. The UN had observers along the coast during the truce period because neither side was supposed to bring in additional weapons. Of course it was no problem for the Arabs to bring them through their own countries, but Israel's only entry route was by sea. It was decided to land the guns near Netanya, so I gave a party at our house in Tel Mond for the UN observers from the Netanya area. I invited some charming Israeli girls, with instructions that on no account was the party to break up before three in the morning, by which time the guns should have been landed; they were.

Jewish Jerusalem was still under siege, rations were down to one thousand calories a day and there was a danger that the city might have to surrender. At the same time Kibbutz Degania, one of the oldest and most important settlements in the north, had been besieged for several weeks and was largely surrounded by the Syrians, who were attacking it with artillery and tanks. Against this the kibbutz had only rifles, light machine-guns and Molotov cocktails. So far they had fought off the attacks; but now Baratz, a senior member of the kibbutz and an old friend of Ben Gurion, came through the lines to beg for support before the kibbutz was overwhelmed.

When we acquired the four guns through Netanya, Yadin, then Chief of Staff, and I went to Ben Gurion as Commander-in-Chief and asked him whether he wanted the guns sent to Degania or, if possible, to Jerusalem. He replied, 'Two to Degania, two to Jerusalem.' We explained that the four guns, to have any effective firing power at all, should be fired together as a battery. Ben Gurion said he understood, so we asked again, 'Where do you want them sent?' He replied, 'Two to Degania, two to Jerusalem,' and that was that. Two were sent to Jerusalem but because they couldn't get up the so-called Burma Road, which the Israelis had built, they were held up at Latrun and did not reach Jerusalem. The two sent to Degania arrived with some ammunition just as the Syrians were mounting what would probably have been the final assault with a number of tanks and considerable fire-power. Fired over open sights, the first Israeli shell hit the leading Syrian tank, which burst into flames, and a minute or two later another tank was hit. The Syrians retreated and did not come back. The destroyed tank was still to be seen in Degania as a monument a year or two ago.

Subsequently I asked Ben Gurion why, against the advice of Yadin and myself, he had decided to send two guns to Jerusalem and two to Degania and not all four to one place. He replied, 'I knew that even all four together were not much good, they were so old and small, but if you have nothing more than a medium machine-gun and some rifles and you see two pieces of artillery arrive, large compared with any weapons you may have (and you don't know much about artillery), it's a great morale booster and you will fight better for it.'

Ben Gurion did not have the same understanding for finance as he did for war – and peace. He had a wonderful library, covering a wide range of subjects from Jewish history to Chinese philosophy. He had read every book in it and had a remarkably retentive mind. He would on rare occasions make secret visits to England with the purpose of visiting bookshops, particularly Blackwell's in Oxford. David Moushine, his secretary in 1950, told me that on one particular occasion Ben Gurion went to Oxford visiting bookshops to look for old volumes of the classics, which he was at the time studying. After his return to Jerusalem he was proudly showing the carton full of books to the late Eliezer Kaplan, then Minister of Finance, explaining with great glee the 'metziot' (bargains) he had found. Mr Kaplan asked him 'How did you pay for the books?'

'That's simple,' answered Ben Gurion. 'Marcus Sieff paid for them there and I shall return to him the equivalent in Israeli pounds.'

'Do you know that you contravened the foreign currency regulations by doing this?' asked Kaplan.

'I don't see that I did,' replied the Prime Minister. 'Whom does it concern that Marcus paid for the books in England and I paid him back in Israel?'

'It concerns me as Minister of Finance. You broke the law by smuggling currency out of the country.'

To no avail. Ben Gurion just could not accept that he had done something wrong. '*Mize ichpat* (whose concern is it)?' he repeated.

In despair, Kaplan sent for Dolik Horowitz, then Director-general of the Ministry of Finance, to come and explain the contravention committed by Ben Gurion. Horowitz came over from his office and tried his best, but just could not convince Ben Gurion that he had broken the law. Finally, both Kaplan and Horowitz gave up and decided not to prosecute the offender.

I was on good terms with Chaim Weizmann, who had now become Israel's first President. Ben Gurion's and Weizmann's relations were not close. I think Ben Gurion was somewhat jealous of Weizmann, while the latter did not fully appreciate the former's qualities. If any single person could be said to have brought the State of Israel into existence it was Chaim Weizmann. He had secured the Balfour Declaration, which had promised a national home for the Jews in Palestine thirty years previously and which was the first step towards a Jewish state; Ben Gurion was then a sergeant in the British army. It was Weizmann who personally convinced President Truman that the United States should recognize the new State of Israel on 14 May 1948. On the other hand, it was Ben Gurion as Prime Minister and Minister of Defence who led Israel's struggle, first for survival then for victory, against the Arab onslaught. Ben Gurion had been carrying on a political and military struggle in Palestine for many years and emerged as Israel's political and military chief. The President of Israel is a man without political power, though in times of crisis, he can intervene and bring the party leaders together, as President Herzog did recently; at such times his influence can be very important.

Sometimes, when I was going to see Weizmann (the head of whose office at that time was George Weidenfeld, today Lord Weidenfeld), Ben Gurion would ask where I was going. I would say I was going to see the modern Moses. This used to irk him, and he used to say, 'Whom do you mean? Do you mean you're going to see the President?' I used to say, 'Yes,' and he would then ask, 'Who am I?' I would reply, 'You're the modern Joshua,' which didn't please him — he considered Joshua less important than Moses.

Weizmann had always sought agreement with Britain and it had been his fond hope for many years that a Jewish state in Palestine would be an eighth Dominion, closely allied to Britain, helping Britain to guard the Suez Canal — a dream never to be realized. He used to talk to us about it. Weizmann had great faith in Britain; Ben Gurion, though in many ways an admirer of much that was British, didn't trust the British Government, particularly the Foreign Office, as he believed that many of the senior Foreign Office officials had over the thirty years following the Balfour Declaration regarded it as an undertaking Britain should never have entered into. Senior members of the Foreign Office were undoubtedly far from helpful in implementing the Balfour Declaration. Ben Gurion understood this, but Weizmann didn't want to believe it, and in the period leading up to the establishment of the state Weizmann's support for Britain cost him dearly in influence in many Jewish circles, while Ben Gurion's influence increased.

Some two years earlier Ben Gurion, as one of the main Jewish leaders, had come to London to ask Bevin to give that support to the Jewish cause which the Labour Party had pledged. Not only Bevin but virtually every other Labour Party leader — except William Jowitt, the Lord Chancellor — refused to see him. Ben Gurion believed that the British, while telling the world they must and would be neutral between the Jews and Arabs, did a great deal to help the Arabs. He believed that the Labour Government had put Arab oil above their promises and principles. Though a convinced socialist, he was not doctrinaire. Throughout his career he fought the extremists outside and within his own party. He believed in the possibility of peace with the Arabs and strove for it. He thought the British way of life and system of government the best in the world of his day.

It was with Yadin that I met Moshe Dayan. He had been born in Palestine, a Sabra, in 1915. In 1948 he was already wearing his eye patch, covering damage sustained when fighting for the British in the Lebanese/Syrian campaign of 1941. He had joined the Haganah when a boy and had been one of the first volunteers in Wingate's Special Night Squads. Many people thought that he wore his eye patch for the publicity it gave him; in fact he deplored it for just that reason.

He attracted publicity as the candle does the moth, though he was in fact a relatively shy man. Nevertheless he was outspoken in his quiet way and the people of whom he did not approve soon knew it. Even in those early days, when fear for their future made some Israelis aggressive, Dayan was, like Ben Gurion, moderate in his hopes and intentions. He was a farmer, a soldier and a politician; after resigning as chief of staff, he became Minister of Agriculture, then Defence Minister, then Foreign Minister. His aim was peace and security for Israel; he was not an expansionist. His early death was a great loss.

Writing of Dayan makes me think immediately of Shimon Peres, his friend and colleague for many years. Shimon was the youngest of the group, having been born in Poland in 1923. In 1947, when only twenty-four, he was picked out by Ben Gurion and made responsible for arms and manpower at the headquarters of the Haganah. He was only twenty-nine when he became Director-General of the Defence Ministry. When Ben Gurion was Minister of Defence and Commander-in-Chief he owed much to Peres, who was largely responsible before the 1967 Six-Day War for bringing about that close co-operation with the French that led to their supplying the arms which greatly helped Israel's dramatic victory in that war.

In those early days I met and became friendly with both Golda Meir and Abba Eban. In 1948 Golda became Israel's first ambassador to Moscow. I got to know her well in the following year, when she was elected to the Knesset and became Minister of Labour. We got on well partly because she admired Mother's work. In 1965 she withdrew from political life, but was asked to return, reluctantly agreed, and ultimately became Prime Minister. Though she had profound socialist convictions, she was objective. Just before she died, she asked me if I had ever met Mrs Thatcher, who had visited Israel when Secretary of State for Education in Mr Heath's administration. I said I had, but didn't know her well. I said, 'Why do you want to know?'

Her reply was, 'In my view she is the best political leader I have met from Britain since I came into politics.'

'Golda,' I said, 'you're one woman talking about another.'

She replied, 'Marcus, you've known me for over twenty years and you ought to know better than to make a remark like that.'

I apologized.

I got to know Abba Eban when, in 1948, he was Israel's first representative to the United Nations, a post which in 1950 he combined with that of ambassador to Washington. In 1958, after he had been back in Israel for several years, I had close contact with him because he became President of the Weizmann Institute of Science for eight years. Born in Cape Town, Eban came to London when he was six and from school won a scholarship to Cambridge, was President of the Union, took three Firsts and was elected a fellow and tutor of Pembroke College. He is a brilliant orator, Arabic being one of the languages he has mastered. He became Israel's Foreign Minister and her leading diplomat.

Another colleague of the War of Independence with whom I still work was Teddy Kollek, who has now been Mayor of Jerusalem for over twenty years; but more of him later.

CHAPTER EIGHT

AFTER the State of Israel was proclaimed the British Government had begun to bring the armed forces home. To withdraw them all would obviously take some time, but it seemed to Israel observers that the rate of evacuation was strangely slow. It was reported to the Israeli Ministry of Defence that four weeks or so after the announcement of withdrawal there were still some 15,000 troops in the Haifa enclave under General MacMillan. Ben Gurion began to suspect that they were going to remain there. About mid-June he said to me, 'I believe, Marcus, that you British are not going to get out of Israel. Your troops will stay in the Haifa enclave until the Arabs have the knife at our throats, and then the British Government will expect us to go down on our knees and beg you to stay on, take back the mandate and rule Palestine again.' I told him that I didn't share his view. 'Let me go to General MacMillan and ask him what his plans are,' I said. 'I don't know him personally but he knows I'm here, who I am and what I am doing.' So, with Ben Gurion's agreement, I went to see MacMillan. I drove up to Haifa; he received me courteously, offered me a drink and asked what he could do for me. Without further preliminaries I asked him directly if all the British troops were going to be withdrawn. 'Yes,' he replied, 'we shall complete our evacuation in about ten days and I shall be the last serving British soldier to embark.' And indeed he was, as he told me himself many years later. This put the date of the final evacuation at 30 June.

I asked him what he thought of the general situation. He replied, 'There will be heavy fighting. The Jews will win, and so they should.'

'Why?' I asked. 'They are outgunned, outplaned, outmanned, and even though they've pushed back the enemy on two fronts the Arab Legion is still at Latrun, the Syrians are near Degania, the Egyptians are approaching Tel Aviv, and the so-called Liberation Army is still in Galilee.'

'Yes,' said General MacMillan, 'but the Jews have a cause and know what they are fighting for; they are fighting for survival. No matter what the odds are against them they will win. I am sorry we are not helping them.'

'General,' I remarked, 'we're not supposed to be helping either side, we're neutral.'

'We are supposed to be,' he replied, 'but are we?'

We finished our drinks; he then insisted that I should be taken back to my hotel escorted by one of his officers in a jeep. A few minutes after I reached my hotel room and was getting ready to return to Tel Aviv, my door was thrown open and three men burst in. They were from the Irgun Zvai Leumi, the larger of two terrorist organizations – the Stern Gang being the other – both of which at that time operated independently of and to the embarrassment of the official Israeli Government and armed forces. They demanded to know what I had been doing closeted with the commander of the British forces. I told them that I was in Haifa as an emissary of the Prime Minister, that I was now on my way to Tel Aviv to give my report to the Prime Minister in person, that the report was for his ears only, and that in the meantime they had better buzz off. They did.

I saw Ben Gurion the following morning. 'Prime Minister,' I said, 'we, the British, are leaving us, the Jews, in ten days' time and what's more General MacMillan says that we, the Jews, are going to win.'

Ben Gurion said, 'Of course we are going to win. You didn't ever doubt it, did you?'

I replied, 'For the last fortnight I have been wondering how I was going to get out of the country alive.'

On 22 June, during the first ceasefire, I found myself witnessing an incident that could have destroyed the new-born state. The Irgun had purchased in the United States the previous April an LST (tank landing ship), which they named the *Altalena*, and had loaded it with arms, ammunition and explosives of various kinds, destined for the members of their group in Israel. The purchase was made a few days before the state came into being, when total war looked imminent and before a government had been formed. While the *Altalena* was en route for Israel discussions took place between Ben Gurion, the members of his new government and the Irgun about their handing over the *Altalena* and its contents to the authorized government of the country. No decision was reached. The *Altalena* arrived during the first truce at Kfar Vitkin, a few miles north of Tel Aviv, on the evening of 21 June. When the Irgun refused to hand over the vessel or its contents, fighting broke out between the Israel Defence Force (IDF) and the Irgun, in which eight people were killed and twenty-four wounded. The ship was driven off. The following morning it anchored some two or three hundred yards off Tel Aviv. Negotiations went on during the morning for the handing over of the ship and its contents to the government.

That morning I had been to a meeting with Ben Gurion. At midday he dropped me about three or four hundred yards from the sea front in the main street of the city and I started to make my way to the little Kaete Dan Hotel on the front where I was staying. As Ben Gurion drove away machine-guns and rifle fire opened up around me and I had literally to crawl on my hands and knees the last two hundred yards to the hotel. I had been caught in the middle of a battle between the Israeli army and the Irgun. The *Altalena*, still at anchor off the beach, had been attacked and was now on fire. In the hotel, around which the firing continued, were two members of the Irgun, who told me that the ship was full of 500 lb bombs and other highly explosive materials. Remembering the great explosion at Bari, I decided that the nearby streets had better be evacuated. I feared that when the ship blew up there might be heavy casualties. However, the members of the Irgun had greatly exaggerated what was in the ships, describing the 2 lb shells as 500 lb bombs. Eventually the *Altalena* sank, but a further sixteen people were killed and seventy-five wounded in what was almost a civil war, with the Arabs only twenty miles away.

Many members of the Irgun were subsequently arrested. This determined action under Ben Gurion, against what were then splinter groups, established the authority of the month-old Government of Israel and was of historic significance. The Irgun and the Stern Gang were no longer tolerated as independent organizations under their own commanders.

Over the next two months the Israelis advanced on all fronts and the siege of Jerusalem was lifted. On 9 June, some three-and-a-half weeks after the fighting had broken out, the Arabs and Israelis agreed to the month's ceasefire ordered by the Security Council of the United Nations. Hostilities were resumed a month later. Israel's equipment was improving, as was her overall position. When a second ceasefire was accepted by both parties on 18 July the Israeli forces broke out of their perimeters and took the Arab towns of Ramaleh and Lydda (from now on to become their main airport) and captured Nazareth. Tens of thousands of Arabs left their homes. The capacity, or desire, of the Arab states to fight the Jews in Israel was put in doubt. Divisions of opinion in high command of the Arab states were weakening their war effort. The ability of the Israelis to resist any attempt to drive them into the sea was no longer in question.

Ben Gurion knew this would be no more than another lull. He continued to look to improving Israel's defences. In case the Arabs made a large-scale attempt to cut off the supplies and manpower now coming in by sea, he asked me to look at what might be done to strengthen the capabilities of the Israeli navy.

Ministry of Defence
27.7.48

To Marcus Sieff
To The Navy
To General Headquarters

You are requested to examine the state of the navy – from the point of view of structure, system of administration, procedures and discipline, equipment and weaponry, supply and communication, planning, and the operation and efficiency of the navy within the general defence set-up – and to submit your conclusions and recommendations.

You are authorized to call upon any officer or employee of the navy as well as officers of the general headquarters, to hear their testimony and views.

Signed: David Ben Gurion

Later he wrote in his diary:

6.8.48

The navy had fewer trained men, experts and qualifications than any other service, but people with wartime seagoing experience are coming to strengthen it. They are not being treated properly and are becoming disappointed. Sieff suggests to me that Harris should deal with Gahal.... In Sieff's opinion, we should not acquire another refugee ship, but should concentrate on the four we already have and convert them into warships. For combined military and naval operations he suggests Schumacher, who received training for this in the British navy. Klein is enthusiastic, but has had little experience. There is a lack of co-ordination between the navy and the army. [Sieff] thinks that Shilomo Shamir should serve as the liaison between the general staff and the navy and air force. The gunnery school should basically be a joint one for the army, air force and navy. Afterwards, each of them will specialize in its own sphere. That is the routine for radar, communications, etc.

It was at this time that I met Ruth Havilio, whose family had lived in Palestine for several generations. She was a second lieutenant in the Israeli navy, their first woman officer, I think. She was highly intelligent and charming, aged about thirty, and spoke a number of languages, including English, perfectly. She was assigned to help me when I interviewed navy personnel. She prepared summaries of what was said, highlighting those points which she thought would be helpful in the report. When the report was finished, I asked that she be seconded to me and she continued to work as my personal assistant throughout the war period; she had much ability. She thought I ought to improve my limited Hebrew and on the quieter days she insisted that we spoke only Hebrew for one hour. I am afraid that I was a poor pupil but what little I remember today I owe largely to Ruth. After I left Ben Gurion's service I asked for her to be transferred to his office; she became the senior secretary there for a considerable period during his premiership.

Efforts were now being made to get more military aircraft into Israel. Three old Liberator bombers from the United States flew in and some old German Messerschmidt fighters were brought in from Czechoslovakia, their components carried in the bellies of C46 transport planes. These landed by torchlight in the Northern Negev (not far from a main Egyptian fighter base) and their contents were taken to an airfield north of Tel Aviv for assembly. It was here that I met Chaim Weizmann's nephew, Ezer Weizman, later to become an outstanding commander of the Israeli air force and minister of defence. He had volunteered for the R.A.F during World War II, was a fine fighter pilot and had seen service in a number of areas, including Burma. He is a man of great charm and much ability, whom I still see regularly and for whom I have both respect and affection.

Until these fighter planes were operational the Arab bombers, mainly Egyptian, attacked Tel Aviv, and other parts of Israel, with impunity. One morning there were two Arab bombers circling lazily around Tel Aviv dropping a bomb here and there, out of range of the few Israeli machine-guns. One bomb hit a bus queue, causing some twenty casualties. Suddenly two fighters approached from the north of the city. The Arabs at first thought they were Egyptian fighters, but soon discovered that they were Israeli, turned tail and fled to the south. I saw one being shot down over Jaffa; the other was shot down a few miles away over Rehovot. That was the last time Arab planes bombed Tel Aviv.

It was good to have something like an air force and more vehicles on the ground to support them. However, Israel was desperately short of fuel. I had a survey made of the supply position. Before evacuating its Haifa refineries the Shell Oil Company had emptied the oil tanks there, but one of the Israeli engineers advised me that the sludge left at the bottom of the oil tanks would contain some petrol, which could be drained off, at the risk of some damage to the tanks – which were the property of Shell. Sharrett, the Foreign Minister, ever the cautious legalist, told a meeting of the informal group I described earlier that we couldn't take the risk of damaging Shell's property. Ben Gurion said we should chance it; I supported him. The tanks were drained successfully and we squeezed out a few hundred tons of usable fuel. No damage was done to the tanks. This manoeuvre alleviated the fuel shortage for only a short time. Some fuel was bought from Mexico, but much larger supplies were essential if Israel was to survive. So Ben Gurion asked Felix Shinnar, one of the most able Israeli immigrants from Germany, to go to Rumania to buy fuel. He flew in one of the DC3s and bought a considerable amount, for which he paid cash. Israel had no wish to give any of the eastern bloc countries an excuse for obtaining a political *quid pro quo* in return for supplies on credit. Russia had given recognition to Israel with remarkable alacrity in the belief that, cold-shouldered by Britain, Israel might become a valuable Middle Eastern ally. Ben Gurion was conscious of this and deeply suspicious of Russia's motives. The last thing he wanted to do, therefore, was to go cap in hand to any of the eastern bloc countries and ask favours. He made sure that Israel paid for any supplies from the bloc. I discussed with Ben Gurion the desirability of my going back to London to see if Israel could buy oil from the United Kingdom. He thought it a good idea and so I flew home at the end of September.

I had an introduction to Simon Voss, the head of the Trinidad Oil Company, whom I arranged to meet on the Friday following my arrival. I told him what the Israeli position was; he was sympathetic

to my request for supplies, but said he was restricted in the movements his tankers could make. They were not allowed outside the
western hemisphere, which precluded their coming to Israel.
However, because he wanted to help, he at once telephoned Sir Frank
Hopwood, then a senior managing director of Shell, and asked him
to see me. Sir Frank invited me immediately to Shell's head office,
then in the Strand. When I met him, I told him the whole story,
beginning with the draining of the storage tanks at Haifa and ending
with the Israelis' fears of becoming involved in a political *quid pro
quo* if they tried to buy more fuel from the eastern bloc. Sir Frank
told me that Shell was quite willing to sell oil to Israel, but was
prevented from doing so by the Foreign Office. He said I could use
this information if I wished, but that he would prefer me not to reveal
its source unless I felt this really necessary.

An hour later, before leaving London for Israel via Paris, where
the UN was meeting at the Palais de Chaillot on the Middle East
situation, I went to lunch with Father and Simon Marks at the office.
On arrival I found they had a guest, Mr Beeley, later to become Sir
Harold Beeley, our ambassador to Egypt, who was in charge of the
Middle East desk at the Foreign Office and was the Foreign Secretary's
main adviser on Palestine. It was a remarkable coincidence – one of
those coincidences which only happen in real life – since it was he
who was, probably, largely responsible for preventing the sale of
oil to Israel. I asked him if the Foreign Office wanted to give
Russia an entry into the Middle East, a region at that time where
they had little contact and in which they had so far failed to find
any support. He said, 'Of course not; I don't know what you
mean.'

'Why then,' I asked, 'does the Foreign Office refuse to allow British
oil companies to sell oil to Israel? The Israelis will have to turn to
the eastern bloc. Do you realize that your policy could create an
unwilling Russian satellite in the Middle East?'

He affected to be surprised. 'So you really mean what you say,'
he said, 'when you tell me that the Foreign Office has stopped the
sale of oil to Israel? You mustn't believe such canards or fairy tales' –
a phrase I shall remember for the rest of my life.

At that point I felt justified in revealing my source. I told him
about my visit to Shell just an hour and a half earlier and what Sir
Frank Hopwood had said. 'Oh, well,' he said, somewhat embarrassed,

'of course Shell may have asked our advice and we would have had to tell them we thought there was a risk to their tankers in selling oil to the Israelis when Israel was fighting the Arabs. They would be entering a war zone and we couldn't give any protection.' I replied that Haifa appeared risk-free and that ships from many countries were unloading there; but I could see that I would get nowhere by talking to Mr Beeley. I do not think he would have cared a damn if Israel had been wiped out.

That evening I flew to Paris. First thing the next morning I went to the Palais de Chaillot in the hope of seeing Hector McNeil, Minister of State at the Foreign Office, who was leading the British delegation. He and I were friendly and I had found him objective about the Middle East. When I arrived he was speaking. I left a message that I would be grateful if he could see me as I had some important information; I would be at the George V Hotel until two o'clock that afternoon but then I was flying to Israel. He turned up at 1.55 pm, just as I was leaving the hotel. I told him how British policy could create an unwilling Russian satellite in the Middle East. As I spoke the look on his face changed. 'My God,' he said, 'we never looked at it like that. The boss [Ernest Bevin] is arriving in Paris later this afternoon; I'll talk to him.'

I then left for Israel. We were in a semi-freighter aircraft without heating and it was cold. We were held up at Athens overnight and after a most unpleasant journey we reached Lydda the following day. Eli Kirschner, a South African immigrant with whom I worked closely in Israel, greeted me with the news that Shell was negotiating to sell a tanker of oil to Israel; it duly arrived. I think this was one of the turning points in Israel's capacity to fight. I thank God for the resolution and speed with which Ernest Bevin acted on that occasion.

Over the next few months there were periods of ceasefire ordered by the United Nations and supervised as far as possible by the United Nations truce commission. At those times the United Nations mediator, Count Bernadotte, sought to find a basis for a settlement. From time to time the truce was breached, not only by the Arabs but also by the Israelis. Hector McNeil said that once some agreement was reached between the Jews and the Arabs, Britain would give recognition to Israel. I informed Ben Gurion. His diary provides a fuller account of my efforts in London than my memory can:

Wednesday 6.10.48

Marcus Sieff has returned. While in London he saw members of the cabinet: Cripps, Lord Addison, Bevan, Shinwell, Dalton, Hector McNeil, and also a number of Conservatives: Lord Salisbury [Cranborne], Eden, Amery, Stanley, Macmillan, Walter Elliot [members of the shadow cabinet], Duncan Sandys [Churchill's son-in-law], as well as a number of Liberals: Clement Davies, Lord Samuel.... He also saw the leaders of the Board of Trade, defence ministry people, people from *The Times*, Mosley, Lord Layton, Crookshank [*News Chronicle*], various other people, newspapers, the manager of Shell and the head of the Federation of British Industries.

Cripps was sympathetic. In general, there was indifference at first, but then they began to show some interest. Others also revealed a conscience. Sieff presented a memorandum to them, and it was also sent to Churchill. They will acknowledge the State of Israel after a decision has been taken by the United Nations. Eden admitted in conversation that the [Arab] League is ruined. Churchill, Attlee, Douglas [the American ambassador] and Eden have influence with Bevin. The quarrel between Britain and Egypt continues to grow. The British regard Farouk as impossible. He wants to create a ferment in the Middle East, in order to divert public attention from domestic troubles. Bevin wanted to send more arms to Transjordan and Iraq, but the cabinet voted him down. So long as Israel does not make war, they will not allow arms to be sent to Transjordan.

America is hand in glove with Britain on Near East questions. Actually, Britain is leading America in the region.

The British want a UN decision to settle the matter and will then accord *de jure* recognition. McNeil told Marcus that it will not be easy to get Bernadotte's report accepted by the UN as it stands....

The Federation of Industries people are prepared to send a delegation to Israel to discuss indirect relations. It is to be hoped that our military victory, the suppression of the *Altalena* and the measures taken against terrorism will have a favourable effect in Britain.

These months, September and October, put a great strain on Israeli relations with Britain and the United States. On 17 September Count Bernadotte, the United Nations mediator, had been assassinated in Jerusalem by Zionist terrorists calling themselves members of the Fatherland Front. Some hundreds of these Sternists were put in gaol as a result. Most of them overpowered their guards and escaped on 9 October. In the next few days an Israeli military convoy passed through Egyptian-held territory in the Negev to relieve two isolated Jewish settlements and was attacked by Egyptian troops. Israeli troops responded with an offensive, as a result of which the Egyptian-occupied area was much reduced and Beersheba was captured. Though it was only a week or so since I had come back to Israel from London, it was decided that I should return at once to solicit all possible understanding and support for Israel, and urge the cause of recognition on the British Government.

November and December 1948 were — once again — not good months to be in London defending the Israeli cause. On 4 November the security council issued a cease-fire order, which the Israelis ignored. Fighting broke out in Galilee, where Israeli forces attacked the remainder of the Arab Liberation Army and drove it over the Lebanese frontier. In December the Negev had still not been handed to the Arabs, as had been prescribed by Count Bernadotte's report; and an Egyptian brigade was still cut off at Faluja. The number of Arabs displaced by the fighting now amounted to 600,000. The Israeli Government stated repeatedly that it could not permit the return of these unfortunate people except under the terms of a final peace settlement to which it could agree. Subsequently hundreds of thousands of Jews were driven or fled from Arab countries to settle in Israel, more in number than the Arabs who fled from or were driven out of Israel. But, whereas the Israelis integrated the Jewish refugees, and most of them became valuable citizens, the Arab governments, despite their wealth and large, relatively uninhabited territories, refused to try to settle and integrate the Palestinian refugees. They were kept in squalid, sometimes appalling, conditions to become a rallying cause for continued hostility towards Israel, and were frequently encouraged to retaliate by terrorist action and murderous attacks.

In spite of this, the cards in London were stacked against the Israelis. Again I saw several leading members of the government and the opposition. Dick Crossman, a leading Labour MP, whom I got to know well, had at the end of the Second World War favoured the Arabs, but in 1946, as a result of his membership of the Anglo–American committee on Palestine, appointed by President Truman and Prime Minister Attlee, he changed his views and became a lifelong friend of Israel. He tried to get me an interview with the Prime Minister and at least succeeded in persuading one of the Prime Minister's private secretaries to write to the Foreign Office asking if Attlee ought to give me a hearing. Eddie Tomkins, later to become a friend of mine, who had a distinguished diplomatic career, replied from the Foreign Office to Number 10 as follows:

16 November 1948

PRIME MINISTER'S
Personal Case

I must apologize for the delay in replying to your letter of the 10th November enclosing a letter from Mr Crossman to the Prime Minister and a memorandum prepared by Colonel Marcus Sieff. I am afraid little is known here about Colonel Sieff except that his father is an influential member of Marks and Spencer, one of whose directors, Mr Simon Marks, has been most assiduous in his support of the Jewish cause. Colonel Sieff has been very active in canvassing influential support for his views, and copies of his earlier memorandum were circulated to a number of prominent people including the Chancellor of the Exchequer and Lord Henderson.

The aim of Colonel Sieff's proposed visit to the Prime Minister would presumably be to emphasize the points made in his memorandum and to urge immediate recognition of the Jewish state and abandonment of the Bernadotte plan in favour of direct Jewish–Arab negotiations. He would be likely to argue that the Jewish state in its present form has come to stay, and that, by recognizing it now, we might strengthen the moderate elements in it at the expense of the potentially Communist ones.

We understand that Colonel Sieff has already had interviews with the Chancellor of the Exchequer and the Minister of Defence. We are prepared to receive him at the Foreign Office at any time he may wish to call but we are inclined to think that it is unnecessary for the Prime Minister to spare time to see him.

I am returning Mr Crossman's letter and the memorandum.

E. E. TOMKINS

J. L. Pumphrey, Esq.,
10 Downing Street.

16 November 1948

To: R. H. S. Crossman M.P.

Thank you very much for sending me Colonel Sieff's memorandum. I think I understand fully the points which he makes.

I gather that he has already seen the Chancellor of the Exchequer and the Minister of Defence. I have so much on hand at present that I do not think it necessary to ask him to come to elaborate his memorandum.

C. R. ATTLEE

Of course I did not think that my seeing Bevin would be any use — that's why I wanted to see Attlee.

On this occasion I stayed in London for about ten days. I saw everybody who would see me: politicians, businessmen, newspaper editors and diplomats; I made little progress. There was some consolation and encouragement in the *Observer*, with a powerful leader advocating recognition forthwith.

During one of my visits to London I met Lord Beaverbrook. I phoned his secretary seeking an appointment and was asked to go the following evening at five-thirty to Arlington House. On arrival I was shown into a room where Lord Beaverbrook sat in a dressing-gown suffering from an attack of asthma; lined against the wall he had several editors or deputy editors of his various newspapers, from whom he was tearing off strips. I remember my embarrassment; I made to leave the room, but he called me back, dismissed the members of his staff and asked the question that I had been asked on several occasions by people when I met them for the first time: 'Are you any relation of Israel Sieff?'

'Yes,' I said, 'he is my father.' I explained that I had a good knowledge of what was happening in Israel and told him why I didn't think the British press were being objective. He began to write down some of the points I was making and I knew from what he read back that he wasn't getting it right. I said, 'Lord Beaverbrook, I have a memorandum here which states the facts and might be helpful.' He took the memorandum and said, 'This will do; we'll use it.'

He then asked me if I saw Father often. I said, 'Yes, almost daily.' He rang the bell and, when his man came, he said, 'Bring me a bottle of Perrier-Jouet '29.' I thought I was making progress. However, when the bottle arrived I had second thoughts, because he said, 'I once crossed the Atlantic on the same ship as your father and we talked a great deal; I much enjoyed his company but somehow or other I don't think he approves of me these days and we never meet.' Still hoping that I was going to get editorial support from his newspapers, I made some weak remark like, 'I'm sure you're wrong, Lord Beaverbrook, there must be some misunderstanding.'

'Anyway,' he said, 'your father enjoys good wine. Please see him tomorrow, give him this bottle of champagne with my good wishes, and tell him that at six o'clock tomorrow evening I shall open a similar bottle and drink to his health.' The following day at six o'clock Father and I opened Beaverbrook's bottle of champagne and drank his health. Forty-eight hours later there was a leader, I think in the *Express*, largely based on the memorandum I had given Lord Beaverbrook.

I returned to Israel for four weeks before coming back again to London early in the new year. Meanwhile the Israelis were rapidly gaining the upper hand. In seven days of fighting they had broken through the Egyptian army's positions in southern Palestine and the road to Sinai now lay open. The bulk of the Egyptian forces had been pushed into the Gaza area. When the Egyptian Government asked for a ceasefire on 5 January the Israelis agreed; the fighting stopped on 7 January.

I was now back in London. On the Saturday I went to the cinema with Jon Kimche, the well-known British journalist and commentator on Israeli and international affairs, with whom I had spent much time in Israel, where he did a first-class job. When we came out I bought an evening paper, the *Star*, to see what had happened to Manchester United. Its headline read, 'JEWS SHOOT DOWN 5 RAF PLANES'. The other two evening papers had similar headlines. This was after the ceasefire; Jon Kimche and I were stunned. It came at the very time when I was again trying to get the British Government to recognize Israel. I couldn't believe that the Israelis, however great the provocation, could have been so stupid as to shoot down British planes when they had obviously won their War of Independence.

On the Sunday morning all the major British newspapers came out with headlines generally hostile to Israel, with the exception of the *Observer*. They, while reporting, and querying, the incident, printed a leader which had been written before it occurred and which argued that Britain should try to reach agreement with, and recognize, Israel. On that Sunday the *People*, which had a very large circulation, carried the headline, 'BEVIN ASKS EMPIRE AID TO STOP ISRAEL REDS'. Since many of them had experienced life under Soviet domination, no nation was less 'red' than the Israelis.

The news that followed the first reports of the incident was grim. According to Israeli sources, their pilots had assumed that these British aircraft were Arab. They were flying with Egyptian planes. The British Government responded to the incident by ordering the movement of a British brigade to Aqaba; an aircraft carrier was put under orders to sail from Malta; British troops were embarked on a cruiser at Tobruk, and the British Government made an angry protest to the Israeli Government. The Israelis rejected this and complained that the decision to despatch troops to Aqaba proved Britain's prejudice in the conflict of interests in Palestine. They in turn made an angry protest to the United Nations against Britain's 'unilateral intervention'.

While Jon and I were wondering what could have happened, it suddenly struck us that under the terms of the Anglo–Egyptian Treaty of 1936 British planes were not permitted to fly far outside the Suez Canal zone. What then were these British planes doing so far away from their limits? Had the treaty been scrapped? Kimche immediately rang the duty officer at the Foreign Office; he explained who he was, an accredited journalist, and asked what had happened. Was it true that the Egyptians had abrogated the 1936 Anglo–Egyptian treaty? The officer at the Foreign Office said, 'No, but some British planes have been flying over Sinai.' This, Kimche and I said, meant that British planes must have been 200 to 300 miles away from the Canal zone. Piecing together what we knew, we concluded that British planes had obviously, whether they intended it or not, flown provocatively with Egyptian planes over Israeli air space, or at any rate well outside their permitted area. We felt sure that this could not have happened had not orders for such an operation come from a very senior level.

On the Sunday morning, 10 January, I went to see Nye Bevan, a friend of the family and a member of the cabinet. He greeted me with: 'It's a pretty mess, isn't it?' I asked him if there would be a cabinet meeting to discuss this incident. 'No,' he said. When I went back to see him later that day he told me there would be a meeting of the defence committee the next morning. I asked, 'Why the defence committee and not the cabinet?'

'Well,' he said, 'a cabinet meeting would include people like me, who would certainly look at the problem objectively and in a way not unfriendly to Israel: a meeting of the defence committee would not only exclude me but also Stafford Cripps, who, although not particularly friendly to Israel, is certainly objective. On the other hand the Foreign Secretary sits on the defence committee and, as you know, Ernest Bevin is not too enamoured of the new State of Israel.'

I knew that one member of the defence committee was the Secretary of State for War, Manny Shinwell. I'd had talks with his parliamentary private secretary, George Wigg. So I sent George a note on what I thought had happened to the R.A.F. planes and why. By now I had more information, which turned out to be largely right. Apparently twelve Egyptian fighters, accompanied by five British planes, had flown over the area in question. Four Israeli planes were flying high above them. The Israeli pilots thought that the planes below were all Egyptian and were making a raid. They came down on them out of the sun and attacked. In the course of this attack the Egyptian planes left the area and the British planes and one Egyptian plane were shot down. I am told that Manny Shinwell vigorously took up this version of events with Bevin. The British planes, he argued, had been flying in the company of Egyptian planes which had been behaving as though they were conducting a raid, so the Israelis could not be blamed for the consequences.

Parliament reassembled on 18 January, when Churchill asked Bevin to make a statement on recent events in the Middle East. Mr Bevin said that he would make a full statement the following week, on 26 January, when a full debate on the Middle East would be held.

As soon as I found out what had happened I prepared a memorandum, dated 10 January 1949, based on the information Jon Kimche and I had acquired. The following are some extracts:

1. Five British planes, four Spitfires and one Tempest, have been shot down by Israeli planes or anti-aircraft fire.

2. According to an Air Ministry communiqué, issued Saturday 8 January, five R.A.F. planes were shot down inside the Egyptian border by Jewish planes. The communiqué states that British planes from the Suez Canal zone have been carrying out reconnaissance to ascertain the depth and scale of Jewish incursions into Egyptian territory. It is stated that these reconnaissances have been strictly confined to the Egyptian side of the frontier and that British planes had received orders to avoid combat.

3. An Israeli communiqué, issued Friday evening 7 January, stated that three Egyptian planes were shot down in dogfights, and two Spitfires destroyed, out of a formation of twelve which strafed Jewish lines northeast of Gaza. This would be within that area of Palestine allocated to the Jews under the UN partition of 1947.

5. It is established that no formal warning was given to the Israelis that British planes of the same type and with markings similar to Egyptian planes (red, white and blue roundels – British; white and green roundels– Egyptian) would be operating on the Egyptian/Israeli frontier.

10. The Foreign Office statement on the Israeli air force gave its strength last June, at the time of the first truce, as approximately forty planes, including four fighters and four converted bombers. According to the statement, the air force has now developed to approximately one hundred and twenty planes, including forty fighters (mainly supplied from Czechoslovakia) and thirty bombers. The Foreign Office continues that the air crews are mainly Czechs, Poles and Eastern Europeans, trained in Czechoslovakia.

11. I know from personal experience that in June the fighters were repaired Egyptian Spitfires which the Jews had shot down, and the remainder of the air force consisted mainly of Austers — 90 mph, unarmed, artillery-spotting planes — sold as scrap by British war disposal to the Jews. The Jews cannibalized these unserviceable planes and got some into the air. At this period the Arabs possessed 100–150 fighters and fighter-bombers, mainly Spitfires and forty to fifty bombers....

13. In my two visits to Israel I met personally a very large number of the air crews. They consisted almost entirely of Palestinian-born Jews, trained in the R.A.F. during the war, and Jewish volunteers from the U.S.A. and the Empire, who fought in the allied air forces.

Naturally there had been some development of the Israeli air force since May. At the time the state proclaimed there was no air force. They now had a few Spitfires, some Messerschmidts and three Liberator bombers. But the Foreign Office estimate of the strength of the Israeli air force was so exaggerated as to be nonsense, and their report that the air crews mainly came from Eastern Europe was equally misleading.

During the two weeks preceding the debate on 26 January, I saw some sixty people. There was a sudden swing of opinion. Chaim Weizmann made an appeal to the British people to use their influence to bring about peace and reconciliation in the Middle East. The *Manchester Guardian* had two leaders which were critical of the Foreign Office and the *Observer* had a leader saying that Britain should recognize the State of Israel forthwith. The *News of the World* published an article by Bob Boothby which was headed STOP THIS MIDDLE EAST MADNESS, and which attacked the Government's policy. In the meantime Dick Crossman was in Israel interviewing the British pilots who had been shot down and hearing their story. As a result of these enquiries he wrote his famous article in the *Sunday Pictorial*, I ACCUSE BEVIN. By Sunday 16 January newspapers with a circulation of many millions had swung round and had attacked the Government's Middle East policy. During the final week I saw Nye

Bevan every day and eventually he said, 'I don't know which is going to last longer, my whisky or your crisis, but at the rate you are drinking my whisky it will be finished before your crisis is resolved.'

The debate on the 26th was opened by Ernest Bevin. Most people thought that he would express some regret at what had occurred and would make some approach to improving relations with Israel: instead his speech was one-sided, largely devoted to sympathetic support for the Arabs over a wide field and to criticism of Israeli activities and the Israeli government's policies. He showed no understanding for Israel's problems. Churchill spoke next in a dramatic speech castigating Bevin's policy. He was followed by Clem Davies, the leader of the Liberal Party, and by Dick Crossman, who had just returned from Israel; both attacked Foreign Office policy. A number of the speakers made use of the memorandum which I had circulated. The Government, which had a huge majority at that time, came in for some severe criticism from its own supporters, a number of whom abstained and some of whom actually voted against their own Government. The Government, with a majority of 286 over all parties, won this debate by only ninety votes.

I was encouraged to believe, despite Bevin's and the Foreign Office's apparently intransigent position, that progress could be made towards improving relations between Britain and Israel, and I continued throughout the week to have discussions with various leaders. On Friday morning 29 January Ivor Linton, who was the unofficial representative of the Israeli Government in London, rang me and asked if he could come and see me in my flat at twelve o'clock. When he arrived, dressed in a morning coat, he said, 'Have you got a bottle of champagne?'

'Yes,' I replied, 'but why are you dressed in this extraordinary way and what do you want the champagne for?'

He said, 'I've just come from the Foreign Office. Israel has been granted *de facto* recognition by the British Government. In view of the part you played, I thought you ought to be one of the first to know about, and drink to, this historic event.'

CHAPTER NINE

WHEN Britain gave *de facto* recognition to Israel in January 1949 I hoped this would lead to cordial and friendly relations between the two countries and to my returning home to resume my career in Marks & Spencer. My colleagues in Israel asked me to remain there longer. So with the agreement of Father and Simon I decided to stay on for the time being to see if I could be helpful.

Although I have been critical of the Foreign Office for its frequent lack of objectivity, most British ambassadors to Israel were men of quality and, while naturally representing Britain's interests first, a number of them were helpful and friendly. Alexander Knox Helm, Francis Evans, Francis Rundall, the late Patrick Hancock, John Beith, Michael Hadow, John Barnes, Bernard Ledwidge were men of high calibre and many of them retained close ties with Israel after they moved on to other positions.

My main job was to try to help the Israeli Government with the development of its economy. I worked with the new Minister of Industry, a South African who had emigrated to Israel, Jack Geri, an able man. It was essential for the infant state to build an economy sufficient to supply the needs of its growing population and to persuade other countries that there was scope for investment. A strong economy would be one of the bulwarks of Israel's security.

The country's main export at that time was citrus fruit. Marks & Spencer was a large importer of citrus and had knowledge, built up over the years, of what the UK consumer wanted. It was also necessary, if the Israelis were going to build a sound economic base, for them to develop the production and export of industrial as well as agricultural products. I did not think that Israel would be able to compete successfully with the increasing exports of the low-wage developing countries with huge populations. I maintained that she should aim to produce goods of high quality and good value. The high standards of education and scientific and technological research on which Chaim Weizmann had always insisted were a major aid to this type of economic development. Today, thirty-seven years later, though Israel faces major economic problems, a number of her industries are highly innovative and very sophisticated, producing high-technology goods for the world market, scanners for example. At the same time there are a number of industries, also highly sophisticated, which manufacture the most ordinary of products, such as men's underwear. But these items are of such high quality and represent such good value that a large percentage of the production finds a ready market abroad.

One unforeseen but colourful contribution to the expansion of both Israel's population and eventually her economy was the arrival in 1949–50 of Yemeni Jews. I was closely involved in the sometimes tricky but rewarding task of resettling a huge number of these immigrants, many of whom came from a fifteeenth-century world and found it hard to cope at first with life in Israel.

The export of citrus fruit was growing. I saw a number of ways in which the profits from this could be increased. The Israelis were spending something like $7 million a year on importing timber to make boxes in which to export fruit, which was a huge amount for the infant Israel. Sapir, seriously concerned about investment, asked me if he should finance a packaging plant. I believed that using cardboard cartons would be more efficient and cheaper than using wooden cases. However, there were people with vested interests who opposed the idea, notably those who imported the timber and manufactured the wooden boxes. Eventually the government agreed to invest in Cargal, an existing but not exactly prosperous packaging firm which had recently acquired highly efficient carton-making machinery from Glasgow. Gradually the change from expensive wooden boxes to cheaper cartons came about, and the citrus industry and Israel's balance of payments both benefited. Indeed, Israel became an exporter of cartons for fruit packing to other countries.

There seemed to be no fields of activity in which this new, rapidly expanding small country was not involved – education, agriculture, industry, building, banking and investment. Simon Marks, Father and other members of my family, including Michael Sacher and Teddy Sieff, visited Israel regularly to see how they could help. I spent much time in Israel and my mother and my aunts, Miriam Sacher, Elaine Blond and Tilly Kennedy, also visited regularly and made worthwhile contributions towards solving some of Israel's social problems – which were substantially increased by the huge immigration of the early years.

Because Marks & Spencer, under Simon and Father, was forward-looking we were in close touch with advanced industrial and agricultural technology; we were able to give Israel some useful information on new technological developments. At the same time Marks & Spencer bought increasing quantities of Israeli products, at that time mainly agricultural, though then, as now, it was the firm's policy to buy British. We buy from abroad only when the quality and value we seek cannot be obtained at home, or when the goods, such as semi-tropical or tropical foodstuffs, cannot be produced in the United Kingdom. While keen to improve their performance, the Israeli farmers and manufacturers were not, in these early days, the easiest people to deal with. They were men and women who had fought and won a war against huge odds. They were, with considerable success, absorbing and integrating thousands of Jewish refugees from Arab lands and Europe. This led some of them to believe they did not need help from outsiders, only a chance to do things for themselves. They believed that they knew best; in addition many, still bruised by earlier experiences, were suspicious of foreigners and did not want to co-operate with them.

Over the next two years work for the new state was my first priority, but I gradually developed a pattern of spending more time in Britain and less in Israel. Somehow or other, even after Israel had established an embassy in London, there seemed to be room for an unofficial link between Israel and the British Government. By now I knew most of the Israeli political leaders and was able unofficially to convey their views to the members of the British Government and vice versa. Anthony Eden, Leo Amery, Aneurin Bevan, Harold Wilson, George Brown and George Thomas were some of the British political leaders with whom I had contact over the years; they gave me sound advice.

My family was friendly with the Lovats, the leading Catholic family of Scotland. I was very friendly with Hugh Fraser, Lord Lovat's younger brother. The Lovats had a reputation for bravery; the Lovat Scouts were a famous commando unit in World War II, of which Hugh had been an outstanding member. I well recall Hugh's marriage to Antonia, the noted writer and daughter of Lord Longford, in 1956. Antonia Fraser (now married to Harold Pinter) was, and still is, a beautiful woman, but it was a wedding where the men almost matched the women for glamour in their kilts and sporrans, with dirks in the side of their hose. Hugh was a Tory Member of Parliament and was later Secretary of State for Air in Harold Macmillan's Government. He spent a few days with me in Israel soon after the state had been created. He was impressed with what he saw and the courage and determination of the people, and told me that when he returned he intended to speak in a Middle East debate in which Israel would figure prominently. He said, 'Of course, Marcus, don't expect me to make a Zionist-type speech.'

'I don't expect anything of you,' I said, 'but at least I know you will talk with some knowledge of what's going on there.'

He made a speech which I found welcome and heartwarming, explaining some of Israel's problems in a most constructive way. Hugh regularly visited Israel and was never slow to criticize Israeli policy and actions when he thought them wrong, but he was a true and consistent friend of Israel no matter what the circumstances or whether his partisanship might damage his political career.

Another great friend of Israel, both when he was in the Lower House and in the Lords, was Frank Byers. He too made an important contribution in many ways to better British/Israeli understanding. He worked tirelessly to his dying day to overturn Britain's partial compliance with the Arab states' boycott regulations. He was chairman of the Anglo/Israel Association, a responsibility which Joan Byers, his widow, has now taken on. Both Hugh Fraser and Frank Byers died whilst I was writing this book; I miss them greatly. Their deaths are a great loss for Israel and for better Anglo/Israeli relations.

Other people with whom I worked at this time were Julian Amery and Sir Winston Churchill's grandson, the so-called 'young Winston', both of whom have followed family tradition in believing that what they are doing is right for Britain. Among people from whom I received good advice was James de Rothschild. He was the son of Baron Edmond de Rothschild, the French head of the Rothschild family, but established his home in England in the early years of the twentieth century and took British nationality. He had a distinguished military career in the 1914–18 war. He was a man of great generosity, supporting many worthwhile causes, both at home and abroad, and was throughout his life firmly behind Palestine and later Israel. The charitable foundation he set up has done outstanding work in many areas, including education. It was his generosity which provided the funds for the building of Israel's magnificent Knesset (Houses of Parliament).

During Israel's War of Independence I made the acquaintance of a number of people with whom I became close friends. One special couple was the Ebners; he had emigrated from Rumania, she from Czechoslovakia, in the 1930s. Dolphi was a successful businessman and an excellent amateur pianist; his wife Lola was a smart, attractive woman with a strong personality. She became a famous *couturière* and was an invaluable unofficial ambassador for Israel; she was most helpful to me when I wanted to meet people unoffically.

I remember that in May 1950 Dr Weizmann, then President, gave a party to celebrate the second anniversary of Israel's independence; the Ebners were to drive me to his home in Rehovot. When I arrived at their apartment in Tel Aviv, I heard the piano being played beautifully. I thought to myself, my God, Dolphi is much better than I thought, he is a very gifted player – but when I walked into the drawing-room I found the pianist was none other than the famous Hephziba Menuhin, Yehudi Menuhin's sister. She was my partner for the evening, and a delightful one she was too. Alas, she is no longer with us.

I continued to have regular meetings in Israel with Ben Gurion, Eshkol and Sapir. Ben Gurion wanted me to settle permanently in Israel, but I declined. When he asked me why, I explained, 'Well, I think I can be of more use to Israel by keeping myself *au fait* with what is happening here and trying to explain developments to our leaders at home, and it is my intention to resume my career with Marks & Spencer, while still maintaining close contact with Israel.'

'I would have preferred,' he replied, 'to hear you say that you had decided to settle in Israel to look after British interests here. That would be better for us.'

I thanked him, but said it wasn't on.

Once I asked Ben Gurion to give me an autographed picture of himself, but he replied, 'It's not my habit to give photographs of myself.'

'It's not,' I said, 'that I particularly want a photograph of you for myself personally; however, I have a certain need for it. Sometimes in London I want to discuss an Israeli problem with somebody but do not want to raise the topic myself. The fact that your picture is there often provokes a discussion about Israel.'

'Ah,' said Ben Gurion with a smile, 'they recognize me, do they?'

'No,' I replied, 'they don't. But your photo is diplayed next to that of a friend of mine, Rosalind Russell, the actress, and when people ask if that's Rosalind Russell and I say "yes", they then ask who is the white-haired old man next to her. I tell them it's Mr Ben Gurion. That's how the conversation about Israel starts.'

Ben Gurion laughed.

I returned from Israel in the early months of 1951, when Simon said I had to make up my mind whether I was coming back to continue my career with Marks & Spencer or giving it up for good. I had continued to keep in touch with Elsa; I flew twice to New York to see her and she visited me in London. I made frequent phone calls to her, an undertaking which was in those days both tedious and expensive. It was difficult enough to phone New York from London – to do so from Israel was a gigantic task.

On my return to London we married, but things did not work out as we had hoped. She had been successful in her business career and was being regularly promoted in Seligman & Latz. We both had strong characters and, despite the fact that we got on well in many ways, our life together was far from peaceful. She preferred New York to London; we separated after eighteen months, and shortly afterwards divorced.

CHAPTER TEN

WHEN I rejoined the firm in 1951, clothing shortages and food rationing still persisted; we had not yet been able to rebuild the majority of the destroyed and bomb-damaged stores; all this limited our progress. We looked forward to the day when we could overcome these difficulties. One priority was to develop our food business, which, having started to make progress in 1936, had been impeded by wartime rationing. In the 1950s, as the availability of goods improved and rationing ended, we gradually removed the cafeterias from the stores; although a profitable operation, they took up much space which could be better used for the development of our traditional clothing and our new and expanding food departments.

As soon as I returned from Israel Simon made it clear that I was to concentrate on developing the food division. I was given the status of a senior executive but not put on the board until 1954, when Simon and Father decided I was up to it; there was no nepotism. My office was in the block above our Marble Arch store. At this time the company's headquarters were split over three sites, with some offices in Baker Street in the old Michael House, some in wartime Nissen huts in Paddington Street just off Baker Street, and others above the store. To be near my work I bought a flat from Stewart Granger, the actor, a mile away in Hyde Park Gate, into which Elsa and I moved in 1951.

I now began in a systematic way to learn more about the business from Simon and Father. My first preoccupation was to understand and apply the business philosophy and principles they had developed over the years. These are best summarized like this:

1. Offer customers, under the company's brand name, St Michael, a selected range of high-quality, well-designed and attractive merchandise at reasonable prices which represent good value.

2. Encourage suppliers to use the most modern and efficient techniques of production based on the latest developments in science and technology.

3. With the co-operation of our suppliers, enforce high standards of quality control.

4. Wherever possible find United Kingdom sources of supply.

5. Simplify operational procedures so that the business runs reasonably efficiently.

6. Foster good human relations with staff, customers and suppliers.

The procedure by which these principles were put into effect was quite demanding, both mentally and physically; not only did it occupy a large part of each working day and night but it also extended into most weekends as well. There was virtually a constant dialogue between Simon, Father, Teddy and me, with my brother Michael often joining in. These were the days when I began to feel Simon's personality very strongly; he was a leader in his field, acknowledged throughout the world as outstanding in the art of shopkeeping, and I learned much from him. When not visiting suppliers or stores, I lunched regularly in the office with Simon and Father and some of the other directors. I continued to spend many weekends with Simon in Sunningdale or with Father in his Berkshire cottage. We talked a lot of 'shop'.

There was a regular Monday morning meeting, chaired by Simon, with the directors and some senior executives, often largely taken up by Simon reviewing the errors of omission and commission he had discovered during the weekend; many of these would be the result of his Friday afternoon drive from Marble Arch to Sunningdale on the 'Royal Route'. Simon's eye for a badly finished skirt or a pair of trousers with puckered seams was hawklike; he seemed to sense even tiny imperfections from yards away. He would bring the offending merchandise to the office on Monday morning and slap it on the table; his language was often brutally frank. He was not gifted with an even temper where faulty or poor quality goods were concerned, and he never compromised. 'How did this crap ever get on our counters?' would be a typical remark. 'How did this muck pass the manufacturer's and our quality control? How did this rubbish get past the manager and staff?' He spoke and behaved as though he had been personally insulted. Indeed, he so deeply identified himself with what we sold that to take every shortcoming personally was natural to him. He expected a thorough investigation to be made into any fault he reported, and that was what he got. It was no use hoping that the matter would pass out of his recollection; his memory was excellent. He was, moreover, a great believer in repetition and had no hesitation in repeating himself, and the more he did so the more scathing he could become. If a lesson didn't go home the first or second time, he didn't hesitate to bring it up a third time. Undoubtedly Marks & Spencer's high quality standards owe much to Simon's persistence and insistence; his influence in this field continues to this day.

It didn't take me long to discover that he was more interested in the development of the clothing than of the food departments; he really cared for and understood the textile business. This was not just because it was highly successful; he sometimes liked lines which sold slowly. For instance he loved leather and was always trying to develop good leather handbags, but for some reason handbags were never successful in the post-war years. He did not really like food, certainly at this time; one reason for this subconscious resistance to the food group was his fear that its introduction might change the nature of Marks & Spencer's business. His attitude towards food faced me with some problems, since I was charged with the expansion of the food departments.

One day, when I had announced with pride the introduction of a new range of canned foods, he pounced on me and said, 'You're not going to turn me into a grocer.'

'I haven't the slightest intention of doing so,' I replied.

'Well, you're not going to, Marcus, and I'll tell you another thing. When I leave here, I shall leave feet first and that's the only way I'm going out.' These turned out to be prophetic words.

Simon's attitude to the food business was not the result of a prejudice against food as such. It is true that he lived plainly, but he lived well. Though he enjoyed the occasional bottle of wine, he did not have Father's gourmet tastes. His attitude towards the food departments came, I think, from a fear that Marks & Spencer, if it went in for food in a big way, might come to resemble the food supermarkets which were beginning to develop. However, sharp and critical though his tongue was and sweeping as were his views, Simon never harboured his moods and never pushed his prejudices to a point where they held back the business. He could contrive an explosion and in a few minutes behave as though it had never happened. He and I had something of this in common, which is why, I suppose, while from time to time we were eyeball to eyeball, we more often saw eye to eye.

He enjoyed his tennis and took a limited interest in horse-racing;

he was greatly concerned with developments in Palestine and then Israel; but his overriding preoccupation was how to improve the business. This was his driving force, but its mainspring was improving efficiency rather than making a fortune. He was a rich man and enjoyed living well. Yet, with the exception of the fine paintings and *objets d'art* with which he and his wife Miriam surrounded themselves, he could not be described as living extravagantly. He enjoyed occasional holidays on chartered yachts and a week or two relaxing in the sunshine of the South of France, and he kept a good table, but nobody who observed him closely would say that these things were anywhere near as important to him as the desire to run, and improve, a great enterprise which would benefit the public.

Politically he was Conservative; he thought that the nationalization policies of the Labour governments of 1945–1951 had been bad for Britain and that the left-wing members of the Labour Party were a great danger to the country. Yet he was friendly with some Labour leaders, particularly Nye Bevan, who was, as I have said, a close friend of Father.

If Simon had an explicit theory of management it was what is called today MBWA, that is management by walking about – to look, listen and learn. We were much helped in the application of this by the change in our method of running the business which we introduced in 1956/57 as a result of 'Operation Simplification'. It gave senior management much more time to visit the buying departments and get out and see what was happening in the stores and at our suppliers and to talk to staff and customers. I shall enlarge on this operation later.

Simon was never deskbound; his main objective was to see what was happening in the stores, which goods were selling, which were not, to talk to junior staff, in particular sales assistants, and to hear the views of customers. He, like every member of the family active in the company, wanted all employees to understand that it was a family-run business; his aim was that those who ran it should be known to as many of the staff as possible and that everyone understood that their welfare was his, and the board's, concern; in all this he set a first-class example. So successfully did Simon implement this policy that it was natural for employees to feel that they all belonged to the Marks & Spencer family.

When I said earlier that Simon wanted to see his business as efficient as he could make it rather than just amass money for himself, I should have added that there was one special reason for his desiring wealth: it was part of his moral code to help good causes. These were many and their range varied greatly. For instance, Simon was one of the founders of the pre-war Cadet Corps and became involved peripherally with the R.A.F. Another of his interests was the Royal College of Surgeons. One of its prominent members was Archie McIndoe, who achieved fame for the wonderful work he did in plastic surgery on badly burned airmen during and after the war. Simon got to know Archie through his sister Elaine. Archie was a man of great ability, frankness and charm, and was good company. Simon and he became close friends and Archie explained to Simon the possibilities and potential for this area of surgery. The college itself had been destroyed during the war. As a result of their friendship, Simon gave substantial continued support, first for its rebuilding and then in helping to maintain it, an example which the family and Marks & Spencer follow to this day. This gesture was characteristic of Simon, who was a generous giver to many other worthwhile causes, both at home and in Palestine. It is part of Jewish tradition, indeed of Jewish religion, to help one's fellow men, but there was more than that to Simon's generosity. He genuinely enjoyed giving and particularly liked to give where his instinct took him.

During the 1950s my relationship with Simon grew closer; it was marked by a mutual affection. This was not just because we were members of the same family, though Simon was fond of his relatives; it was mutual because I liked his forthrightness, his devotion to his work and responsibilities, and his concern for his staff; I also had great respect for him as a business leader. I think he liked me because I stood up to him. When it came to business, Simon was as tough with members of the family as with anyone else; on the other hand, if you stuck to your guns and he saw that you had a point, he respected you. I think too that he thought well of my war record and appreciated the work I had done in the early years of Israel's independence. But there was in Simon's attitude towards me a certain ambivalence. I was now making considerable progress in Marks & Spencer and was perhaps the most active member of my generation of the family, but I was not Simon's son. If Simon had a failing, it was that he was inclined to lavish too much attention on his closest relations. He had two children, Hannah and Michael, my double cousins, both of whom he spoiled, certainly in the material sense. He did not extend this spoiling to me; I received limited praise from him, but plenty of criticism, much of it expressed in vigorous language. As a result I learned a great deal more.

His attitude to my development of the food department in the 1950s could be maddening; one day he might be supportive, another day, to say the least, discouraging. On one occasion in 1953 he said to me, 'I think you're doing a good job in foods, Marcus; you've got a turnover of £17 million. If you keep at it, one day we might have a £50 million turnover in foods.' I thought about this remark when I retired as chairman in 1984 and the food turnover was £1.1 billion. However, within a few days of that remark he was angrily telling me again, 'Don't think you can turn me into a grocer.' When he was in this mood his pet aversion was the canned goods department. One evening we left the Baker Street office and walked down to the Marble Arch store just before closing time to have a look at what was going one. As we came up to the store Simon was saying that canned goods were not really our business; I decided to employ a technique which I used with him from time to time, generally with success, though to be safe I used it sparingly. 'Simon,' I said, 'maybe you're right. The best thing we can do is get out of canned goods altogether.' We were by this time just outside the store; it was closing time and the porter had almost closed the door. Simon quickly thrust his foot inside. 'Marcus,' he said, 'let's just keep our foot in canned goods like I've got mine in this door.' Canned goods and groceries are still with us; in fact they are developing considerably.

Since I have mentioned the growth of the Marks & Spencer food department I should say at this point how much I was helped in building it up by Alec Miller. Alec, who was 6'4" and built in proportion, started his working life as a bank clerk, but decided it wasn't for him. Then, though he was so tall and had large feet to match his height, he took up ballroom dancing and used to go to tea dances at one of the Kensington hotels. He turned professional, eventually winning the world ballroom dancing championship, which gave him sufficient income to have a good standard of living. However, he decided there was really no long-term future in this occupation, even for a world champion, and he joined Marks & Spencer at a much lower level of income, but making a valuable contribution to its progress. Simon, who was a small man, about 5'7", didn't much care for tall men and, though deep down he appreciated Alec's work, he found it difficult to be warm towards him.

Some of Simon's views on food were the result of his attitude to change. He would not have been successful if he had not been ready to adapt, but he was by nature conservative. It often took him time to modify his attitude to a suggested innovation, but it happened more quickly when he thought the innovation was his own idea. An example of this is the way he behaved about my introduction of self-service and multiple tills or checkouts into the food section. This form of selling is commonplace today, but was then a novelty. As an experiment I introduced this at two or three stores, including Slough on the 'Royal Route'. One Friday afternoon Simon went there on his way to Sunningdale. On the following Monday morning he summoned me to his office and exploded, 'You're not turning me into a grocer, least of all into a self-service grocer. I'm not having this system; get it out.' I removed the new system from those stores which I thought Simon might visit and extended it to those stores he was less likely to see, convinced that eventually it would establish itself as the best way for customers to select and pay for their goods at a reasonable speed.

Some time later Simon was in Leeds to receive an honorary degree. It was just before the Whitsun bank holiday, which was a busy time for food sales, and Leeds was operating the new self-service system. While he was in the city, Simon visited the store and when he came back to London he called me in. 'You know, Marcus,' he said, 'Leeds has developed a first-class system of food display and payment. There are tills outside the food area and the customers take their food to the tills in trolleys or baskets. It cuts down on time and it's more convenient and efficient – it's an excellent idea. I think we ought to put it in to more stores.'

'It sounds marvellous,' I said. 'I'll go and look at it with store operations personnel and work out the best way to extend it.'

Sometimes we had differences about political issues; he was no reactionary, indeed his Conservatism was liberal, but I can't imagine him voting for any other party. He was a great patriot and believed in the British Empire. Like Chaim Weizmann, he hoped Palestine would become the eighth Dominion. I was then on the left wing of the Conservative Party and there were elements of the party's philosophy in those days which did not appeal to me. Simon strongly deplored nationalization; though I was never a supporter of nationalization, I remembered what had happened in the 1929/31 depression and I had also seen something of the results of nepotism in top business management, which so often led to the mismanagement and decay of many worthwhile and important businesses, leading to increased unemployment. Equally, many employers did not understand the importance of treating their employees decently — what I call today implementing a policy of good human relations at work. I had seen the rejection of reasonable demands put forward by moderate trade union leaders and how this rejection had led to such men being replaced by those with extreme ideas. All this led me to question some Conservative tenets. When I spoke about my misgivings, Simon was inclined to say, 'You are young, one day you'll learn better.' Notwithstanding his Conservative loyalties, my readiness to question them, and our somewhat differing political views, Simon and I did not seriously clash on political issues. I think this was because he put personality above party.

When I was busy lobbying for the recognition of the State of Israel, I had found a sympathetic listener and supporter in Aneurin Bevan, as the reader may recall, and the friendship continued. One evening I took Nye to have a pre-dinner drink with Simon at his Grosvenor Square flat. It so happened that Simon had invited ten true-blue Tory guests to dinner; because he had so much enjoyed his drink with Nye he asked us to stay and eat. We did so. Nye was in brilliant form and largely monopolized the conversation to the pleasure and interest of his fellow guests. He talked much good sense as well as putting forward, constructively and with moderation, certain Labour principles. Simon was impressed, even though he did not agree, and admitted that Nye made a major contribution to the evening's success.

Virtually nobody around Simon, whether a member of the family or a colleague in the company, was spared his criticism or his occasional irascibility. This treatment could be extended to his sisters and their offspring, but one exception was Father; he could do no wrong. Simon respected his views and his judgment; a gentle word from him could swiftly bring relief to a victim of Simon's wrath.

Looking back on that period, and bearing in mind what I have since been told, I think that how he treated me was partly, if not mainly, due to his growing feeling that one day I would succeed him as chief executive – not immediately, but eventually. He did not have any personal objection to me as a potential Marks & Spencer's chief executive; it was more that, like many leaders of genius, he did not like the idea of being succeeded *by anybody* – of moving away from centre-stage. Nor was it that he wanted his son to succeed him; it was clear early on that Michael, the present Lord Marks, did not have the inclination or qualifications to become a full-time business executive. Simon's son-in-law, Alec Lerner, who had started life as a doctor, and was very competent, but was not sufficiently equipped with store executive experience. Michael, my older brother, made the board before I did; he was good in business, had a great knowledge of clothing and first-class relations with people. He was popular and respected inside and outside the business, but he was not as ambitious, or perhaps as pushy, as I was. Eventually I was promoted over his head, but he was never jealous – or, if he was, he certainly never showed it: our relationship has always been close. Simon's nephew, Michael Sacher, who later became vice-chairman and joint managing director, also had much ability and a dry sense of humour. He has made a major contribution to the business. Gabriel, Michael's younger brother, did not have that round-the-clock devotion to business which Simon considered essential. My uncle Teddy, Father's younger brother, who in years was half-way between my generation and Simon's and Father's, *was* in the mainstream for the succession. He followed Father as chairman and showed great flair, particularly in the whole textile field, a most important area.

Outside the family there were several very able people, including Jan Lewando, a few years older than I, who had started in Marks & Spencer as a management trainee and had made excellent progress; he joined the main board well before I did. For a short time we were rivals for the top place, but Jan decided to leave and accepted the post of chairman and chief executive of the Viyella Carrington group.

I think that in the last few years of his life, though I didn't appreciate it at the time, both Simon and Father were sure that I would eventually become chairman and chief executive. It was possibly because of this that I sometimes received tougher treatment from Simon than anybody else, both in private and in the presence of board colleagues.

It was shortly after I was made a director that I paid a store visit which was to have long-term, and beneficial, effects on the future of the company. I referred earlier to the practice we developed in the early 1930s whereby all management recruits, other than tech-nologists or specialists, who hoped to make a career in head office had first to spend two years working in the stores finding out what the business was all about. This rule, as far as I am personally concerned, has only been broken once. That was over thirty years ago, in 1954, when one Saturday morning I visited the Oxford store. As we left the food department to look at other parts of the store the manager, Mr Gibson, said, 'If Mr Rayner didn't know much about the food department, you must make allowances. He has only been there a week. He's a new recruit – he only joined us a few months ago.' In fact I had been most impressed with Mr Rayner's knowledge and suggestions, and went back to talk to him. I found out that he had studied at Selwyn College, Cambridge, with a view to taking holy orders but had decided it was not for him. He had then set up in a retail fancy goods business in his home town of Norwich, but, having decided there was not adequate scope, he joined Marks & Spencer.

On the following Monday morning at head office I went to the director of personnel, Norman Laski, my uncle by marriage, and to Cedric Woolf, the head of store operations. I said I would like Derek Rayner brought into the food group. They refused: he hadn't spent his two years in the stores. 'Well, it's a very good rule but good rules are made to be broken on occasion and this is such an occasion,' I replied. They still didn't agree, but I insisted. They asked if I was agreeable to leaving Derek Rayner in Oxford to help in the store over the holiday period – it was then June – after he had had his own holidays he could come into head office, probably at the beginning of October. I said, 'Yes,' but they were annoyed with my seeming to put a pistol at their heads.

A few weeks later, on a visit to the Watford store, I saw an apparently familiar figure on the first floor. It was Derek Rayner. I asked him what he was doing. He said he had been transferred to Watford shortly after my visit to Oxford. The day was again a Saturday; on the following Monday in head office I played merry hell and said that, unless Derek Rayner was in head office by the following Monday, I would take up the matter with the chairman. He was in by the following Monday. That young man is now Lord Rayner, chairman and chief executive of Marks & Spencer.

It was at this time that I was involved in the exercise which I have already mentioned which became known as 'Operation Simplification'. One day I went to Simon's office and found an expert on computers there — I think he was an IBM representative. He had come to us to explain why we should install computers. We had no computers then, nor in fact did we make use of them until some years later. Simon began by asking our visitor what the computer could do. He replied, 'Virtually everything.' Simon turned to me and said, 'Well, we don't want everything — what do we really want? It's time we had a good look at the business to see what systems we have that are no longer necessary and what we really need.' Our expenses at that time were mounting rapidly and eating up much of our concomitant increase in profits.

The following day Simon was in the Reading store just as it was closing and found a number of girls filling in what we called catalogue cards, which gave details of sizes, colours, sales, stock position, on order position, and other information on virtually every line in the business. Store staff then produced fortnightly checking lists which gave total sales and stock and stock on order on each line; these were done in great detail and then sent to head office. The amount of form filling, figure compilation and other data which had to be written out by hand was already very large, and growing. On the following Monday Simon called a meeting and said, 'We have developed a number of crutches on which the business apparently depends; we must examine the whole operation with a view to simplifying it and throwing away our crutches.' He then told me to organize a team to examine our administrative and operational system to see what was absolutely necessary and what could be cut out; he believed that a great deal of our paperwork was unnecessary.

My team consisted of a store operations executive, a merchandise executive, a divisional superintendent — someone who had overall responsibility for about twenty stores in an area — and the chief accountant. I co-opted others as and when I needed them. I had co-operation and help from all except the chief accountant.

I remember early in the exercise visiting a small millinery department: a distributor was going through a seven-page checking list, or trying to; in the end he threw it into the wastepaper basket. 'No value to you?', I asked.

'No,' he said, 'it's far too long, it's impossible to use.'

I then asked, 'How do you distribute your stocks to the stores?'

He explained his method, which was certainly simpler and no less efficient than using the cumbersome checking list prepared with so much labour in the stores.

My team, in small groups or singly, examined various facets of the business and we had fortnightly meetings to discuss what could be cut out or where we could put in a more efficient system. At the beginning I informed every member of staff that we wanted their ideas on how to make the business simpler and more efficient, and that no one would lose his job, whatever the result. Suggestions poured in. I remember on one occasion discussing with a store manager and his office and stockroom staff what was called the pink slip. This was a form prepared in triplicate detailing goods received (for which the store already had an advice); one copy went back to head office, one copy was retained in the receiving/stockroom and the third went to the store office. All the information could be found in existing documents, so I made the experiment of eliminating the pink slip in four stores. I worked on the principle of if in doubt throw it out; you can always bring it back but, if you don't throw it out, you will never know whether a particular form or document was necessary in the first place.

I visited three of the four stores at the end of the month and asked the managers and staff concerned whether they had missed these pink slips; they all said, 'No, and don't ever bring them back.' At our next meeting the chief accountant stated that it was essential to restore the pink slips to the stores from which they had been eliminated; I asked him how he knew: had he visited the stores? He said he hadn't, but his local accountants had told him they were essential. I was fairly sure that he had told his local accountants what they were to say. I made it clear that I had visited the stores and, as the store personnel were all in favour of elimination, the pink slip should now be eliminated from all stores – and it was. This cut out six million pieces of paper a year.

In those days it was easier to get a visa to go to Russia than it was for a member of the sales staff to go into the stockroom, which was protected with walls like a fortress; when they wanted stock, the sales staff had to complete stock order forms and give them to the stockroom staff, who would – eventually – bring the goods down to the counters, providing they could read the often barely legible order forms. In most stores there were many times of the day when the sales staff were not busy. So I said that at these times the sales staff should, from now on, go to the stockroom in an orderly and organized way and bring down their own goods for their departments. The chief accountant opposed this: it would lead to a huge increase in stealing. I said, 'Nonsense, ninety-nine per cent of our staff are honest and the one per cent will steal anyhow.' By removing the stockroom walls we created greater space for stock, which enabled us to operate more efficiently. There was no increase in stealing.

One day, when I was driving with the chief accountant between Birmingham and Coventry, I stopped the car and said to him, 'You are not playing your part in this operation, or, if you are, it is in a negative way. What have you in mind?'

He replied, 'I'm standing on the sidelines to pick up the pieces when you have finished destroying the business.'

When I got back to the office, I went to Simon and said, 'I can't deal with the chief accountant. You must.' He said he didn't think he could either. The gentleman ended up with a golden handshake and, as rumour has it, set himself up as an independent accountant who had carried out Marks & Spencer's simplification operation — which by then had become nationally known.

By the time we finished we had cut out some twenty-six million forms and documents, had eliminated several hundred time-clocks — resulting in better punctuality — had sold off 1,000 filing cabinets, and had put the business in better shape.

When I saw what was happening after 'Operation Simplification' had been in existence for a few weeks, I banned all recruitment of personnel throughout head office and the stores because I could see that we were going to have a large surplus of staff. In view of our policy, and the promise I had made the staff at the beginning of the operation that no one would lose his job, the only way we could adjust numbers downwards was by people reaching retirement age or leaving us for other reasons. Since ninety per cent of our staff are women, we have a larger turnover than a firm which employs a majority of men but already, because of the good conditions under which staff worked and the various benefits they received in addition to their salaries, staff turnover was small. The opening up of stockrooms and allowing sales staff to fetch their own stock had made 1,000 stockroom assistants surplus. When I was asked what we should do with them, I replied, 'Offer them jobs on the sales floor.' At the end of a few months 950 were working on the sales floor, training as sales assistants or supervisors, according to their qualifications, but fifty, who had been working in the stockrooms for many years, did not want to move. I was asked what we should do with these fifty, now largely passengers. 'Well,' I said, 'we've had ninety-five per cent success. Don't let's be greedy, just leave them where they are.' Over the next six months a few decided, because they were bored, to take early retirement or just left us; the rest came down to work on the sales floor.

Turnover in 1955 was £108 million; in 1960 it was £148 million (there was little inflation during those years). Staff numbers in 1955 were 26,400; in 1960 they were 22,400. Service and efficiency had not suffered. Turnover had increased in that period by thirty-six per cent while staff had fallen by fifteen per cent; we had reduced the prices of most major lines and substantially increased salaries, benefits and profits.

It gave me much pleasure when my son David joined the company in October 1957; he spent two years in various stores, as I had done. He became an alternate director in 1968, a full director in 1972, had a variety of responsibilities, and became a successful director of personnel in 1975.

In the late 1950s I was director in charge of three divisions — store operations, personnel and foods. During December, in the pre-Christmas period, store sales increase hugely; it is our practice just before closing time each evening to fill the counters with substantial quantities of goods to meet the following morning's demand. On one occasion during December Teddy Sieff, who was the assistant managing director, developed a bad attack of flu. He told me on the telephone that before he had taken to his bed he had visited one or two stores in the evening and found that some were not replenishing the counter stocks sufficiently. I was to send a message to all stores asking the managers to ensure that there was plenty of stock put on display at closing time to meet the demand next morning. That weekend I was staying with Father; on Friday evening the phone rang and I picked it up; it was Simon. He had been visiting stores on his way to Sunningdale and just before closing time went to Hounslow, where the manager, with excessive zeal, had filled up the men's socks counter, a big seller in the pre-Christmas period, so that it was like a mountain; the counter looked a mess. When he asked the manager why, the latter showed him a copy of my telegram. Simon asked me about my instructions and why I had sent a message when it wasn't my responsibility anyway. He blasted me good and proper. I was furious but kept my temper, merely pointing out that it came within my responsibility as director of store operations. (I didn't say that Teddy had asked me to send the message.) Simon then said he wanted to talk to Father. When he'd finished, I said to Father, 'I'm not taking this; I'm going to resign.'

Father said, 'If that's how you feel then resign, but don't be over hasty.'

During the weekend I composed a letter of resignation, which I proposed to give Simon on Monday morning.

We had the normal Monday morning directors/executives meeting going over the problems, faults and so on that had been uncovered at the weekend, but Simon made no reference to the incident with the Hounslow manager. When the meeting broke up and I was about to give the letter to Simon's secretary, with a sinking feeling, Simon said, 'Stay just a minute, Marcus.' Then he put his arm round my shoulder and without making any reference to the telephone conversation said, 'Let's forget all about it, shall we?' And that was the end of my proposed resignation.

It was under Simon's chairmanship and because of my closeness to him that I learned a great deal about the business. I was given a breadth of experience which was not given to most others of my generation. I learned much in my capacity as director of personnel, further developing in a practical way the policy of good treatment of staff which had started in the early 1930s. It was during this time that I coined the phrase which I have used often since – 'good human relations at work' as opposed to 'good industrial relations', because we are human beings at work, not industrial beings. Even in those days we had some 500 people in the personnel department, mainly spread throughout the stores in the role of staff managers, or, as they were then called, staff manageresses, whose responsibility was to look after the well-being, development and progress of the fifty to sixty staff in their care and to take part in the operational management of the store. We found that if staff managers were not involved in practical store management they became remote from what was happening in the business.

Store operations was concerned with the ranges the stores carried as well as with the layout and their general administration and efficient running. As director both of personnel and store operations it was essential for me to visit stores regularly and frequently, including, as far as possible, the more remote shops which did not receive the same attention as those in London and the main cities. It was important to ensure that these stores did not feel cut off and that staff at head office, particularly those leading the business, were as concerned with their progress and well-being, whether they were small or medium-sized, as with that of the larger premises. This entailed a great deal of travelling. If it was an organized visit, the store managers would be informed in advance, but many visits were made off the cuff when I was in the district, perhaps visiting a supplier; I then went in unannounced. I found that if I told a manager in advance that I was likely to visit the store and for some reason I didn't turn up, instead of creating relief it often caused disappointment.

This nearly happened when I was visiting the south-west division. I took the night train to Falmouth, had a bath and brush-up at the hotel and then went with the divisional executive, Ray Bentley, to the Falmouth store. From Falmouth we went on to Plymouth, where we spent longer than intended, then from Plymouth to Torquay. We were ending up with a dinner at Exeter for all the managers on the division and the divisional team. We had planned to go to Newton Abbot en route from Torquay to Exeter, but we were late arriving at Torquay and I was so tired that I said to Mr Bentley, 'I think I must leave out Newton Abbot because it's late and we shall probably arrive after closing time. I'm tired, and I have to host the dinner.'

He said, 'Mr Sieff, you must go to Newton Abbot; they will be upset if you don't – they have made all sorts of preparations.'

'Well,' I said, 'give me an example of what you mean or a convincing reason why I should go.'

He said, 'Every sales assistant in the store has had her hair specially done for your visit.'

'All right,' I replied, 'I'll go, but we shall arrive after closing time. Please phone the manager and explain that we are going to be late and I don't want anybody to stay specially for me. I want to make it clear that those who have responsibilities at home or dates should keep them.'

We arrived at Newton Abbot shortly after closing time to find that all the staff had stayed, except one, who had gone to look after her baby. As they had all stayed, I had to say a few words to every member of the staff; fortunately Newton Abbot was a small store and there were not many people to talk to. Even so it took quite a long time and I was not in very good form for hosting the dinner, which didn't start until nine o'clock.

I generally began a visit to a store by looking at the goods reception area and the stockrooms, from where I went on to the sales floor. At each point I talked to various members of the staff and possibly one or two customers. One can learn a great deal about the desirability of goods and other matters from the information that sales staff give; when they say goods will sell well five times out of six they are right, and when they say something is going to be a slow seller they are equally right. I usually ended up in the manager's office with the senior members of the store management team, giving them the opportunity to raise any questions they might have, and taking the opportunity of telling them our plans for the period ahead.

I was lucky when I became director of personnel and store operations in having a splendid team of people with whom to work. We were learning all the time how to do better, not least in relation to staff welfare. This, it will be remembered, we really started to develop systematically and thoroughly in the early 1930s; over the years we have made much progress. Provision of medical and dental care and good meals at low prices was followed by the introduction of chiropody and hairdressing. If their work entails standing for a large part of the day many people greatly value the facility for having their feet looked after in the store; if women are going out in the evening, they often like to have their hair done. Because we found that some of our staff were still giving up their lunch break to go to the hairdresser, we installed a hairdressing unit for the staff in every store so that they could have their lunch under the drier.

In dealing with various staff problems we found that, providing a decision was made quickly, the person concerned was generally satisfied. Hence we delegated responsibility to the local store manager and his team to deal with personnel problems – inevitable from time to time – and encouraged them to act quickly and generously but not precipitately. The local manager, in case of need, could make an immediate grant or loan of up to £100 or extend sick pay beyond the normal time, if there was a valid reason. This immediate response to individual needs is an important feature of our caring policy.

There are some cases with which local management are not allowed to deal. Such instances include long-term leave of absence due to illness, staff looking after elderly dependants, or staff needing loans because, through lack of budgetary understanding, they get themselves into financial difficulties. To deal with these problems a welfare committee was set up in 1933 and has met weekly ever since, providing there are cases for discussion. The welfare committee is asked to take a decision within a week; if that is not possible, they are requested to contact the individual concerned so that he or she knows that the problem is being looked at; again speed is of the essence. The members of the welfare committee are recruited from the senior members of our personnel and staff management departments, the pensions department, and store staff managers who may be visiting head office at that particular time. Our staff welfare activities, combined with decent and progressive salaries and, in recent years, profit-sharing, have resulted in a devoted, hard-working and involved staff and the absence of industrial strife.

One case stands out in my memory. Some twenty-five years ago the staff manageress of one of the stores reported the predicament of a cleaner who had been working at the store for twenty years. This particular lady was always cheerful and had become one of the most popular members of the store staff. One day, however, she came in to work silent and depressed. The staff manageress asked her if there was anything wrong. 'No,' she replied, but again the following day she was very quiet – not at all her usual cheerful self. The staff manageress eventually discovered that the cleaner and her husband, both of modest backgrounds and incomes, had worked hard, and I supposed scraped, to give their son a good education: he had become a qualified engineer and had found a job in South America, where he had fallen in love with a local girl, whom he was now going to marry. He didn't have the money to bring his parents out for the wedding and they couldn't afford to pay for the trip themselves. This was the cause of our cleaning lady's depression. The staff manageress recommended that we should give the cleaner time off and pay her expenses to go to the wedding. The welfare committee, after its deliberations, agreed. The cleaner was given a fortnight's leave; her fare and expenses were paid; and off she went to South America for her son's wedding.

I cited this as an example of 'good human relations at work' to the head of a major firm. He said, 'You must be mad to do it for a cleaner.'

'If,' I asked, 'you had an executive in your organization who, for some reason or another, was short of money and had a similar problem to that of the cleaner's family, would you not allow him the time off and give or loan him the money?'

'Ah,' he replied, 'an executive, that would be different. Yes, I would.'

I said, 'Please tell me why such privileges should be given to an executive and not to a cleaner who has given many years loyal and faithful service.'

He did not give me a satisfactory answer.

It has always been our policy to encourage our suppliers to adopt a similar approach to our own as regards their employees, modified to suit the conditions of work. The establishment of decent conditions in addition to fair rates of pay and respect for the individual undoubtedly has been an important factor in our suppliers' increasing efficiency and productivity, and in their comparative lack of industrial strife. They have in turn been able to improve the value they offer and so to increase demand for their products. This has stood both us and them in good stead.

You can tell a great deal about the general standards of a firm by looking at those maintained in their washrooms and lavatories. If they are poor, standards in the factory as a whole will often be poor. When visiting suppliers, I nearly always asked to see the toilet facilities, and some members of the management team used to say, 'Look out — here comes Dan, Dan, the lavatory man.'

The policy of establishing good human relations at work is a continuing process. An interesting example of such development originated in 1958. That year I wanted Simon to visit East Kent Packers in Faversham, the fruit co-operative with whom we were developing a substantial apple business. The route took us through Dartford; Simon decided to have a look at the Dartford store, which was being rebuilt. We had acquired it many years previously; despite some modernization it was still old-fashioned. It is our custom when rebuilding a store to continue trading in one part while the reconstruction work goes on in another. Dartford was a major job and was going to take a year and a half. At the time we visited it about fifty per cent of the rebuilding had been completed.

When we got back to the car Simon, who never missed an opportunity, said, 'I must go to the loo.' It was pouring with rain. Instead of returning to the store, where the staff lavatories were excellent, he went to the area nearby, where the workmen had their so-called facilities. Bricklayers and carpenters were sitting having their lunch — doorstep sandwiches and billycans of tea — under a tarpaulin hung over two girders from which the rain was cascading down. The lavatory was a primitive chemical closet. As he got back into the car Simon said, 'You know, Marcus, we can't have people working for us for whom there are two standards; some of these Bovis people will be on the site for a few months, some for the whole year and a half. We would not tolerate such facilities, or lack of them, in any of our stores, wherever they are situated, large or small. Although these people work for Bovis or their sub-contractors they are really working for us.'

On the following Monday we arranged to meet the heads of Bovis—Keith Joseph and the Vincents. We discussed the problem and asked them to put forward suggestions for decent facilities for the staff. They were responsive and quick; before the end of the week they produced a plan under which, wherever they were building a new store for us or extending an existing store, the first buildings to go up would be temporary but decent accommodation for their employees. This would consist of a proper cloakroom/changing-room with washing and lavatory facilities and a canteen for the preparation of hot meals which could be eaten in reasonable comfort. Because a lot of the work was outdoors there would be facilities for drying clothes. These additions added some one per cent to our building costs.

Bovis, with whom we had been working already for some twenty-five years, had always done a good job, but their performance since 1957 has been outstanding. During this time they have completed some 750 jobs, the cost of which is about £500 million. With one exception, which involved a well-known troublemaker who took work with them under a false name, no job has been handed over to us later than the originally agreed completion date; some have been ready several weeks, some several months in advance. From time to time we have checked the cost of Bovis' work against that of one or two other major building firms. None could compete; yet Bovis has been one of the most profitable firms in the industry. Bovis told us a few weeks after they had first provided their staff with decent facilities that productivity on the site had increased, casual labour turnover had decreased, and as a result costs were lower. This is an example of the benefits of creating better facilities at work – still not sufficiently appreciated by many people in top management.

It was in the 1950s that a number of young people emerged who today are the senior members of the board. I have already written about Derek Rayner, the present chairman. Henry Lewis, who became a managing director and has just retired, joined Marks & Spencer in 1950 and Brian Howard, now deputy chairman and joint managing director, joined in 1951. Henry went to head office after two years in stores and Brian after three. Both started in the clothing side, and then had a period in the food groups; both made important contributions to the business. Their progress speeded up when Teddy Sieff developed the concept of a merchandiser working alongside the selector or buyer; both Henry and Brian quickly established themselves as first-class merchandisers and became group executives and then members of the board.

Another recruit who joined in 1953 was a young man of seventeen called Richard Greenbury, godson of my solicitor, Raymond Gardiner. Rick was first class at sport; he was Wimbledon standard in tennis, though I don't think he got far beyond the first round. Slazenger offered him a job. He was also a fine soccer player and was offered a job by Arsenal, but he decided to join us. He too has made a valuable contribution to the business during his career, not only having been in charge of various merchandise departments – clothing, home furnishings and foods – but also having had a spell as the head of our store operations, building and equipment. Today he is joint managing director, with overall responsibility for personnel, store operations, store building development and equipment. With our huge building and equipment programme, which will cost over £1,500 million over the next five years, he has wide responsibilities and authority.

Simon, who had been made a peer in 1961, suffered a series of minor heart attacks in the early 1960s, but he continued, when he was back on his feet, to come regularly to the office and, though he limited his activities, he remained very much the overall boss of the business. By this time it was becoming increasingly hard to convince him that a certain action was the right course to take; this delayed worthwhile developments. He had never been easy to deal with but he had always been held in high regard and, despite his critical approach, in much affection. His illness, however, made him more difficult to work with. Father, therefore, played an important role at this time; he didn't want, because of Simon's illness, to distress him in any way, but equally he didn't want to see the business held back, and he was able to persuade Simon that certain developments should take place with which Simon was not initially in agreement.

Before Simon's illness his dining-room was on the seventh floor and could comfortably seat ten people; he now had a small dining-room built on the first floor, next to his office, which could hold four or five people. When I was at head office and didn't have a specific engagement, I generally lunched with him. One day in 1964 he said to me, 'Are you lunching with me today, Marcus?'

'No, I've got Woodrow Wyatt coming.'

'Well, bring Woodrow,' he said.

When Woodrow arrived, I told him that we were lunching with Simon and warned him that he had become rather difficult and argumentative and he must be prepared for it. Simon, Father, Woodrow and I lunched together and Simon was reasonable, charming, courteous and an excellent host. When I was seeing Woodrow off, he remarked, 'I don't understand what you said about Simon – he was in terrific form – in fact I have never seen him in a better mood.' I had to agree.

A few minutes after Woodrow had left I was in my office on the sixth floor when Bruce Goodman, one of my co-directors, phoned to ask me to come to Simon's office. When I got there, Simon was lying on a stretcher covered with a blanket with his feet sticking out; Father was sitting by the stretcher quietly weeping. When Woodrow and I had left him after lunch Simon had gone with my brother Michael into the rainwear and coat department and had made a number of critical but justified remarks about the finish of some of the garments. He then said to Michael, 'Let's go back to my office.' As Michael was opening the door he felt a hand slide down his back; Simon had collapsed on the floor. Within a few seconds he had died from a massive heart attack. I thought to myself as he was carried out that he went as he would have wished and as he had prophesied he would when he had told me, years before, that when he left the business it would be feet first. It was the end of an era.

That remains an unhappy memory. But there were happy ones too from those years. One of the pleasures I remember was another visit to Covent Garden. Although I have little knowledge of music, in various forms it has given me much pleasure. In 1956 the Bolshoi Ballet visited London for the first time and I was lucky to be present at the opening gala evening. The atmosphere was electric; many of us thought this visit indicated the beginning of détente between Russia and the West. It was a white tie, bemedalled affair, with the much bejewelled ladies wearing their latest gowns. The Bolshoi gave a superb performance of *Romeo and Juliet*, with Ulanova dancing Juliet. I think she was in her middle forties, but she danced and acted so well that she was like a girl of fourteen or fifteen. The male dancers were wonderful. I had never seen such dynamic and virile male ballet dancing before; it was thrilling. In the interval I ran into William Jowitt, the former Lord Chancellor, who was getting on in years. I said, 'Don't they dance superbly?'

'But Marcus,' he said, 'they were always very good.'

'I don't remember them,' I said.

'You must remember them — they danced so well before the war.'

I said, 'I don't remember them before the war.'

'Yes,' he said, 'don't you remember the famous Russian ballet company here before the war?'

'When?' I asked.

He said, 'Just before the war — in 1912.'

I pointed out that, as I had only been born in 1913, there was good reason for my memory failure. Lord Jowitt was referring to Diaghilev's Ballets Russes, who first performed in London at Covent Garden in 1911.

Elsa and I had divorced in 1953. I had been friendly for a number of years with Brenda Beith, who was an aspiring actress, pretty, charming and very popular. Brenda had been born in China; she and her family were caught by the Japanese in the early days of the war, and spent three-and-a-half years in Chapei Prison Camp, Shanghai. Her uncle,

Ian Hay Beith, became a well-known playwright under the name of Ian Hay; this may have been one of the reasons why Brenda wanted to be an actress.

When I was courting Brenda, she was in a play starring Yvonne Arnaud. She had one line to say at the end of the play, which was, 'Good evening, madam.' It was a toss-up whether the curtain came down before or after she said it. From time to time I would go to the theatre before the show was over and give her a drink in the pub just across the alleyway from the stage-door. I remember that on one occasion Murray MacDonald, the director, walked into the pub when we were having a drink, and tore strips off her. She didn't attempt to defend herself, but I said, 'Look, she is not going to be on for another three-quarters of an hour – I can't see why you are being so rough about it.'

'She is understudying one of the leads,' he said. 'How does she know what's happening on stage?'

I said it was all my fault and apologized, but I don't think it did Brenda's stage career much good.

Brenda and I married in 1956. That Christmas we went to St Moritz. Brenda was knocked down by a truck when we were watching the bob-sleighing and badly hurt. She had to spend several weeks in the nursing home; I was left on my own in the hotel and felt that I couldn't take part in winter sports, at which I was a poor performer, in case I was hurt and couldn't be around for Brenda. In the bar of the Palace Hotel I made the acquaintance of Bill and Betty de Vigier. Bill at that time was building up the Acrow Engineering Company. I remember discussing with him the wooden stockroom racks in our stores; this was about 1.00 am, sitting at the bar. He said, 'You shouldn't have wooden racks, you should have steel. We can produce the right racks for you.'

I retorted, 'Well, show me what you mean.'

I was impressed when seventy-two hours later he showed me sketches, plans and specifications for a steel rack which his office had sent to St Moritz. When I got back to the office, the building department examined the drawings, ordered a prototype and we have been using Acrow racks ever since, though Acrow UK no longer exists. Bill, who is a most dynamic man, and Betty, a charming and attractive lady, are close friends to this day. We have spent many happy holidays together.

Amanda, Brenda's and my daughter, was born in 1958. Brenda and I separated in 1961 and later were divorced. It was I who had been difficult and it had been my fault, but we remain good friends, which is important because of Amanda, who had naturally been upset at our separation. Brenda always maintained that when we married and she got rid of her acting aspirations, I saved her from a fate worse than death.

CHAPTER ELEVEN

{   }

SIMON'S ill-health and inability to work at full blast had, as I have said, made him frustrated and over-critical. Because his colleagues refrained from arguing with him the development of the business had been held back somewhat, but when he died in 1964 the momentum was restored.

Many of us had been brought up at Simon's feet, indoctrinated in his philosophy, educated in his skills; we had absorbed his attitudes to the welfare of his employees and his concern for the customer. His pride in the company and his perception of its place in society were ours as well as his; Father, the new chairman of the company, had been Simon's *alter ego* for nearly forty years. It was not surprising then that, though our leader had gone from us, the force he had created and directed moved steadily and strongly on.

From my description of what we did in the late 1950s and early 1960s, largely from the point of view of my own involvement in it, the reader may have gained the impression that the progress of Marks & Spencer was overwhelmingly in organization, administration and the management of personnel. Certainly the personnel policy and principles established by Simon and Father, and further implemented over the years, made an important contribution to our success, because our staff became more dedicated to, and involved in, the business. However, there was much more to Marks & Spencer's evolution than this.

Marks & Spencer changed from being a successful chain of stores into a national institution. The quality, the value for money, the range and attractiveness of St Michael goods were making a great impression on the community. By the time Simon had died there were thousands of families in which the wife and children were largely clothed by Marks & Spencer. A widespread feeling had developed that the value and reliability of our goods were excellent; our reputation for care in handling foodstuffs and for high standards of hygiene had become well known, and was much appreciated by our customers. Increasing numbers approved of our new and better ranges of clothing.

The improvement in the quality of our clothing, still by far the largest section of the business, was due to a number of factors. The war had accelerated scientific and technological progress. Some of this new technology could be applied to improving the raw materials for our garments; a greater range of higher quality fabrics became available, and this led to a better choice of garments and more attractive designs. As we emerged from post-war austerity and rationing, our customers, especially the women, expressed their pleasure at escaping from the years of limited choice by seeking a wider selection of lighter, brighter garments of varied colour and design. Men as well as women wanted to get away from the days when everybody seemed to be in uniform or overalls; they began to buy more and more casual clothing. As my father put it in his memoirs: 'After the war, Simon deduced, women would want light, comfortable clothes, the cheapest of which would not be greatly different to look at from the most expensive. Shop girls were going to expect to look like duchesses – as they had in the WRNS or the ATS – and feel just as comfortable.'

We had set up a design department in 1938, but its major development took place under Hans Schneider, who joined us in 1949. He had a feel for, as well as knowledge of, what our women customers sought, and under his leadership we developed a design team which contributed greatly to the progress of our ladieswear, particularly outerwear – dresses, skirts, blouses, jackets and so on – which within this very large section was the biggest department. We now created a print design department which advised both our own buying departments and our suppliers on types, patterns and colours of prints, and created original designs for our dresses, scarves and other garments. Simon kept in touch with what was being produced for the leading fashion houses in London and on the Continent, and in this his wife Miriam, who had very good taste and dressed well, was a great help. As a result we found that our garments, at one time largely bought by working girls and the lower income groups, were being bought in ever-increasing quantities by women of the middle class and those with higher incomes.

The development of the Welfare State, it was said by someone at the time, played a part in the changing demand and the consequent production of new types of goods. Lawrence Thompson wrote in the *News Chronicle* in 1955: 'Before the Welfare State there were broadly two classes of consumers, the middle class who had the money, and the working class who hadn't. Now there is only one class and I am told ... that many a débutante wears a Marks & Spencer nylon slip beneath her Dior dress as if she were just a Gateshead factory girl.' Full employment in the 1950s led to increased purchasing power. More than any other supplier of clothing Marks & Spencer was prominently associated with what was a social revolution in miniature. Working with our suppliers, we were leaders in developing the new manmade clothing fibres, with the advantage of their easy care. As my father said, 'We got off to a fast start and it made all the difference.'

In all this we were helping to bring about that democratization of demand which has been a feature of post-war Britain and which should have helped to produce a less jealously divided society. Between 1950 and 1966 Marks & Spencer doubled its share of the national clothing market from five to ten per cent, and in the decade between 1956 and 1966 our profits trebled. Our sales of clothing and food between 1956 and 1966 increased from £119 million to £238 million, a 100% increase; inflation during this period increased by thirty-two per cent. In real terms there was a big increase in the volume of the goods we sold.

My father was deeply shaken by Simon's death but he recorded in his memoirs: 'Since he died, I have in one sense felt a freer person; my decisions and judgements are not related to those of anybody else as they were to Simon's.' Father, wise man that he was, did not attempt in the three years of his chairmanship to move into areas in which he knew he did not have Simon's gifts. Although he supervised the business generally, he gave increasing responsibility for the development of our clothing and textile side to his younger brother Teddy, who had a great feel for fabrics and clothing; Teddy was ably supported by my brother Michael and by Jan Lewando. I, meanwhile, concentrated on the development of the growing food department.

One aspect of the development of the food business was the improvement in the standards of hygiene which we encouraged at our food manufacturers; this improvement extended to the farms who supplied fresh produce directly to our stores or products to our food manufacturers for processing. In some cases our 'encouragement' was regarded as a nuisance, but most of our food suppliers approved and co-operated willingly. Simon was almost neurotic about cleanliness and hygiene and he had transmitted this valuable obsession to all of us in the food group; I was ably assisted by Nathan Goldenberg, an outstanding food technologist, nationally recognized.

Goldenberg, as I said earlier, was mentally incapable of any form of compromise in the fields he considered important. On one ocasion we started business with a world-famous and long-established family biscuit firm. The head of the business didn't approve of their making biscuits for Marks & Spencer under the St Michael brand name. Goldenberg, on the other hand, wasn't certain that the standards of hygiene in the main biscuit factory were good enough. One night he stayed on there, and after the ovens had been closed down he went back with one of the supplier's younger executives into that part of the plant where the ovens were situated. He had all the lights switched on, whereupon hundreds of red ants, with which the floor was alive, scurried back beneath the ovens. These creatures thrived on the heat and enjoyed the scraps which fell on the floor during the process of manufacture. We immediately ceased business with this supplier. What had happened during Goldenberg's nocturnal visit became known; the chairman asked for a resumption of business with us — a request to which we agreed only when we were sure that they had improved their standards to meet our exacting specifications.

We had been raising our own standards all the time. The basis of our policy was the training of staff in personal cleanliness and hygiene; the educational programme by which this was done centred on the inculcation of an attitude of mind. In the foreward to the handbook on hygiene circulated in Marks & Spencer's kitchens and dining rooms we stated: 'Hygiene is part of our philosophy.... It is based on each person recognizing his individual responsibility for carrying out the rules of clean food handling and the "clean as you go" principle. By the phrase "clean as you go" we insist that at all times the employee should give his mind to removing any kind of dirt.'

There were strict rules in our kitchens and dining rooms governing the safe storage of food and the conditions under which it was cooked and served. Equally strict rules were agreed with our food suppliers, both on the farm and in the processing plants. It was rewarding to find that some of our employees wanted to reproduce similar standards of hygiene at home; complaints were received from some mothers about the demands made on them by their daughters. One mother wrote,

'She even expects me to wash my hands before making pastry.'

From my enthusiasm for the development of the food side of Marks & Spencer there sprang, in the early 1960s, before Simon's death, a determination to purchase food produced in Britain. Simon and Father were both very patriotic. They had inherited a love for their country and a pride in being British from their fathers. My father enjoyed telling the tale of how, as a little boy, he saw Queen Victoria when she visited Manchester. My grandfather pushed his way through the crowds until his view was blocked by a huge man in labourer's clothes; the man, an Irishman, turned round and truculently demanded to know what my grandfather was pushing for. 'I want my little boy to see the Queen,' my grandfather said diffidently, in his foreign accent.

'What's the Queen to you?' demanded the Irishman.

'She is my Queen,' said my grandfather, 'I'm a British citizen.'

'Well, she's my Queen too,' said the Irishman and, moving to make room for my grandfather, he lifted up my father and put him on his shoulders so that he could see the Queen.

The policy of buying British was long established by the time I decided to apply it to our growing food department. Its application in this area was not without problems. In the 1960s we were selling a carrot called the Amsterdam forcing carrot, which was, as the name indicates, grown in Holland; it was of excellent quality and sold well. I suggested that we grow the Amsterdam carrot in Britain, but the experts said that it could not be grown in British soil. I found this hard to believe when in the eastern counties we had a soil and climate similar to the Dutch. Our technologists believed that it could be grown in Britain. The first attempt was made by the late Lord (Julian) Melchett and Dr Roseen, whom we used as a consultant. A disused airfield on Julian Melchett's land was ploughed up for the purpose, but the experiment was a failure.

I then met a Lincolnshire farmer, Tim Tinsley, married to a Dutch lady who was a first-class technologist. I remember my first visit well; it was bitterly cold, with a terrible wind, and there seemed to be nothing in the way of protection between the flat Lincolnshire fields and the icy blast from the Russian steppes. Mr Tinsley farmed about 2000 acres; he and his wife believed they could grow the Amsterdam forcing carrot; we asked them to have a go. They grew it exceedingly well and from that modest beginning a great business has developed between Tinsley and Marks & Spencer over the last seventeen years.

At the start they employed twenty people on the farm; their turnover with us in the first year was £84,000. Their turnover with us in 1986 will be about £20 million, but it was not all in carrots, though they are an important item. The size of their farm has grown to 4,000 acres; they process many of the fresh vegetables they produce into salads and pre-packed ready-to-eat dishes. Much of the raw materials they grow themselves or sub-contract to neighbouring farms. The number of people employed on their farm and in the farm processing plants has increased from twenty to 1,100. This shows what can be done when the farmer co-operates closely with his customer, producing what the customer wants. We encourage our food suppliers to develop good standards of working conditions, welfare and wages for their employees, just as we do our major clothing manufacturers. The most successful are those who have implemented such a policy.

But we were not always successful in persuading all our suppliers to agree to establishing the standards we believed essential and so we had to cease business with a number of them. At one time we did business with a famous firm in the Midlands which produced excellent cooked meats for us. They had been established for over 250 years and had a national, if not an international, reputation. The original family was still running the business, and they made it clear, after I had visited them a couple of times, that they preferred me not to go on Wednesdays and Thursdays in the winter as those were the days on which they hunted or shot.

The area of the factory in which the St Michael products were cooked and processed was clean, with good standards, but elsewhere conditions were poor: the walls ran with moisture, the men's cloak-rooms and lavatories were dirty and dilapidated, in fact Dickensian. I told them that they couldn't have two standards on their premises; eventually the bad would drive out the good. I asked them to get things right. They were polite and said that they saw my point. I thought that would be that but, when I went back two months later, I found little had changed. This time I gave them an ultimatum: if they did not deal with the situation, we would cease to do business with them. 'You can't do that,' they retorted, 'we've become one of your biggest food suppliers.' They thought we could not afford to stop doing business with them, and therefore did not take me at my word. I told them I'd be back in four weeks; I was. I said, 'We cease to do business with you on Monday.'

'We don't believe you,' they said. They weren't so polite now. 'You'll never cut out a million pounds' worth of business just like that.'

I told them we would. 'One day you'll run into serious trouble if you try to go on like this,' I said. 'We might as well stop trading with you now as wait for the inevitable. Anyhow, we don't want to put any of our customers at risk of eventually buying contaminated food.'

We ceased business with them that Monday. Soon afterwards that long-established business collapsed; its operations were taken over by another large organization, but it wasn't successful and 1,500 people lost their jobs. The original business had collapsed because the owners, rather than spending enough time and effort looking after it, preferred to indulge themselves in the hunting field and on other pleasures, and didn't build up alternative management to operate the plant efficiently.

It took us some time to replace the supplies we lost, but eventually we were able to do so and meet the growing demand – partly from British and partly from Danish sources, where our requirements on conditions of production were fully met.

Whenever we have taken decisions such as the one above, which have caused us short-term problems, we have benefited in the medium and longer term; while, whenever we have compromised on our principles, we and our customers have been the losers.

In the 1960s an ever-increasing proportion of frozen poultry was being sold, much of poor quality. We believed there was a demand for a high-quality fresh bird though the price might be more. At first we had difficulty in finding a suitable supplier, but eventually Colonel Corbett, a former Tory M P, who chaired a farmers' co-operative in Hereford, Sun Valley Poultry, said he would supply us with fresh poultry. He did a first-class job and this was the beginning of a major development, which ultimately led to our becoming the largest seller of poultry in the country.

In 1959 I started the practice of selecting bright, energetic young men and making them my personal assistants. They generally spent from eighteen months to two years with me and, if they were successful and did a good job, they went on to more responsible senior positions within the company than they had held when they joined me. An exception to this rule was Simon Susman, who returned to South Africa to become head of the food group at Woolworths, with whom we continue to have close ties. Frank Hirst and Don Trangmar became members of the board, and Alan Lambert, Andrew Stone, Chris Littmoden and Geoff Dart are all senior executives, just below board level. My last PA was Ronnie Jacobson. He was with me for a large part of the time during which I was writing this book. He showed much patience, for which I thank him. I found their help very useful and most of them broadened their experience of the business, which they subsequently found of value. I recommend this as a method of speeding up the development of people with potential who have already gained some modest experience at relatively junior levels. One of the best of my PAs was the first, Bob Thornton; he did an excellent job and had great ability, but decided that there was possibly more scope for him in other pastures. He left the business in 1961 and eventually became the chairman and chief executive of the Debenham group, from which he has recently retired.

CHAPTER TWELVE

{   }

IN the late 1950s I met Lily Moretzki (née Spatz); she was exceptionally attractive and intelligent. We married in 1963 and our daughter, Daniela, was born in 1965. Lily came from Lvov, that part of Poland which used to belong to the Austro-Hungarian Empire, then called Lemberg. Her father, who was in the timber business, owned forests and was well-to-do with a house in Lvov and another in the country.

Lily is Jewish; her mother was a Zionist, but her father had no interest in Zionism or indeed in Palestine. He was a Polish patriot, who did not see, or want to see, what was happening in Germany and Europe after Hitler took power. When the war broke out and Germany invaded Poland, Lily's father said that Britain and France would come to Poland's aid and Germany would soon be defeated; there was nothing to worry about – the family could stay in Lvov. Soon afterwards his illusions were rudely shattered when the Germans began to make substantial advances into Poland and bombed Lvov heavily. Lily's first memory of the war is of fires and bombing in her home town. Her father decided it would be best for the family to leave Lvov, an important city, and go to the country until the war was over; they managed to get away.

With her father, mother and brother Lily moved to a village near the Rumanian border. The Germans were advancing further and further into Poland from the north-west; then Russia attacked Poland from the east. At this point Lily's father decided that they should try to escape across the border into Rumania. They could take with them only what they could carry; fortunately they had brought with them some gold coins and jewellery because when they got to the border, the Rumanian police shouted at them, 'Jews, go back.' A bribe changed the attitude of one of the border guards and they were allowed to cross, in company with many thousands of people fleeing from the advancing Germans. They were sent to a camp for refugees, where the Jews were segregated. Again by bribes Lily's father managed to get his family out of the camp to Bucharest, where Lily went to the Lycée Français.

Lily's father did not want to go to Palestine; he tried to obtain a visa for the United States, where his brother had lived for some time, but was refused. In the end he succeeded in getting papers which enabled the family to emigrate to Palestine. They were lucky to be on the last boat which left Europe legally for that haven, in 1940. Lily was brought up in Palestine for the next eight years. She was educated in Israel and at Geneva University, where she studied under the famous Professor Rappard and took a degree in political and economic science. Afterwards she studied for a Master's degree at the London School of Economics.

Following the death of her first husband at an early age from cancer, in Canada, she returned to London. She was deeply depressed, until a friend helped her to obtain a job with the Israeli diplomatic service. I first met her when she was working in the Israeli embassy in London. She is a woman of tremendous ability, energy and drive, and we have been happily married for twenty-three years. Lily has provided invaluable help and encouragement to me in my work in many ways.

The day we were married was cold and snowy. We were going to Barbados for our honeymoon and, since the plane did not leave until eight o'clock that night, my brother Michael and his wife Daphne gave a little cocktail party for us en route to Heathrow airport, at which I had several drinks. Michael decided to come and see us off. The flight was delayed by the snow, so I had a few more drinks. There weren't any jet passenger planes in those days and the journey to Barbados took about seventeen hours. I didn't sleep much on the plane and had another drink or two. When we arrived at the hotel in Barbados the following afternoon, we were greeted with a rum punch from the management, which I drank. I was tired, but decided to go for a walk, as I knew Victor Rothschild had a house a few hundred yards away on the beach. He was there. He and his wife Tess congratulated me and insisted that I had a drink, another excellent rum punch, to celebrate the occasion. I walked somewhat unsteadily back to the hotel, cleaned up and went down with Lily for dinner. It was a warm evening, the restaurant was most pleasant and I ordered a bottle of white burgundy. We each had a glass, I toasted my bride, and within seconds the room began to revolve at an ever-increasing pace. Lily helped me back to our bedroom and got me to bed; I awoke twelve hours later, luckily without a hangover.

So the first night of our marriage was spent in a plane and the second night I was tight. Hardly an auspicious beginning, but perhaps that's part of the reason why it has generally gone so well for twenty-three years.

For the next five or six years we went in January or February to Barbados to stay with Victor and Tess. For a serious shopkeeper no time is more demanding than the October/November/December period prior to Christmas, so among the many things I have to be grateful to Victor and Tess for is their regular hospitality following the most exhausting period of the year. We always had a marvellous time – plenty of sun, swimming, relaxation and good conversation. It was our main holiday of the year and I think was one reason why, on the whole, I have kept reasonably well and pretty active.

It was in Barbados, too, that we became friendly with Charlie and Jeryl Smith-Ryland. Charlie has been the Chairman of the Council of the Royal Agricultural Society for many years and it was largely due to him and Francis Pemberton that I became President of the R.A.S.E. twenty years later in 1984–5.

In 1964, when Christopher Soames was Minister of Agriculture, he phoned me one day and said, 'Marcus, will Marks & Spencer endow a chair in agricultural marketing at Wye College?' I said, 'No, we won't.' He then said he would like to come and talk about it, so I invited him to lunch. He arrived so well briefed and with such a hearty appetite – I can remember to this day watching a plate of smoked salmon disappear with incredible rapidity – that I was lost in admiration on both counts. At the end of the meal I said, 'Look here, Christopher, we will endow half the chair providing farmers, and it must be farmers, endow the other half; this way they will take an active interest in the chair, which they may not if all the money is put up by outsiders.' After the chair had been established there was a lunch in the Houses of Parliament, at which I was asked to say a few words. When I had finished, a member of a well-known farming family got up to reply and said, 'I have listened to Mr Sieff with amazement. Since when must we farmers grow what the consumer wants? The consumer must take what we grow.' He was pulled down by his colleagues, but I am afraid that this attitude is still quite prevalent in industry and agriculture to this day.

In January 1966 I spoke at the twentieth Oxford Farming Conference with the theme, 'The Expanding Market for Quality Products'. I described to the largely farming audience the progress we had made, in co-operation with progressive farmers, farm groups, and food processors, in expanding the market for quality food products; I talked about fruit, vegetables, poultry, fresh and canned meat products and eggs, and explained that our customers were prepared to pay a premium for high-quality products which looked well and were virtually waste-free, but which, above all, were enjoyable to eat. I explained to the audience that members of our board, senior executives and their families regularly ate at home the foodstuffs we sold; that we believed if the food wasn't good enough for us and our families then it wasn't good enough for anybody – certainly not for our customers. We applied the same principle to our clothing and other departments, and do so to this day. It is one way of helping to maintain high quality standards. Of course we made and still make many mistakes.

Another speech, three years later, dealt with the subject of good human relations at work. The occasion was the annual conference of the Institute of Directors at the Albert Hall. I was the unknown in a distinguished group of speakers which included Iain McLeod, the Shadow Chancellor of the Exchequer, a man of great ability whose premature death was a great loss to the country; Ronald Reagan, who had previously been Governor of California; Barbara Castle, then a member of the cabinet with responsibility for employment and productivity; Sir John Betjeman, the poet; and Sir Derek Pritchard, the president of the Institute of Directors.

Barbara Castle devoted part of her talk to the importance of good industrial relations and made a number of justified criticisms of top management's remoteness from the majority of their employees. She ended her talk by saying: 'We have got to recognize whether we like it or not, that real power now resides in the workshops and on the office floor.' This was largely true, but some shop stewards on the far left regarded their power as a licence to create trouble, whether justified or not; the authority of the foremen, many of whom were excellent, was largely undermined.

The views which I expressed in my own speech – which I entitled 'Human Relations – Success or Failure' – were, predictably perhaps, rather different from Barbara Castle's. Here is part of what I said:

I believe that one of the most important problems which industry faces today is the development of good human relations – the relationship which management establishes with each and every individual who works in any particular organization, and I include in this all types of management, be it government, nationalized industry, trade union or private enterprise.

The outlook is depressing unless we tackle the problems of developing better human relations more sympathetically, more professionally, more persistently and on a wider scale. Such relations cannot be imposed on industry from outside, by government for example, though government tries to do it from time to time. It is generally unsuccessful and highly undesirable. . . . Good human relations can only develop if top management believes in its importance and then sees that such a philosophy is dynamically implemented.

Management must care for the people they employ in all aspects of their daily work. Now I am not talking about sentimentality and 'do gooders', but about care in a sensible way, which we have found brings a response, with few exceptions, from all grades of staff. This response expresses itself in loyalty to the firm, co-operation with management, greater labour stability and a willing acceptance of new and more modern methods. The majority of workers under such conditions take pride in doing a good job. All this results in greater productivity and higher profits. This enables management both to provide all those facilities which make for a contented and hard-working staff, and to pay better wages based on genuinely increased productivity. So it is of benefit to the individual, the firm and the national effort.

We employ some 500 people trained in staff management whose primary responsibility is the well-being of our 30,000 staff; that is one per sixty. It is their job to see that the board's policy is implemented down the line. Every member of the staff is personally known by and has regular contact with somebody who is concerned with his or her well-being and progress. In every store, for example, we have a manager and a staff manageress. The staff manageress is not a remote staff officer sitting in a little room upstairs. She knows her staff well and is integrated into the commercial life of the store.

I went on to explain the view that businessmen had paid too much attention to machines and systems, too little to people. I then explained how a policy such as the one I had been expounding expressed itself materially:

First, in a progressive wage policy. Unless wages are satisfactory and increasing, there will be no improvement in productivity and human relations will be poor. But management must also see that staff amenities are good – staff dining rooms, kitchens, recreation rooms, cloakrooms and lavatories.... These amenities should be of such a nature that executives are pleased to take advantage of them when they are on the factory floor.... If the facilities provided are not good enough for top management, then they are not good enough for staff.... How many of us eat from time to time in the staff canteen, visit the staff cloakrooms, use the staff lavatories? There is no substitute for personal visits to the shopfloor with seeing eyes and hearing ears....

Despite the National Health Service, there is much left undone and much scope for medical care at work, as you all know. My company has long provided advisory medical and dental services ... a chiropody service ...and a system of testing for cervical and breast cancer.... These welfare activities are small things ... but ... show people that management cares for them and is trying to study their personal problems....

The word 'welfare' has an old-fashioned sound reminiscent of the Victorian era, but ... people do have troubles and it is a fundamental part of a good staff policy to be able unobtrusively and above all speedily to give help and advice where needed. The essence of any good welfare scheme is prevention rather than cure. I wish that more attention was given to the preventive aspect in the industrial scene, where bureaucratic delays in solving minor problems and grievances result all too often in major industrial strife....

I quoted Thomas Watson Junior, the chairman of IBM, who, in his book *A Business and its Beliefs – The Ideas that Helped Build IBM,* wrote:

There is simply no substitute for good human relations and for the high morale they bring. It takes good people to do the jobs necessary to reach your profit goals. But good people alone are not enough. No matter how good your people may be, if they don't really like the business, if they don't feel totally involved in it, or if they don't think they're being treated fairly – it's awfully hard to get a business off the ground. Good human relations are easy to talk about. The real lesson, I think, is that you must work at them all the time time and make sure your managers are working with you.

I concluded:

If private enterprise is to play the important role of which it is capable and which is so vital for the national effort and economy, I think it is one of the responsibilities of all of us here to see that the principles I have enumerated are applied, modified, of course, to suit those businesses with which you are concerned. If we do not do this, the effectiveness and value of private enterprise will diminish. Then the state in one form or another will assume an increasing degree of ownership and control over that type of industry which, properly managed, private enterprise can operate more efficiently and more humanely. Such a development could be costly to the nation.

Regrettably, eighty per cent of what I said in 1969 about top management's failure to implement a policy of good human relations still largely applies today.

Though Simon, my father, Teddy and others had many times spoken in public about our concern for what other people called 'industrial relations', and though Father's speeches in the House of Lords – he was created a life peer in 1966 – had drawn considerable attention to the subject, it was my speech to the Institute of Directors which, mainly due no doubt to the temper of the times, focused attention on the Marks & Spencer approach to the importance of good human relations in industry. This led to a certain amount of public attention being paid to me. It was not all complimentary. Many people, including some of my friends, thought I was 'soft' on industrial relations, naive, obsessive, paternalistic and/or boring. I came in for criticism.

Despite this, it is undoubtedly true that today more top management follows the policy and implements the principles about which I spoke, but they are still a minority. That minority includes a number of the most successful and profitable industrial and commercial organizations in the world. I do not understand why more leaders in economic fields in the widest sense do not understand the value of good human relations at work. IBM, for instance, is a great international company, very much in the public eye. They implement a policy of good human relations at work. They employ 395,000 people; in 1985 they had sales of $49 billion, and profits of $6 billion after tax. They have virtually no industrial strife. Why do not other companies follow their example?

Some, I am glad to say did – eventually. The outstandingly capable chief executive of one of our biggest manufacturing companies used to say to me when we discussed our policies and developments together, 'You know, Marcus, I think you are a bit soft the way you treat your staff and the amount of money you spend on staff benefits.'

I replied, 'We may be soft, but if you look at our profits they are not bad.'

Unlike us he was unionized, his huge staff being divided among several unions; from time to time he suffered from industrial strife. One day he remarked, 'Marcus, there may be something in the way you do things; are you prepared to have a look at our firm's operations?'

I seconded to them one of our top personnel executives, Paul Smith. Over a period of two months he visited eight of their factories, their headquarters, and one of their training centres. The first thing he found was that there was no common personnel policy. Morale in one or two factories was good, at others indifferent, and at some poor. Paul Smith produced a first-class report, critical but constructive; here are some extracts from it:

The personnel function is totally dominated by industrial relations. Whilst this is perfectly understandable in their culture, one was left wondering just how many of the fires that had to be put out would ever have ignited in the first place with a greater consideration of the human side of management. It was the technical side of personnel work rather than the humanitarian that was more in evidence, and the people employed in this function reflected this company requirement in their approach. An attitude of caring was not prevalent and I think would have been regarded as 'soft'. I met only one personnel manager who actually talked about their needs and problems.

There was a lot of responsibility for personnel matters vested in first-line management. Whilst this enriches their job considerably beyond that of a similar level in Marks & Spencer, it seems odd that minimal attention has been paid to training these people to deal with this aspect of their work.

There was a fairly widespread feeling amongst the personnel people I met that their work was not highly regarded by the chief executive.

Paul Smith stressed there were certain activities in the organization from which Marks & Spencer could learn — for instance, about decentralization: Marks & Spencer is very centralized — but he concluded: 'However, I remain convinced that the cause of many industrial problems is a lack of understanding of what people's needs are. Whether a company is capital or labour intensive, the human element will become more critical. To debate whether the problem is best handled by an effective personnel department or line management trained to understand human behaviour is irrelevant. It is more important to ensure that somehow the needs of all those employed are understood and satisfied if at all possible.'

He asked me what he should do with his report. I replied, 'Send it to the chief executive of the firm.'

The latter phoned me a week later: 'Marcus, have you read the report on us?'

'Yes,' I said, 'bloody good isn't it?'

'Are you prepared to go on helping?' he asked.

'Yes, what do you want?'

He said, 'I would like you to second Paul Smith to us for a couple of years.'

'Nothing doing,' I replied, 'we can't spare him, but we are prepared to continue to co-operate with whoever you nominate; we shall try to be helpful working with him or her.'

A few months later I was lunching with the chief executive in his office. The tone of our conversation was very different from previous lunches. He said, 'You know, Marcus, I have personnel problems in three factories. One is due to a shop steward who is determined to create trouble. We shall have trouble in that plant until we get rid of him. The trouble at the other two factories is entirely due to the stupidity of management who do not know how to treat their staff.'

Between 1960 and 1970 Marks & Spencer's food sales increased from £24 million to £97 million. In the second half of the 1960s we began to develop a national system of food depots and transport which enabled us to ensure that the products from the farms and food processors who supplied us could reach all our stores throughout Great Britain within thirty-six hours in prime condition under the appropriate temperatures – ambient, chilled or freezing.

An obvious example of this concern with quality is the development of our winter tomatoes. We found in the winter that the quality of those we imported from the Canary Islands was often poor; although they were nicely coloured they were often bladdery and lacked flavour. The sale of tomatoes was important to us. I said to Jim Lane, in charge of our produce department, 'Unless we can improve the quality of our winter tomatoes, we shall have to eliminate the line even though sales are considerable. What are your views?' He visited the Canary Islands in the middle of the season and on his return reported that the tomatoes were picked green and unripe, thrown by the pickers into baskets, sometimes quite a few feet away, and then left to stand on the quay waiting for shipment by sea to the United Kingdom. They coloured up in the hot sun; those that had been bruised when thrown into the baskets became bladdery as they ripened; all the tomatoes were tasteless and of poor quality.

I asked Jim Lane what he thought we should do. 'Bring them in by air,' he replied. As far as we knew nobody had airlifted tomatoes to this country before, or for that matter anywhere else.

I said, 'Won't this add greatly to the cost?'

'Yes,' he said, 'it will; in fact it will add about fifty per cent to our selling price but we shall have a decent tomato!'

We then brought in our first load, a Britannia full of tomatoes. The selling price was 1/6d (7½p) per pound; the selling price of those brought by sea was 1/- (5p) per pound.

Just after the first plane-load arrived I was going to Wye Agricultural College in Kent to give a talk; on the way I called in at our Maidstone store. There on the counter were the shipped and air-freighted tomatoes side by side with a price differential of fifty per cent. Both tomatoes were red in colour; the only indication that one was different from the other was that the air-freighted tomatoes had a ticket which said, 'Transported by air for freshness and flavour'; otherwise both looked the same. I said to the sales assistant, 'I don't suppose you sell many of those at 1/6d against those at 1/-.' She replied, 'Mr Sieff, if you once taste the tomatoes brought by air you'll never buy a tomato brought by sea again.' She was right – and our customers soon realized it.

One evening early in 1970 Ted Heath, the leader of the Conservative Party, asked some ten people to dinner at his flat in Albany; the only politician apart from the host, if I remember rightly, was Robert Carr, the rest of the guests being concerned with industry and commerce. Among the people there were George Cole, then chairman of Unilever, Val Duncan, chairman of RTZ, and one of the directors of Shell Oil. The dinner was delicious and the wine so outstanding that I asked to see the bottle; I remember to this day that it was a Cheval Blanc '45. When dinner was finished, Ted Heath made an outstanding short speech, saying that when – not if – he became Prime Minister it was his intention to work more closely with industry than previous governments had done. To make this co-operation effective he wanted us each to second to government for a minimum of two years a top-class person from our businesses.

He asked George Cole what he thought about the idea; I remember his reply. 'Well, it's a good idea, Ted, but we couldn't afford to second anybody for two years from the main board of Unilever. I am sure we would find someone down the line in one of our subsidiaries to take on this role.'

Ted Heath then turned to Val Duncan and asked what he thought. I intervened at that point and said, 'Do you mind if I say something?' He agreed. 'Your first-class dinner, excellent talk, good idea and outstanding wine will be wasted if, having decided to support it, we don't loan to the government the people we can't really afford.'

I went back to the office and spoke to Teddy and Father. I said there were three people who might be able to do the job: Jan Lewando, Derek Rayner or myself (I was never modest), but since I was taking on more responsibilities in the business in the near future and Jan, who was older than me, was getting on, I thought we should second Derek Rayner. Teddy said, 'What have you done? You can't commit us like that.'

I retorted, 'I have committed us and I think Derek Rayner, if he is willing, should go.'

Derek Rayner went to work with Ted Heath after the Conservatives won the 1970 General Election. He was assigned the task of examining defence procurement and making recommendations. He completed this assignment in one year and was invited to stay to implement his recommendations as Chief Executive, Procurement Executive in the Ministry of Defence. He returned to Marks & Spencer in 1973 and was appointed a managing director. When Mrs Thatcher became Prime Minister, she asked Derek to become her adviser on improving efficiency and eliminating wastage in government departments—a role he carried out most effectively from 1979 to 1983.

But life was not all Marks & Spencer, head office and visits to stores, to suppliers and to Israel. In the late 1950s and early 1960s I became a keen trout fisherman. Lily and I have a house on the farm which Father built up over many years. A small river runs through the farm into the Kennet, which over the last twenty-five years had become a very good trout stream. We are surrounded by friends on the farm. My sister Judith, who married an Israeli, Abrasha Shechterman, now lives in Israel, but her greatest friend, Ursula (Ushy) Adam, who married Peter Adam, a German refugee who served in Intelligence during the war, has a house on the farm. It was Peter who taught me the pleasure of fishing. Regrettably he died in the early 1960s, but his son-in-law, Peter Kleeman, who is married to Carola, also has a house near ours and continues to be my fishing companion.

Lily and I have a full social life with a wide circle of friends from many walks of life: friends from childhood days, people who became friends as a result of business connections, friends from the political sphere. Over the years I have maintained an active interest in Israel, always hoping that in some way or another I might be able to make a minor contribution to peace between Israel and her Arab neighbours. (I also have friends from those countries.) One particular friendship we developed at this time was with the publisher George Weidenfeld, a very cultured and highly intelligent man. He is consistent in the most constructive way, whether it is popular or not, in his support of Israel; since he became a member of the House of Lords he has spoken regularly and persuasively in debates concerning the Middle East.

CHAPTER THIRTEEN

I HAVE visited Israel regularly since returning to England in 1951, generally three times a year and largely for three purposes: first, to assist members of both the British and Israeli Governments, who sometimes wish to convey messages to each other through unofficial channels; second, to try and help Israel in her economic development; third, because I was becoming more active in the affairs of the Weizmann Institute of Science.

After one of my visits in 1953 I prepared a memorandum entitled 'Stability in the Middle East', the main points of which referred to the continued Arab hostility towards Israel and the opposition at that time of the Arab governments towards Britain as well. I quote the first two paragraphs below:

1. Stability in the Middle East continues to be an aim to be pursued in the interests of world peace. British policy since 1918 has sought consistently to establish close co-operation with the Arab successor states, who, it was believed, would act in unity under the leadership of Great Britain. This policy has not proved successful, especially during the war years of 1939–1945. The Arab states only show some measure of unity in opposing British or any other non-Arab powers' leadership or guidance, or in hostility against Israel. There is no combined Arab effort for economic development of the region or for the establishment of stability or for effective military co-ordination. Governments are unstable, intrigue and revolution are frequent and the maintenance of power largely depends on the whipping-up of mob emotion against the non-Arab powers who have, or have had, influence in the region. The declared intention of the present Egyptian government is the removal of British authority from the area.

2. Turkey and Israel alone in the Middle East are politically stable and developing along western lines. Recently, British ties with Turkey have been considerably strengthened. Our relations with Israel have, however, made only limited progress.

I then went on to discuss Israel's economic problems and development. The final paragraph of the memorandum read as follows:

14. If, however, the present negotiations for an agreement between

Great Britain and Egypt are not successful, it would be still more important, in the circumstances that would be likely to follow, for Great Britain to establish a closer understanding with Israel. Such co-operation would be of great value in maintaining an effective degree of British influence in the area.

I gave this memorandum wide circulation: recipients included the Prime Minister, Sir Winston Churchill, and, of course, the Foreign Office. Subsequently I was told the reactions of a number of senior members of the Foreign Office, all of whom considered the memorandum one-sided and far too favourable to Israel. One senior member of the Foreign Office, Peter Ramsbotham, later to become British ambassador in Washington, commented thus:

Mr. Marcus Sieff is a director of his family's firm of Marks and Spencer. . . . He is a very sincere man and genuinely believes in Israel's future. . . . The attached memorandum will, no doubt, have been given a fairly wide circulation here in influential quarters. It is well written but, of course, far too optimistic about Israel's economic prospects.

It is far too early to state categorically (para 8) that Israel is 'a viable economy'. Present evidence is to the contrary, I think. Para 12 ignores the fact that M.E. crude oil is, in fact, going to Haifa and the amounts will be increased this year (unless we can persuade the oil companies to stop it) — but perhaps this omission is just as well!

The lesson for us is at para 14.

P. Ramsbotham

18/5

Perhaps I was too optimistic about Israel's economy but, despite her present economic problems, she has made and makes remarkable economic progress in many areas.

In October 1957 I went with my then wife Brenda to Jerusalem to see Ben Gurion, then still Prime Minister. As soon as I arrived at the hotel I phoned Ben Gurion at his home, to be told by Paula, his wife, who had just returned from the hospital, that a bomb — it turned out to be a hand-grenade — had been thrown into the Knesset chamber from the visitors' gallery, slightly wounding five of the ministers, including the Prime Minister, and seriously wounding Mr Shapira, the Minister for Religious Affairs. It had been thrown by a twenty-five-year-old Iraqi Jew who was mentally unbalanced.

Having been told by Paula that Ben Gurion wished to see me, I went with Brenda next morning to the hospital, where a large crowd was milling around outside. We were escorted to Ben Gurion's room; his wrists and legs were bandaged, but he was in good form. His first question was to enquire whether I had ever been injured by a hand-grenade.

During the course of our discussion he asked me whether I could help over one or two matters in which the United Kingdom was involved; I promised to do my best. Meanwhile two officers concerned with military affairs and security came in to get emergency documents, made necessary by the grenade attack, signed by Ben Gurion. I had been there about half an hour and thought it was time to leave. I was looking for a way of leaving politely when in came a man wearing the usual military dress of short-sleeved shirt and khaki shorts. I knew his face well, but couldn't remember his name. We shook hands warmly and Ben Gurion remarked, 'I see you two know each other.' I said, 'Yes,' and took the opportunity to leave. The crowd outside the hospital had grown considerably and I said to Brenda, 'I know the old man is popular, but I didn't realize how popular.'

She replied, 'Don't be silly, they're not gathered here just because of Ben Gurion but because of Danny Kaye.'

'What do you mean? Is he here?'

'What are you talking about?' she asked. 'You and he shook hands warmly in Ben Gurion's room and chatted just before you left; I saw you through the door.'

It was only then that I realized that the man I had thought was another member of the military staff was Danny Kaye. I had never met him in my life but I had seen his face many times on the screen. It was the beginning of a friendship which continued for many years, though I have seen little of him recently.

In 1956, following continuous Arab terrorist incursions into Israeli territory, which resulted in many casualties, Israel attacked the Egyptian forces in Sinai and Gaza and defeated them in what was called 'the 100 hours' war'. Israel at the same time occupied the Gaza Strip. Under international pressure Israel had to give up these territories; UN observers were stationed on the agreed ceasefire line in the Negev between Israel and Egypt. Nasser refused any form of peace negotiations. He built up the Egyptian armed forces, including the air force, and in 1967 announced that it was his intention to drive the Israelis into the sea. He started to assemble a number of divisions in Sinai, just south of the ceasefire line, and then proceeded, in spite of international protest, including that of the British government, to blockade the entrance to the Gulf of Aqaba, Israel's main line of communication with East Africa and the Far East. Transit through the Suez Canal was already barred to Israeli ships, again contrary to international law. Despite further protests Nasser continued with his arms build-up and his threats to wipe out Israel.

A number of us believed that Israel's survival was at risk. I remember having discussions with Victor Rothschild on Saturday 3 June, two days before war broke out; we sent messages to Harold Wilson, the Prime Minister, and, I think, to Robert Strauss at the American Democratic Convention, asking them to use their influence to prevent Nasser carrying out his threats. War was obviously imminent, and on Monday 5 June it erupted, with Israel making a pre-emptive air strike which wiped out a major part of the Egyptian air force. Despite this initial setback, Nasser announced great victories. In the first days of that week Israel's friends in London believed the Egyptian communiqués and were deeply concerned that Israel would be defeated and destroyed. A number of us wanted to get to Israel as quickly as possible to see if we could be of any help. Six of us went: Scottie Morrison, Jacob, the son of Victor Rothschild, Stuart Young, the late chairman of the BBC, Hyman Kreitman of Tesco, David Susman of Woolworth South Africa, and I. When we arrived in Israel on the Wednesday evening we were hugely relieved to find the military situation very different from what we had expected. The Israelis were well on the way to victory; they were driving the Egyptians out of Sinai and had repelled a Jordanian attack.

I learned later that initially Nasser not only claimed great victories but also told King Hussein of Jordan that if he did not join in the attack on Israel he would not share in the fruits of victory, and implied that he would be considered a traitor to the Arab cause. The Israelis had sent messages to King Hussein, who at that time occupied the West Bank and half of Jerusalem, that Israel would not take any action against Jordan, whatever the outcome of the war, providing he did not intervene. Regrettably King Hussein believed Nasser's false claims of victory and his threat that, unless he acted, Jordan would not reap any benefits from that victory, so he attacked Israel from the West Bank and the Jordanian-held part of Jerusalem; but by the end of the week the Egyptians had been routed and the Jordanians driven back. Israel then took control of the whole of Jerusalem and the West Bank, and occupied Sinai down to the Suez Canal.

On Saturday 12 June I went to Eshkol's office – he was then Prime Minister. I was told he was on his own but, when I entered, I found him in battledress, sitting with a general whom I didn't know. He had just returned from Kuneitra on the Golan Heights, and he and the Prime Minister were discussing the proposed ceasefire line. I apologized and started to back out, but Eshkol said, 'Sit down, Marcus.' He turned to the general and said, 'We had better talk in English because Marcus's Hebrew is so bad.' After they had finished talking, I congratulated him on Israel's victory, but he said he was very worried: 'We now have the whole of Jerusalem – and the world will not forgive us.'

'Why?' I asked. 'Is it the intention of the Israelis to take action against Arabs or Christians in Jerusalem?'

He said, 'No.'

'Are you going to prevent Christians, Moslems or Jews from worshipping at their holy places?'

'No, we are not. It is our desire to live in peace in this formerly divided city and to grant maximum freedom to all.'

I said, 'Well, in that case theoretically you should have nothing to worry about in governing Jerusalem, but of course you are probably right – the world will not forgive Israel for its victory. Israel's public relations have always been and still are appalling. I suggest you establish a ministry of public relations, not just to explain what you intend to do in Jerusalem but also to explain Israel's overall policy, particularly with regard to your desire for peace and compromise with your Arab neighbours, which is so poorly understood by the world at large and so deliberately misrepresented by most Arab leaders.'

An attempt was in fact made to set up such a ministry, but the Israeli Foreign Office has always controlled foreign public relations, though it has not done a good job, and it soon saw off this project.

Prior to the Six-Day War I believed that if divided Jerusalem were ever united it would be one of the most difficult places in the world in which to maintain peaceful co-existence because of the enmity between Arabs and Jews; I believed that the Christian holy places could be a further source of friction. I was wrong. I did not envy

Teddy Kollek, who has been Mayor of Jerusalem for twenty years since the city was reunited; but I have watched how the Arabs and Jews in their previously divided city have, in general, co-operated under Teddy Kollek's outstanding leadership. It would be quite wrong to say that all is harmony, but there is no safer place in the Middle East today than Jerusalem, where Jews, Arabs and Christians live together in peace. Despite occasional minor setbacks, co-operation between the different creeds improves, and whenever I go to Jerusalem I see progress which would not have been achieved without Teddy Kollek's leadership. What he has achieved in Jerusalem is an outstanding example of how people can live together peacefully even when all the circumstances appear to be conducive to strife. Teddy Kollek has now been re-elected four times, with much support from the Arab citizens. All Jews, Moslems and Christians are in his debt.

One of the most able Israelis with whom I have become friendly in the last ten years is David Kimche, the Director-General for several years now of Israel's Foreign Office. He has experience and commonsense; he is a wise man, fulfilling well a difficult role. Israel is lucky to have people like Teddy Kollek and David Kimche.

It would, however, be misleading of me to give the impression that I both got on with and thought well of all Israelis in government or other positions of authority − or indeed they of me. There were a number whom I thought extreme in their views, with whom I had little in common and whom I could in no way influence. Often they did not even want to talk to me − nor I, in the end, to them.

During this time I was becoming closely involved in the activities of the Weizmann Institute of Science. It had grown considerably since its foundation in 1934, and was by that time acquiring an international reputation. It received help and co-operation from many distinguished scientists, Jewish and non-Jewish, from many different countries. Its activities were supported by government grants, grants from technological and scientific companies which were interested in its work, and donations from its friends and supporters abroad. I had become chairman of the Weizmann Institute Foundation in the UK in 1956, following the untimely death of Siegmund Gestetner, who had played a major role in helping the Weizmann Institute to get on its feet, and together with his wife, Henny, had already done a great deal for Israel, work which she continues to this day. At the same time I became a member of the institute's international board of governors. I continued as chairman of the Weizmann Institute Foundation in the United Kingdom until 1972, when I was succeeded by Derrick Kleeman, who had become involved in Israeli affairs because of his affection and admiration for Father.

I described earlier how the Weizmann Institute started life as the Daniel Sieff Institute at the suggestion of Dr Weizmann, following my brother Daniel's early death, and how Weizmann became its first head. The institute soon began to make a worthwhile contribution to scientific knowledge and to the development of Israel, where certain of its discoveries were applied. In 1944 a number of Weizmann's friends asked him what he would like for his seventieth birthday present. He said he didn't want one, whereupon his American friends, who were also leading supporters of the institute, declared, 'Look, chief, we are going to give you a seventieth birthday present, so you might as well have something you want.' He said, 'If you want to do something for me, enlarge the Sieff Institute.'

Meyer Weisgal, a man of excellence, journalist, wit, writer and theatrical producer, had become Weizmann's right-hand man. Meyer had many talents, one being a flair for fund-raising for worthwhile causes. There is a Yiddish word for a fund-raiser — *schnorrer* — and the actual raising of funds is called *schnorrerei*. Meyer was a *schnorrer* of genius. He said to Weizmann: 'Chief, if we were to ask people to contribute money to enlarge the Sieff Institute the reply would be, "Let the Sieffs, the Marks and the Sachers enlarge their own institute." But if we were to change the name to the Weizmann Institute then it would be a different matter — I think we could get the substantial funds which are so necessary to expand the institute's work.'

Weizmann replied, 'The Sieffs and their family founded the Daniel Sieff Institute at my suggestion and request and I have no intention of allowing the name to be changed. I don't want the matter raised again, and that's that.'

'Okay,' said Weisgal, 'I won't raise the matter again.' He then proceeded to telephone Father in London. He said, 'You know, Israel, if we can change the name of the Sieff Institute to the Weizman Institute I could raise $1 million' ($1 million was a huge amount in those days).

Father replied, 'By all means change the name, but don't sell Weizmann short; I believe you could raise $5 million.' And $5 million was raised, which provided the funds for a number of new laboratories, important equipment and other facilities for the institute.

It used to be said that if there had been a Nobel prize for *schnorrerei* there would have been only one candidate, Meyer Weisgal, and that this was the only occasion when he underbid his hand.

Weisgal's widow, Shirley, is a lovely, charming and amusing lady. Weisgal himself was an entertaining raconteur, though sometimes his tales were somewhat risqué. He used to tell the story of how he asked Shirley's father for his daughter's hand in marriage, to which the reply was: 'Why not? – you've had everything else.'

Dr Chaim Weizmann died in 1952 but over the next twenty years the institute went from strength to strength. Weisgal became the chancellor. The chairman of the international board of governors at that time was a dedicated American from Boston, Dewey Stone. The following is an extract from the institute's annual report, issued in the summer of 1967.

We have always reported briefly on the board meetings – but in this editorial we should like, for once, to pay public tribute specifically to our governors for the quality of their endeavours on our behalf, and for the kind of intellectual climate which they have done so much to create, and maintain, during their meetings. All of us draw sustenance of many kinds from them, and we hope that they find their reward in the words of the overall conclusion of the Rabi-Wiesner survey commission, that 'the Weizmann Institute is one of the world's truly eminent scientific research centers'.

The commission referred to in the report was set up in 1965. It was headed by Professors Rabi of Columbia University and by Jerome Wiesner, who later became the head of MIT (Massachusetts Institute of Technology). Both men were governors of the institute. The commission had twenty-six members from many countries, most of whom were distinguished scientists of international reputation. They covered all the disciplines in which the Weizmann Institute was engaged. The purpose of the commission was to recommend, if necessary, changes in scientific policy, shifts in emphasis, and possible reorganization. The commission's final report recommended certain changes in direction, but said that in general the work of the institute was first class. When the commission had completed its work, I attended a meeting with six of its leading members, each from a different world-famous scientific institution; one of them said that the Weizmann Institute was now among the world's six leading institutes of scientific research. I looked around innocently and said, 'Gentlemen, you represent six of the world's great institutions – which one of you now comes after the Weizmann Institute?' Silence followed.

In 1962 I had been elected deputy chairman of the board of governors of the Weizmann Institute. In 1966 my father was to be the main speaker at the most important fund-raising event in the institute's calendar, the annual New York dinner, which is usually attended by about 1,000 supporters and guests. Father was taken ill just before he was due to go to New York and so I was asked to take his place. It was the first time I had spoken to so large an audience. What I had to say was concerned largely with how the family got to know Chaim Weizmann in 1913, his influence on the family, the founding of the institute and what we believed it could achieve for science in general, for Israel in particular, and, above all, for peace. My speech was well received and no doubt this was part of the reason why I was elected chairman of the international board of governors in 1976, with considerable American support.

My fund-raising efforts for the Weizmann Institute took a rather unusual turn with the late Garfield Weston. I first met Garfield in the mid-1930s, when he started to develop the Weston Biscuit Company in the United Kingdom. He was a Canadian of outstanding ability and built up a huge commercial empire with world-wide interests. He bought the department store, Fortnum & Mason, in London, where he had his headquarters. His sons – Garry in London and Galen in Canada – follow in their father's footsteps to ensure further development of this great organization. I got on well with Garfield from the beginning, despite the fact that I had a feeling that he was slightly anti-Semitic and rather mean in spite of his wealth. I was to be proved totally wrong. Though there were often long intervals between our meetings, we always picked up where we had left off.

Marks & Spencer has for many years had a substantial and growing business with Associated British Foods, the Westons' British operation. Early in 1967 Garfield invited me to lunch. I thought it would probably be a business meeting with him and one or two of his colleagues, but I found we were alone; he did not want to talk business. During lunch I found out that a large part of the Weston fortune was tied up in a charitable foundation, from which donations were generally given anonymously. I asked him why. He told me that when he had made a large charitable donation at the beginning of World War II he had received so many letters afterwards, some serious but the majority of a begging nature, that he had decided in future largely to adopt the policy of anonymity.

He asked me if I knew the head of a large South African milling company he had just bought. I said I did and asked why he raised the question. He said, and I remember the phrase well, 'He is the finest type of Jew; I propose to put him on my central board.' The phrase 'finest type of Jew' slightly irritated me, but I said nothing. He then started to talk about the debt Christianity owed to Judaism. When he finished I said, 'You are a lucky man, Garfield, you live in a time when you can start paying off the debt.' He said, 'What do you mean?' I told him something about the various hospitals, universities and research institutions in Israel, and said that perhaps he would like to give them some of the support they so badly needed. He said he would think about it. On my return to my office I wrote thanking him for the lunch and reminding him of what we had discussed. My letter was acknowledged by his secretary, who said Mr Weston had left on a world tour.

I heard nothing for several months. Then one day he telephoned me. I imagined he wanted to discuss some business problem, but he said, 'Marcus, I have been thinking about our conversation' – I wondered what conversation he was referring to – 'I would like to do a little something for Israel to help one or other of those causes about which you spoke to me.' I thought, 'How nice, he's going to give a donation, maybe £3,000 or £4,000.' He continued, 'I would like to give something in the way of an endowment for the Weizmann Institute.' When he said 'endowment' I thought, 'Well, that is going to mean a lot, at least £50,000.' I asked, 'What would you like to do, Garfield?' He said, 'I would like to give a quarter of a million pounds for an Israeli fund to be used for endowment purposes, as you think fit.' He continued, 'I know you are a busy man but I have my solicitor here ' – who happened to be a friend of mine, Mr Kramer – 'and I am instructing him. Do you think you could spare him five minutes today?'

'For a quarter of a million pounds, Garfield,' I said, 'Mr Kramer can have tea with me this afternoon.' And this was the beginning of the

Garfield Weston Israeli Foundation, which has given money not only to the Weizmann Institute of Science but also to other projects, including some concerned with Jewish/Arab co-operation and with child welfare. On a number of occasions subsequently Garfield gave additional large donations to various worthwhile causes after he had visited Israel himself.

Many years later Garfield invited me to lunch, during which he told me something about how he had built up his great world-wide commercial empire. He was also very complimentary about Marks & Spencer. He then asked if there was anything I wanted from him, to which I replied, 'No, nothing.' He asked again. I said, 'No.' As he was taking me to the lift he said, 'Are you sure there is nothing I can do for you?'

'Nothing,' I replied.

He said, 'Would you mind if I gave another £100,000 for research at the Weizmann Institute?'

I replied, 'Of course I wouldn't mind; I would be delighted.'

The following day I wrote to thank Garfield for the lunch and for his further generous support for the institute. I received a letter back from his secretary saying that Mr Weston had left for Canada but had instructed her to write and say how much he had enjoyed the lunch. Four days later he died in Toronto.

He was a man of great ability and generosity, one of those who took care that a substantial proportion of the wealth he created was used for the benefit of people in very different and less fortunate circumstances, or for research for the benefit of mankind. He is an example to many other men of substance.

CHAPTER FOURTEEN

{ }

I HAD been appointed assistant managing director of Marks & Spencer in 1965 and joint managing director in 1967. This led to wider responsibilities, but I still retained direct responsibility for the personnel department and the development of the food group. In 1972 I became chairman and chief executive; Teddy became president. It was for me a moment of fulfilment; it had long been my ambition to lead the company in which I had grown up and for which I had officially worked for thirty-seven years, with breaks during World War II and the two-and-a-half years I had spent in Israel. I had no intention of making any changes in our principles except, possibly, to emphasize even more their value, but I did intend to experiment with new departments and I foresaw a growing overseas development.

My mentors had been Simon and Father. They agreed on the principles but each emphasized particular areas: Simon the vital importance of offering goods which represented high quality and good value, Father the importance of good human relations with staff, customers and suppliers. They had transformed the business from the modest chain of shops and small stores to Britain's leading retailer with a national, in fact to some extent international, reputation. Simon had led the way; but the manner in which Simon led and somewhat autocratically controlled the business was not suitable as it became bigger. The development of able leaders and executives with delegated responsibility was essential; anyway I was no Simon or Father and didn't have their abilities.

There was no reason for changing long-established principles which had proved to work well; my main targets, in addition to developing able leaders with greater responsibilities, were first, further to develop production in the United Kingdom and so increase employment at home; second, to improve human relations, not only in our own business but also with our suppliers, and encourage them to do likewise in their own organizations; third, to increase our involvement with and contribution to the communities in which we traded; and fourth, to develop Marks & Spencer overseas. In all this

I was most ably supported by my brother Michael and by Michael Sacher, joint managing directors; by Derek Rayner, Brian Howard, Henry Lewis, Rick Greenbury and a number of younger people, who today largely control the business and are leading it to new heights. At that time we had no non-executive directors; all were executive and were responsible for various sections of the business. The managing directors were responsible for a number of groups, which were headed by executive directors, some of whom headed one major group, some two smaller groups, others personnel, technology, building, store development and operations, finance and administration. The largest merchandise group was ladies' outerwear, which covered dresses, blouses, skirts, jackets, coats and rainwear. A smaller group was ladies' underwear: slips, briefs, bras and girdles, nightdresses and dressing-gowns. Menswear was a modest-sized group, steadily growing, covering both outerwear and underwear. Women's, men's and children's footwear were put with fancy goods. Foods also was a growing group. Each director had a team of executives who headed departments in major sections.

Over the years our technologists, headed by a director, had developed into valuable members of the different merchandise teams and worked closely with the departments concerned. This group, with its supporting staff, numbered some 300. They were not back-room boys but members of the buying teams; they worked with our clothing, fabric and food suppliers, and with farmers, monitoring quality, developing new materials and food dishes, co-operating in new methods of production and developing new lines. They played, and continue to play, an important role. Some of our major suppliers had good scientific and technological teams, but many had not. We had encouraged them all over many years to develop and strengthen their technological teams, and the majority did so, to our mutual advantage.

My relationship with Teddy was excellent. His knowledge of fabric, and of textiles in particular, was encyclopaedic. His advice and suggestions were generally wise; we did not always agree but, when I came to a decision, no one supported me more loyally.

One of the ways in which I implemented my policy was by making more visits to stores and suppliers, and I was happy that in general my relationship both with store staff and suppliers' management became closer and more friendly. We were and still are a centralized business, though we listen carefully to our store divisional executives' and store management's suggestions for improvement, but it was the responsibility of the executives at head office to decide on the catalogue we ran, the new lines we introduced, the lines to be eliminated, production programmes and the amounts to be distributed to each store. We have always made mistakes; generally we were quick enough to recognize them before they created substantial losses, though from time to time we were late in realizing and admitting our mistakes and reducing production of or eliminating slow-selling items. Sometimes we had favourites which, had we looked at them objectively, we would have cleared out much earlier.

My normal week began with the Monday morning meeting of directors; then I had informal conversations with top executives, followed by visits to a number of the merchandise departments to look at the current and developing ranges of goods. Every week I looked at the sales of new trial lines of clothing, foodstuffs and goods in other departments and listened to recommendations from my colleagues: whether the lines should be developed for national distribution or continued for the moment as trials, or, based on poor initial sales and store comments, eliminated immediately. Then there were meetings with our suppliers — some in Baker Street, some at their factories — and visits to our stores throughout the country. These were generally on Thursdays, Fridays and Saturdays. There were also formal shows in the early autumn of the proposed ranges for the following spring, and in the early spring of the proposed autumn ranges, particularly of ladies' fashions. The preliminary range of styles and colours had to be prepared twelve months in advance.

I opened each Monday meeting with an account of what I had seen in the stores the previous week. I put the emphasis on what was wrong, rather than what was right. The Monday morning meeting ranged more widely than it did in Simon's day, partly because the company's activities had broadened and partly because I did not have Simon's autocratic conception of the chief executive's role. The meeting would review the past week across the board — plans, problems, ups and downs — and we would look forward to the weeks ahead; anybody present could raise any matter he wished. One of the items which often came up for discussion was our policy always to seek sources of production at home, which, as I said, it was my intention to intensify. A number of these developments stand out.

We decided in 1971 to develop a men's suits department; to our dismay we found that the manufacture of men's suits in the United Kingdom had virtually ceased, famous names such as Burtons having closed nearly all their plants. We could find only one manufacturer in the United Kingdom at that time capable of supplying us. This was Activon, a subsidiary of the Daks-Simpson group. They started to produce for us in 1972 in a modest way with one hundred employees, doing an excellent job. We had to import the rest of our suits, mainly from Scandinavia, Italy and Israel. Of our modest first year's sales 10% were home produced, 90% came from abroad.

In 1971 I was visiting our Newcastle store and ran into Sandy Dewhirst, whose grandfather, Isaac Dewhirst, had loaned my grandfather, Michael Marks, that famous £5 in 1884 with which he started 'Marks's Penny Stall'. Dewhirst was still a privately owned family company. They made a number of clothing items for us; we took the bulk of their production, in fact some 90% – not something we like to do normally because it means one has a moral responsibility to keep the firm going however good or bad their performance. However, Dewhirst has always been an excellent supplier and our relationship has been close for over one hundred years. Sandy said to me, 'Marcus, we have a good deal of cash, have you any suggestions how we can use it further to develop our business?' 'Well,' I replied, 'you do a good job in a number of menswear items, but you have never been involved in suit production. It is our intention to develop a men's suit department, where we believe there is considerable potential, but we can find only one manufacturer in the United Kingdom. If you decide to go into suit production I think you will have to import technology from Scandinavia, Italy or Israel, because it has largely disappeared in this country. We could help with design.' (We already had as a consultant to our menswear group a leading Italian designer, Angelo Vittucci, who later fought a courageous battle for many years against cancer.)

Sandy and his colleagues decided to go ahead, brought in a technologist from Sweden, and opened their first plant in Sunderland in 1973. It was, like all their other plants, a first-class factory with modern machinery and excellent working conditions and staff facilities. Dewhirst did a good job and steadily improved. In 1980 they opened their second suit factory for us, and in 1985 a third. They employ nearly 1,000 people today in their suit plants in Sunderland, where unemployment at the time of writing is over 20%.

At the same time Activon continued to develop. Demand has increased so much that, despite the introduction of the most modern methods of production, such as computer grading and cutting, they now have some 600 or 700 people employed in their suit plant in Lanarkshire. In addition some 300 people are engaged in the UK making the fabric for our suits. Today we have a large and growing suit department, for which 60% of the items are produced at home, 40% abroad. If we did not have a policy of seeking production in the United Kingdom we would have continued to buy 90% of our suits from abroad, which would have meant nearly 2,000 more unemployed at home.

A further example of developing production at home is ladies' footwear. We have had a footwear department for a long time, a large part of which, for many years, was slippers, but while the business overall was developing, the footwear department at the end of the 1970s was making no progress; in fact it was retrogressing. In the United Kingdom today more than 50% of all ladies' footwear is imported; less than 50% is home produced. Imports come mainly from the Far East, Spain and South America. In 1980 Edward Rayne, the head of Rayne Shoes, became our footwear consultant. He was also a director of the Debenham group and responsible for Lotus Ltd, their footwear company, which was in trouble. Lotus's sales had diminished, they had closed one factory and the number of people they employed at their Stafford factory had fallen drastically. I asked Bob Thornton, chairman and chief executive of Debenhams, and Eddie Rayne, whether they would like to try and work with us to build up a footwear business. They said they would.

In 1980 I invited the heads of our four main British suppliers, Lambert Howarth in Lancashire, Fiona Footwear Industries in Wales, Peter Black in Yorkshire, and Lotus, to lunch with me. I suggested they came at 11.30 am for a discussion prior to lunch. I did not tell any of them that the others would be there. To their surprise the four men found themselves in a room with Derek Rayner, the executives, the head selectors of our footwear group, and me. I then said to them, 'Gentlemen, please tell us what is wrong with our footwear.' Absolute silence followed; a minute in such circumstances seems like an age. I said, 'Gentlemen, I have asked you to lunch; you won't get any until you tell us where we are going wrong. If you are worried that by pointing out our mistakes before my colleagues responsible for our footwear group they may take it out on you subsequently, forget it. At the rate we're going, in five years from now we won't *have* a footwear department.'

Monty Sumray, the head of Fiona Footwear, then started the ball rolling, saying we were marketing too stylish a product, and one which was altogether too expensive. A valuable discussion followed; they all earned their lunch. It was the beginning of a transformation of the footwear department, which in the last five years has trebled its sales and has been highly profitable, both to our suppliers and to ourselves. Our business with Lotus has increased sixteen-fold during this period and despite the introduction at their Stafford factory of modern machinery the numbers employed have increased from 200 to 600 and the company has gone from a loss to a substantial profit. Fiona Footwear spent over £5 million on a new plant in South Wales which opened in 1986. Despite the introduction of modern labour-saving machinery demand for their products has increased so sub-stantially that they had to engage a further 150 people to cope with the increased demand. Our suppliers are producing footwear of first-class quality and value, which three or four years ago we were told could never be made in the United Kingdom. We still have to im-port some ladies' footwear, but nearly 80% is produced in the UK. In the country as a whole less than 50% is produced at home — why?

Another example of our development of production at home is the humble lettuce. In the 1970s most of the lettuce produced at home was soft and rather floppy; even when fresh such a lettuce would not keep. At that time our customers were developing a taste for what we called the crispheart lettuce, which we imported from California; demand was growing. It was brought in by air — a very costly business, and getting more so. Although it was expensive compared with the British lettuce — two and a half times the price — the crispheart has much more body and you can eat some of it, put the rest back in the fridge, and it will be perfectly good a day or two later.

We thought that, at least during the summer months, it should be possible to grow the crispheart at home. The experts told us it could not be done. Based on past experience we did not accept this. We arranged for a potential supplier and one of our technologists to go to California to study the technology, growing techniques, varieties and other relevant factors. Starting in 1977 we and our suppliers made experiments over a two-year period, ultimately found the right answer, and started successful commercial production in 1979. Crispheart lettuce now represents more than 25% of all the lettuce grown in the United Kingdom. Our own sales run into some millions of pounds; as a result more employment has been created. British supplies are available only during the summer and early autumn months, so to supplement what we obtain from California we have encouraged development in Spain and Israel.

Another example of what can be produced at home is men's woven shirts. Again less than 50% of such shirts sold in this country are home produced; the rest are imported. Our own shirt department has been steadily expanding and we are by far the largest sellers of shirts in the country. 100% of the shirts we sell today are home produced. Our manufacturers find it a profitable business and are substantially increasing their capacity, and again, despite labour-saving methods of production, are taking on more employees.

In the last ten years we have developed a substantial business in cosmetics and toiletries. Initially a large proportion of these were imported, but today some 95% of our business in this area is British produced. One of our fastest growing suppliers is a Yorkshire firm now employing 2,000 people which was founded in 1947 by a German refugee, whose name it bears: Peter Black. His work has been carried on by his two sons, Gordon and Thomas, who now operate eleven first-class plants in areas of high unemployment.

The further development of medium-size and large firms to which I have referred is not the only way to create employment. Small businesses employing few people can be helped to grow quite rapidly if they produce goods that the customer wants. One such example is the Carpenters' Workshop in Barnstaple. The business was set up in 1979 by Mr Pedwell and the two Martins; one had been encouraged by his wife, who had found that there were few good wooden products made in the UK. They began with four skilled employees. They said they would like to sell their products in Marks & Spencer, so we placed a trial order for some wooden towel-rails; they were well-made and sold well, so we worked with them to produce a range of products for the house. I visited the Carpenters' Workshop at the beginning of 1985. The staff has grown over the five-year period from seven to eighty-five. They have blended skilled craftsmanship with modern machinery and are developing a substantial business. They have just rented an additional factory to provide for future expansion. Our turnover with them is increasing.

The sale of smoked salmon is among the new items we have developed in recent years. In 1976 David Stapleton set up Pinneys in South West Scotland to smoke, slice and pre-pack salmon; he had seven employees. At first our business with him was very modest, but the quality and value of his product is so good that the business has grown substantially. We are Pinneys's major customer and our turnover this year with them will be about £8 million. In turn, the number of employees has grown from seven to over 350.

What a pity that more members of senior management in the United Kingdom do not understand what can be produced at home, make this their policy, and be prepared to be patient and persistent in implementing it.

Overall, we import about 10% of our goods. Once our overseas suppliers have organized themselves to do business with us, and providing they maintain quality and value and are innovative, we feel the same moral obligation to them as we do to our British suppliers. But we have encouraged them, when it is beneficial to both them and us, to set up processing and finishing plants in the United Kingdom. For example, after the demise of the British firm producing our cooked meats, to which I referred earlier – the long-established business which collapsed because of poor management – our main source of supply of cooked meats, particularly ham, the biggest item, was a Danish firm called JAKA, who produced, sliced and packed in Denmark. JAKA still supplies much of our ham, but today it is sent in bulk to this country and sliced and packed at two JAKA plants in New Brighton.

One of our major fish suppliers is Rahbefisk in Denmark, a first-class operation run by Poul Rahbek Hansen, who has become a close friend of mine. After discussions with us some two years ago he set up a factory in Redditch which is making progress and now employs one hundred people.

Two leading Israeli textile and clothing firms manufacture high quality goods for us. Polgat, in Kiryat Gat in the Northern Negev, makes a variety of clothing for us, including men's suits, all of which used to be finished and pressed in Israel and shipped to the UK, which was expensive. Nowadays virtually all their garments are packed and sent in bulk to Skelmersdale in Lancashire, where 300 people are employed in finishing and pressing, and sewing buttons on, a whole range of their garments, including suits, and in despatching them to our stores.

The history of Polgat is fascinating. When I first knew the area of Kiryat back in 1948, during Israel's War of Independence, it was desert sand. Nobody lived there. A few years later a small village grew up. Towards the end of the 1960s Israel Pollak, an outstanding man who had gone to Israel from Poland via Chile, and his immediate family set up a small textile plant, which has now developed into a huge, diversified textile operation, starting with the wool, cotton or manmade fibre and ending with the finished garments. Today they employ – in excellent conditions – some 6,000 people, including Jews from forty countries and many Arabs. In general their products are very good. They are our largest overseas supplier. Kiryat Gat is now a town of thirty thousand.

Delta, another Israeli firm, which makes men's and women's underwear and knitted T-shirts, set up a plant two years ago in Lesmahagow, Scotland, to which they send fine-quality fabric knitted in Israel. They now employ 160 people there and are already exporting from Lesmahagow to Europe. Delta started as recently as the 1970s. In Israel the organization employs nearly 2,000 people in various plants, which are among the most sophisticated and modern in the world, again with first-class facilities, with Jews and Arabs working together under exactly the same conditions, and without friction.

Overall, our overseas suppliers have eleven plants in this country, processing a variety of imported goods for us and providing employment to some 3,700 people. Generally the heads of these firms praise their British workers for their productivity and performance. This is partly due to the decent conditions in the factories and the humane approach of management to their employees.

For many years I have looked back with amusement at one particular development of overseas production in this country. In 1956 I was staying with Rosalind Russell in Beverly Hills. One afternoon at tea I was given a piece of cake which I found delicious.

I said to Ros, 'Your cook is remarkable, but I didn't know she was that good.'

'What do you mean?' she asked.

I said, 'Well, this cake is outstanding.'

She said, 'Don't be silly, Marcus, this is a frozen cake bought in a supermarket.'

In those days a number of us in the firm were very much against frozen foods; I was surprised to find that a frozen cake could be of such high quality. I told Ros so. She said, 'Look, I'm not filming tomorrow, let's go round the supermarkets and buy some frozen cakes.' So off we went to three or four supermarkets, bought a range of cakes and sampled them. The packaging in every case was glamorous, but the only cake that was any good was the brand given to me by Ros the day before, which again was first class. I thought I would follow this up. The cake, I learned, was baked in 'The Kitchens of Sara Lee', a bakery in Chicago, controlled at that time by a man called Charlie Lubin. I gained an introduction and on my way back to New York stopped off at Chicago. We took to each other at once, and he showed me around his bakery. It was fairly large and beautifully equipped, the quality of the raw materials was first class, the standards of hygiene excellent. Charlie Lubin was justifiably proud of his operation, products and plant.

Two or three days later I was sitting at dinner next to Nate Cummings, an old friend of the family and the head of a large organization, Consolidated Foods. 'I hear you visited "The Kitchens of Sara Lee" the other day,' he said. 'What did you think of the operation?'

'It's first class,' I said, 'why do you ask?'

'We bought Sara Lee yesterday,' he replied, 'and now I'm thinking about what we should do with it.' I asked him if it was making a profit.

'A good profit,' he said.

'Nate,' said I, 'you're a marvellous organizer and a financial wizard, but so far as I know you know nothing about baking cakes. If I were you, I'd just leave Charlie Lubin to go on baking those cakes.'

Charlie Lubin was left to get on with his business, which he further developed. He is now over eighty and still dynamic, though he no longer directly controls Sara Lee. Nate Cummings died recently, in his late eighties, but was very active until his death; under his presidency of the huge Consolidated Foods organization Sara Lee expanded enormously. In 1983 I went to see its new site, fifty-two acres of it, with superb factories set in beautiful grounds.

From the early days Nate wanted Marks & Spencer to sell Sara Lee products. Their quality was high and we were ready to do so but there was an obstacle: we were prepared to sell his products only under the St Michael name and they were prepared to sell only under the name of Sara Lee. We couldn't agree, so eventually I said to Nate, 'Well, you won't have any problem in making progress without Marks & Spencer's custom; as for us, it will be a struggle, but somehow we shall survive without Sara Lee cakes.' From time to time he tried again to get us to sell his cakes, but agreement always broke down on the question of whose name they should be sold under.

Six or seven years ago he phoned me, saying he was at the Dorchester and would like me to have breakfast with him. Over coffee he said, 'Have you thought again about Marks & Spencer selling Sara Lee cakes?'

I said, 'Yes, particularly since your telephone call, but only under the St Michael label.'

'Well,' he said, 'it would be nice to have our cakes on your counters. What about a large "St Michael" with a small "by The Kitchens of Sara Lee"?'

'No,' I said, 'if we put your name on the label all our other suppliers will want us to do the same.'

'Well,' he said, 'I'm going back to see if I can do something about it.'

He rang two days later from New York and said that the board of Consolidated Foods had finally agreed to experiment with supplying cakes with the St Michael name on the wrapper. We ordered a trial quantity from the United States and sold them at the price we thought we would ask if they had been baked in the UK. They sold well. In consequence Sara Lee took over and rebuilt an old bakery in Yorkshire which, when they started, employed seventy people; it now employs 350, supplying a number of customers, of whom we are the prime one. Credit for this success is due to Rosalind Russell – and also, I suppose, to Charlie Lubin's mother, who baked the first of those cakes in the family kitchen.

Incidentally, when Charlie first visited Marks & Spencer thirty years ago, as he was leaving my office he said he was on his way for his first visit to Israel. I talked to him about Israel in general and about the Weizmann Institute in particular, and asked him to visit it; he did. The result was that Charlie has taken a keen interest in the institute, particularly in the work being done in agriculture and wheat culture, and has substantially and generously supported a project which, if successful, will greatly increase the protein content of wheat, for the benefit of mankind in general and the hungry in particular; and all this is the result of my eating a cake of outstanding quality thirty years ago.

Prior to and during the early years of my chairmanship a number of our leading and most efficient suppliers, particularly in the textile field, made considerable investments in the most modern equipment and new factories. They greatly increased their production capacity, but if their investments were to pay off they needed to make use of a high percentage of their increased capacity. In general these suppliers were the most efficient and quality-conscious, and, providing they were working at a high level of productivity, the ones who produced the best value. A number of other suppliers, some of whom we had been doing business with for a considerable time, were falling by the wayside: because of lack of good management and/or investment, or failure to develop, they were simply not up to it. But precisely because we had been doing business with them for many years we could not cut them off abruptly, so we gave them warning, sometimes two years or more, and said that unless they could improve their performance we would either have to reduce our business or cease doing business with them altogether. If it came to this point we gave them not only considerable notice but also substantial financial help as well, to enable them to deal with redundancy payments and for other purposes. Nevertheless, my colleagues and I very much disliked having to cease business with these firms.

As chairman I continued our already established practice of expanding our retailing in Britain, more by increasing the size of existing stores than by adding new ones. The reason for this preference was that, as we widened the ranges of existing goods for sale and introduced new items, the individual stores needed more space in which to display their goods. There was, however, one case in which I decided, after reflection, that a new store should be opened. My method of site selection was unusual. Evelyn de Rothschild, as deputy chairman of the Milton Keynes Development Corporation, thought that Marks & Spencer should have a store there. Because it was an isolated centre, or appeared to be, I decided against this idea. Evelyn, however, suggested that we go and have a look at the Milton Keynes area from a helicopter. This was the first time I had used a helicopter for such a purpose. From the air it could be seen that Milton Keynes was surrounded, at a distance, by a number of large and growing satellite villages. The helicopter gave us a bird's eye view of the potential. As a result of that reconnaissance we chose a site; we opened our Milton Keynes store in 1980 and today it is one of our most successful new stores.

In the second half of the 1970s we introduced various items of homeware, such as bedding — sheets, blankets, pillows and duvets — towels, crockery, kitchen goods, cosmetics and toiletries, books and stationery. My successor has extended the range. Generally our introductions have been worthwhile, though of course, there have been failures. As a result of our policies we now deal with 489 manufacturers of clothing and general merchandise, and 464 food suppliers.

During my fifty years in the business, and particularly in the last twenty, I became friendly with many of our suppliers' executives, and over the years visited most of their factories, food processing plants and farms. Without the co-operation of some of our major suppliers over the years our progress would have been limited.

I have worked with Hector Laing, the chairman and chief executive of the United Biscuits group, for thirty years; he and I are close friends, as indeed are our wives, Marian and Lily. Hector, who is a man of many qualities, does not limit his activities to the development of United Biscuits; we have worked together further to develop UK production generally. He understands the importance of businesses being actively and constructively involved in society, particularly in the communities in which they operate. He is one of the people who believes in the importance of good human relations at work; in this field he sets an example. We started originally in the early post-World War II period to sell McVities famous digestive biscuits under the St Michael label, and United Biscuits now produces for us a wide range of goods, processed foods, chicken products and many other lines. They developed with us chicken Kiev, which has acquired a national reputation. When we were shown that a very high-quality chicken Kiev could be produced on a flow production-line and, providing it was kept chilled, would remain in first-class condition for several days until cooked, we made a trial. Although by our standards it was rather expensive, it sold well on trial. When we decided to give it national distribution I asked what we would call it in the north, in Newcastle for example, and was told, 'Chicken Kiev.' I said, 'You will never sell it up there with a name like that.' I couldn't have been more wrong; it sold well everywhere and now, in its seventh year, continues to be a multi-million pound business.

We have had a long association with Courtaulds, our biggest single supplier, whose business with us continues to develop. I have been friendly with the last three chairmen, Lord Kearton, Sir Arthur Knight and Sir Christopher Hogg. Chris Hogg took over the chairmanship some six years ago at the age of forty-four. Courtaulds was then going through a difficult period and Chris had to make some unpleasant decisions, which resulted in many redundancies, but if he had not made those decisions there might not have been a Courtaulds today. Courtaulds is now a dynamic, developing and profitable company. Chris says generously that if it had not been for Marks & Spencer's co-operation there might well not be a clothing manufacturing division in Courtaulds today. Their sales to us in this area in 1985 exceeded £160 million at cost. The major credit for this development goes to Chris Hogg.

Another long association of ours has been with the Nottingham Manufacturing Company, the largest knitwear producers in the United Kingdom, founded by the Djanoglys, Jews who built up a textile business in Russia but left after the 1917 Revolution and settled in Chemnitz in Germany. Jonathan Djanogly, the father, and his two sons, Simon and Jack, established a ladies' hosiery business there. In the late 1920s or early 1930s we bought some stockings from them. Then came the Nazis, and for the second time the Djanoglys left virtually everything behind and fled from Germany to Czechoslovakia. They intended to set up a plant there; with the money they had left one of the two sons went to the United States to buy machinery to send to Czechoslovakia. One Saturday morning the father and the other son heard a noise, looked out of the hotel window and saw the Communists rushing in from one side of the square and the Nazis from the other, shouting abuse at each other. The father said, 'We left Russia because of the Communists and Germany because of the Nazis – this is no place for us.' They were able, at the last minute, to divert the machinery coming from America to the United Kingdom, where it was dumped in a field near Nottingham. There in the 1930s they built their first British plant; more factories followed. Jonathan Djanogly, Simon and Jack are now dead, but the business has been further developed over many years by Harry Djanogly, Jack's son, into one of the most successful businesses of its kind in the world, which today employs some 13,000 people. Harry, like his father and grandfather before him, both of whom I knew, is a man of ability and quality, and most charitable, supporting many worthwhile causes.

Another textile clothing firm that went through many vicissitudes and financial problems was the Carrington-Viyella complex. David Alliance, who was born in Iran and came here many years ago, took over and built up Vantona, then bought Carrington-Viyella, which he renamed Vantona Viyella, and made it into a highly successful and dynamic firm, utilizing the most modern methods of production. He explained to the trades union leaders what he was doing and how it would preserve and develop employment, and received their full co-operation.

We have many first-class food suppliers – like our textile suppliers too many to name – but there are three to whom I want to pay tribute. Firstly Northern Foods, built up outstandingly well by Nicholas Horsley and Chris Haskins; our turnover with them last year exceeded £120 million. Secondly, Colonel Corbett of Sun Valley Poultry, with whom we started our poultry lines in the 1960s, today a major section in the business. And thirdly, Avana Bakeries, whose great development took place under Julian Hodge, who took over the company when it was on the verge of collapse. Julian, like Garfield Weston, gives generously to worthwhile causes.

Two of Marks & Spencer's important suppliers today developed because we failed to appreciate the abilities of the current heads of these firms when they worked for us. One of them, Peter Wolff, worked in various merchandising sections for a number of years and was a dynamic and talented maverick – the kind of person we still perhaps do not know how to make proper use of. He left us some fifteen years ago to become joint managing director of a small clothing supplier, now S. R. Gent, whose turnover then with us was a few hundred thousand pounds a year. As a result of Peter Wolff's dynamism, our turnover with his firm today is £60 million annually. The second man is Henry Knobil, a fabric technologist who considered he had commercial ability which could be used to great advantage in conjunction with his technological knowledge. His seniors did not believe he had commercial qualities, so he left us and established a knitted-fabric business called Textured Jersey, which now has several factories supplying substantial quantities of fabrics to Marks & Spencer's garment suppliers. In both cases we failed to recognize their potential, but as both had enough initiative to leave the security of jobs with us and establish businesses of their own, perhaps we could claim to have benefited from our mistakes.

One of the most important events which took place in food merchandising during my chairmanship has to do with Sir Isaiah Berlin. Isaiah, as many people know, is, and has been for years, one of the leading academics at Oxford University. He is a philosopher whose knowledge and studies cover a very wide field – he has acquired international fame and recognition. The event is best explained by the correspondence that took place between Isaiah, his wife Aline, and me, in the spring of 1982:

10 April 1982

Dear Marcus,

May I make a pathetic appeal to you? At the centre of my gastronomic life (which greatly matters to me) for some time now has been a delectable product of St Michael – 'smoked almonds' in packets of 75g at 56p. Few things have given me so much gustatory pleasure in my old age as this wonderfully treated form of almond. I used to be able to get them at your store in Oxford. A few months ago, they were no longer there. I went to your store in Oxford Street, and to my great relief was able to buy a supply. A few weeks ago, my supply finished, I went again to the Oxford Street store – the packets were no longer there, and no one could even remember there being such an object on sale. In a state nearing despair, I went to Orchard Street, where to my immense and joyful relief I was able to buy some more packets, but perhaps not enough. Three days ago my day was darkened by the fact that 'smoked almonds' were not obtainable even there — and again, the lady I spoke to professed total ignorance as to what I could possibly mean. I enclose an integument of this sacred object, plus one surviving sample of it. If it is anywhere to be obtained, I should be grateful if you would let me know — it would make a crucial difference to my expectations of pleasure, and ultimately, pleasure itself.

Please forgive me for writing about what may seem trivial to you, but to me...

Yours ever, apologetically,
Isaiah

15 April 1982

Dear Isaiah,

Your letter touched our hearts. All normal work at Michael House ceased yesterday while the board and senior executives studied how to meet your request. These nuts come from America and I am happy to say that a carton, specially packed to remain fresh for a long time, will be delivered next week. We hope that this will give you gustatory pleasure for some time to come.

I am only sorry that our staff to whom you spoke at the stores did not remember them; this is possibly psychological as the nuts did not sell well due to their high price.

When Simon Susman, my assistant, was able to report to me that we would be getting a carton, the board met in thankful prayer, primarily because of being able to meet your demand, as all of us have great respect, and some of us much affection, for you; secondly, because we can now return to work.

Love to Aline, as ever,
Marcus

28 April 1982

Dear Marcus,

Thank you for your letter of 15th April. It arrived when I was abroad, else I should have written at once to say that it rendered me speechless (only, you will be relieved to hear, in your goodness of heart, for one moment) with overwhelming gratitude and deep remorse — the remorse of having inadvertently cost the country and the world a diminution in the productivity of your great firm (something that Mrs T. would have frowned upon, for once with some justice) — still, the saving of a life authorizes us to break all the Commandments save three, according to our ancient faith — and my life you have surely saved from a squalid condition. As for gratitude — there is nothing like the sense of exhilaration at getting so much more than one's due (much nicer than one's due): the joy with which I fell upon those beautiful silver packets containing the precious ambrosia was only equalled by a similar sensation when your late Uncle Simon presented me with no fewer than two shirts and a pair of slacks at what was then your store in Cornmarket in this town, now replaced by some pathetic and implausible imitation known, I think as the Co-op, to which my steps will lead me when I am, as so often, 'not thinking'. Not only were these gifts showered upon me, but I was introduced to no fewer than fifteen employees of the firm on that occasion. Never, anywhere, has there been a more loyal and admiring client than St Michael has in me.

My joy is, of course, mixed with some embarrassment – I had no intention of soliciting such a rich gift, only of learning where I could obtain these nuts; but I should have known you better than not to realize that your generosity would sweep aside my scruples – what can I say, that holds anything nicer than friendship and affection?

And now to my new life, sustained by this divine substance – the years roll off my shoulders.

Yours ever,
   Isaiah

This [enclosed bottle] in gratitude for having 'saved Isaiah's life'!
With love from us both,
   Aline

4 May 1982

Dear Aline,
   To 'save Isaiah's life' is both a privilege and a pleasure – to get such a reward [Chateau Lafite '45] is overwhelming.
   Thank you very much.
   With love,
      Marcus

In my period as chairman I made – or, quite properly, had to take responsibility for – a number of mistakes.

One of them concerned housing for directors. For many years the company had a policy of making loans to executives and management staff to help them purchase their houses, but we were prohibited by law from having a similar scheme for directors. However, there was a legal way of helping them. From 1973 until 1980 the company entered into property transactions with directors to help them maintain homes in or near London. Properties were bought for individual directors and rented to them, or directors' own homes were bought and rented back to them, in order to give the directors some capital.

In some cases directors were given the option to puchase their houses back at their original cost to the company. These transactions were a legally acceptable and tax-effective way of enabling the company to help directors. The transactions were first published in the report and accounts for the year ending 31 March 1982; this was necessary because of changes in company legislation. We then belatedly realized that the company should have notified the Stock Exchange, and sought shareholders' approval, before entering into these transactions.

So in November 1982 I called an extraordinary general meeting to give shareholders the opportunity of considering the transactions. We expected 400 or so shareholders to turn up – the room in the hotel could accommodate about 600; in fact over 1,000 shareholders came, of whom several hundred either had to stand around or sit in the balcony. We had an exceedingly noisy meeting, some shareholders being vociferously for the transaction, some against. At the beginning of the meeting feelings ran high. Then one shareholder got up and said he was the chairman and chief executive of his company; he paid his fellow directors a small salary but added a percentage of the annual profits. He recommended that we should adopt this system and pointed out that if we had done so, the directors' rewards would have far exceeded their present remuneration. He added that he was going to vote for the resolution that would legalize the action we had taken. I thanked him for his suggestion and support, and said that it might well be, if the vote went against the board, that I should shortly be looking for a job; I wanted him to know that he would be the first person to whom I would apply. This amused the shareholders, the majority of whom anyway were sympathetic, and in the end they supported the transactions by a large majority. However, these housing transactions with directors were all wound up, the last in June 1984.

When I took over the chairmanship, and even before, a number of us, including Teddy, thought that the potential scope for further expansion in the UK was limited and we should examine the possibility of developing overseas. Our assumption was quite wrong; our major expansion in the last fifteen years has been and still is in the United Kingdom, and will be in the foreseeable future. But in the early 1970s we began to develop stores in Canada and Europe. In 1972 we started operations in Canada through St Michael Shops of

Canada, a company jointly owned with People's Department Stores, whose head was Abe Gold, a dynamic retailer of ability, though he operated on somewhat different principles to those to which we at Marks & Spencer had become accustomed. We held 50% of the equity. In 1974 we sought to acquire the whole of People's Department Stores share capital, but this was not permitted under government regulations at that time, exercised through FIRA (Foreign Investment Review Agency), though we were allowed to acquire a controlling interest of 55%. People's Stores had a wholly owned subsidiary, D'Allairds, and a controlling interest in Walkers Stores.

We thought we knew all about retailing and that Marks & Spencer's principles and practices in the UK would apply to our Canadian operations. The principles did, although it took time to establish some of them, but the practices were often different, as we learned to our cost.

Our three groups in Canada were the Marks & Spencer Division (previously Walkers Stores), D'Allairds and People's Division. Our aim was to make the Marks & Spencer Division a miniature replica of Marks & Spencer UK; D'Allairds was a chain of shops specializing in clothes for women of thirty-five and older; People's ran a wide range and variety of goods, different from and of lower quality than that to which we had been accustomed. Abe Gold had overall management of the People's Division, while D'Allairds was efficiently run by Robert and Ruth Connolly, but the Marks & Spencer division was a mess. Derek Rayner and I were on the Canadian board, of which I was the chairman. The majority of the directors had to be Canadian citizens. Derek and I visited Canada three or four times a year.

Fortunately D'Allairds and People's were profitable, but not sufficiently to justify the capital we had invested in acquiring the group. There were several reasons for Marks & Spencer's poor performance. First, though all human beings are brothers and sisters under the skin they do not want to clothe themselves in identical gear. The Canadians, we found, favoured casual wear more than we did, and had less use for formal clothing. This was partly due to climate – the extremes of hot and cold – and partly due to their way of life.

Second, we found that goods had to be presented and promoted differently. Our British customers liked the soft sell; the Canadian customer responded to the hard sell. For instance, if in Britain we found it possible to reduce the price of an article we would state on the promotion ticket that the price of this article was being reduced but that this reduction in price did not mean that there was any change in the quality. We found that in Canada this kind of statement had no effect on the customer and sales remained as before, but that if we put up a large ticket with 'regular price $25' slashed through with a bold stroke and underneath 'new reduced price $19.99', sales would soar.

We also discovered that the sober décor of our British stores did not suit Canadians — a lesson we learned from a loyal customer. I received a letter from a gentleman in Scotland who described himself as a devoted Marks & Spencer shopper, owning a few of our shares. He said he had just returned from a tour of Canada, in the course of which he had spent time with his daughter and her husband in Alberta. He had been surprised to find that they didn't do their shopping in their local Marks & Spencer store, and asked why. His daughter explained that, though she occasionally shopped there and didn't dispute the quality and value of the goods, she disliked shopping 'in a hospital ward'. She found our Canadian stores too clinically clean, whereas other stores were bright, colourful and cheerful. Her father had then taken the trouble to do some research during the rest of his stay in Canada. In four Canadian cities he took up a position within fifty yards of the Marks & Spencer store, stopped twenty-four people and asked them if they could direct him to Marks & Spencer. On average only one in four could. I followed up his research with enquiries of my own. As a result we painted the interiors of our Canadian stores in brighter colours and put in mirrors and spotlights on the walls and columns. The result was a warmer, more welcoming atmosphere, and the illusion that the store had been enlarged. Not long after we embarked on this transformation I was in our Bay Street store in Ottawa. A lady came up to me and said, 'You're obviously something to do with Marks & Spencer.'

'Yes,' I replied, 'what can I do for you?'

'I just want to say thank you for enlarging the store and brightening it up,' she said. 'It's so much better than it used to be. I come here regularly now.'

Canadian shoppers were used to paying high prices for high-quality goods, and often not such high-quality goods, in the major department stores, but generally regarded the chain stores, in which category they included us, as stores for low-priced and low-quality merchandise. Gradually, by advertising, more dynamic promotion, and a growing word-of-mouth reputation for quality, we have convinced more customers that we are a good place in which to shop. After many years of disappointing results, 1985 saw a big turn-round in the Marks & Spencer division, from a loss to a profit, and overall profits in the three divisions increased substantially. Our turnover in Canada in the last financial year also increased substantially and, having learned its lessons, our Canadian business should go from strength to strength over the next few years. In 1986 we purchased the balance of the equity we did not own.

Our initial experiences in France were not dissimilar to those in Canada. We started in Paris at the beginning of 1975, with a medium-sized store in Boulevard Haussmann, one of the main shopping streets of the capital, situated opposite Printemps and Galerie Lafayette, which are perhaps the Paris equivalent of Harrods and Selfridges. Business was excellent during the first week or two, but it turned out that the majority of our customers were British expatriates resident in Paris. After they had stocked up, business fell away sharply. But this did not deter us; in September 1975 we opened a store in Lyon, France's second largest city, in a new shopping centre. Here again we were not successful; business was way below expectations. We had to struggle for several years to establish ourselves. We found the French conservative in their shopping habits, but eventually we broke through and have now extended the Paris store four times; it is among our leading stores, still too small but very profitable.

As with Canada, we made our mistakes and had to learn our lessons. We had to provide fitting-rooms, which we do in the UK only in a few remote stores. Our customers in the UK know that, if something doesn't fit when they try it on at home, they can return it to any store and change it or get their money back. French women do not want to take garments home. They want to try on everything on the premises, including underwear. They started to do this in a corner of the sales floor, so we had to provide fitting-rooms. There was another difficulty about having no fitting-rooms which I personally encountered in the Paris store. I was standing a few feet away from a man who was buying a suit, which he wanted to try on. I explained that it was our policy not to have fitting-rooms, but if the suit didn't fit he could bring it back and exchange it or get his money back from his nearest store. He said, 'This is my nearest store. I live 200 kilometres from Paris — it's a hell of a way to come to change a suit.'

We now have seven stores in France, two in Belgium and one in Dublin; our continental operation is steadily improving its profitability. What has been encouraging is that, despite French conservatism, a large proportion of the goods we sell on the Continent are made in the UK and represent a valuable export.

In Boulevard Haussmann we have developed a substantial food business, and here also most of what we sell comes from the UK. This is very rewarding, as Paris is reputed to be the most discriminating eating capital in the world. French bread is justly famous for its freshness and crispness, but we sell several thousand pounds' worth of British bread in Paris every week. The success of our sliced and wholemeal bread was so striking when we introduced it that I did not at first believe the sales figures. Soon after I had seen them I was in Paris and made a point of standing by the bread counter at opening time. Two women came along and one bought two loaves of our bread. The other said, rather scornfully, 'Why do you buy English bread?' The first replied, 'I buy it because the quality is so good and it is so fresh.' The second woman then bought a loaf.

In general our mistake overseas has been our failure to modify policy to suit local conditions. We believed that our British policies and practices would work just as well abroad as at home; we were wrong, and we have learned from our mistakes. In fact the lessons we have learned in Canada and France have relevance to our developments in the United Kingdom, and are being applied successfully here.

CHAPTER FIFTEEN

IT is vitally important to recognize talent and make sure that those who perform well are promoted and given more scope and responsibility. The director of personnel is a key member of the team, but we at Marks & Spencer believe that all directors should be interested in and concerned with the development of the people who work for the company.

I continued to emphasize to myself, and to my colleagues who led the business, the importance of our maintaining and developing our good human relations policy. I found that if people were to be treated as individuals this required more attention as we grew in size and increased in numbers. In 1978 we introduced profit-sharing; staff who had been with us for five years or more were given annually a number of shares in the company — they were, after all, whatever their positions, all making a contribution to its progress. Before we did this I sought advice from one of the country's largest companies, which had operated a profit-sharing scheme for several years, and asked the chairman whether he thought it was worthwhile. 'Yes,' he said, 'but I must warn you, Marcus, that a very large proportion of the shares allocated are sold by our employees within the first six months.' Marks & Spencer has now been operating the profit-sharing scheme for eight years and the percentage of shares sold has been low. When I ask members of the staff what they have done with their shares the majority say: 'I have kept them; I'm looking forward to getting more.'

On one occasion, talking to a warehouseman who had been with us for many years, I asked him whether he had been allocated any shares and if so what he had done with them: had he sold them? He replied, 'No, I haven't. I have put them in trust for my grandson's education.'

While I was chairman I gave a number of talks to various groups, including conferences, schools and colleges, the subject of which was nearly always the importance of good human relations at work. In 1983, at the annual meeting of the National Federation of Building Trades Employers, I returned to the same theme. Afterwards there was a panel discussion and a question-and-answer session. The members of the panel were: John Turner, the president of the Building Employers' Confederation; Les Wood, general secretary of UCATT (the Union of Construction, Allied Trades and Technologists); George Henderson, national secretary of the TGWU; Peter Rainbird, managing director of A. Rainbird & Son, Brentwood; and Don Stradling, director of personnel at John Laing. There were about 180 heads of various building companies present. During the panel discussion one of the trades union leaders said, looking at the audience, 'If you all followed a policy similar to that about which Lord Sieff has spoken I would be worried about my job. But I know I can rely on you to see that I keep it.'

The result of such a policy is not only that many individuals work for us for a long time, but also that we often have several members of one family working for us at the same time. I was at our Poole store recently, where there were several such family groups working. One consisted of three sisters, whose service together now totals just under sixty years, while the daughter of one of them works at head office. Another family there consisted of four sisters, two still working for us, two having left to have children. In addition there were mothers and daughters and mothers and sons. There was one family whose grandmother had worked as a departmental supervisor, and had recently retired after thirty years' service; her daughter and son both worked in the store, and her granddaughter also worked part-time in the store while she attended college.

The best way of keeping in touch with staff is to visit stores and talk to people face-to-face. As the business expands it becomes more difficult to get around all the stores, but it is important that members of the board, in fact all senior head office staff, continue to make these visits. I am happy to say that my successor and my colleagues continue the tradition of store visits, with the result that those who run the business are not just faceless names to the majority of the staff.

Personal contact is equally important as far as our customers are concerned. When I am walking round a store I take the opportunity to talk to one or two people who are shopping, but one of the main methods of knowing what our customers are thinking is by reading their letters and listening to their telephone calls. Our customer liaison department receives about 2,500 letters, parcels and phone calls a week. Many of these letters and calls praise our staff, and sometimes our goods; the majority are critical. They complain, for instance, that our goods have turned out to be unsatisfactory; the ranges are inadequate; we are short of sizes or our colours are poor. Sometimes we are told that staff have been unhelpful or, occasionally, downright rude; sometimes that our store management have behaved in a bloody-minded way. We are, of course, delighted to receive the letters of praise, to which we reply with a thank you, and we make sure that the store staff concerned know and are thanked for what the customers say about them. We take the complaints seriously; the majority are justified. We follow them up and phone or write to and, if appropriate, recompense the customers concerned. If a customer is constructively critical, perhaps covering a wide range of goods, we invite him or her, and sometimes the wife and husband together, to head office as our guests for the day, show them round the departments concerned so they can see what we are doing and make their views known to the executive and selectors concerned. In the old days we used to reply to a letter with a letter, but we found it was more efficient and economical, and much appreciated by the customer, to phone, if we had his or her number, as soon as we received the letter, particularly if it was a complaint. Sometimes we make mistakes. Letters get lost; occasionally our head office staff do not accept justified criticism; but in the main the customers appreciate the trouble we take to deal quickly and properly with the points they raise. Where someone has been poorly treated in a store, we arrange for the store manager to invite the customer in, make his apologies and give the customer tea and whatever recompense is justified.

The conception of the founders and developers of our business was that we should be involved in the well-being of the communities in which we operate. The Articles of Association of 1903 stated our intention 'to support and subscribe to any charitable or public object, and any institution, society, or club which may be connected with any town or place where the company carries on business'. It was a policy which we carried on in a modest way for a long time, but in the last fifteen years we have substantially increased our involvement in the community. Some twelve years ago we established a separate charity department with its own manager and staff. Today we receive over 10,000 letters annually, mostly for worthwhile causes. Although we give substantially, spending in total on community and charitable projects somewhere between £2½ and £3 million a year, if we were to try to support all the worthwhile appeals which reach us the amount we could give each would be very small. Our policy is generally not to support those worthwhile charitable causes which can raise support from other sources relatively quickly and easily, partly because of their emotional appeal; we prefer to support equally worthwhile but less popular causes, for example in the field of health and medicine: Huntington's chorea, autism, deafness, and so on. In the arts we generally support those institutions and activities outside London which find it more difficult to raise funds rather than those which have the glamour of association with the metropolis.

Charity is not the only way in which we 'support ... the place where the company carries on business'. At any one time we have from fifteen to twenty people seconded to community work, for periods of one to five years. Originally most of our secondees came from those nearing retirement, who worked in their local communities using their Marks & Spencer experience to help in various ways. A number of these people were still working well for us, despite the fact that they were getting on in years; others were, frankly, no longer quite up to their job: I suspect that from time to time we did not mind seeing them go, since we were able to replace them with younger and more able people. In recent years, however, we have made a point of not seconding people for community work unless we believe they have the ability and energy to do a worthwhile job. We still second a number of managers approaching retirement to such work, but other secondees are thirty-five to fifty-year-olds, of whose abilities we think highly. We keep in touch with them during their secondments; if they perform well, they gain valuable experience which enables us to promote them on their return to the business. Naturally we continue to pay secondees their salaries and all other entitlements. We were much helped in the development of this operation when in 1977 the late Lord Byers became a consultant to the company on community involvement.

We decided that we would celebrate our centenary in 1984 by asking head office and each store to choose a community project. These projects were vetted by a committee in head office; virtually all the local staffs' choices were approved. As well as our normal allocation for communal and charity purposes, we set aside an additional £3½ million to provide for the proposed projects, all the money if the schemes were modest, the seed money only if they were not.

Store staff began to select their projects towards the end of 1982 and during 1983 so that proper plans could be made for them to be implemented in the 1984 centenary year. What was most heartening was not only the care with which the projects were selected by the store staff, but their enthusiasm; unasked they raised, by their own efforts, funds totalling an additional £600,000. I was particularly impressed by what our store staff did in Belfast. In December 1982 I was going round that store with a supervisor, Maureen Miller, and asked her if they had selected a community project, and did she know anything about it. She said they had, and she did. She told me that the Northern Ireland Council for Orthopaedic Development, which caters for spastics and people with cerebral palsy, lacked proper facilities: at the age of sixteen sufferers from these distressing complaints either had to go into geriatric wards or return home; there was nothing else for them in Northern Ireland. I asked how much seed money head office had allocated. She said, '£27,500, but we are going to raise as much again ourselves.' I took this with a pinch of salt and asked if they had started to raise the money. She said they had been raising funds for a few weeks; so far they had raised more than £4,000.

'How on earth did you do it?' I asked, somewhat surprised.

She said, 'For example, last night we sang Christmas carols in the centre of Belfast and we raised £800.'

I asked, 'Who is we?'

'We were 50% Catholic, 50% Protestant, working together,' she replied.

What a commentary on events in that strife-ridden area. They were marvellously successful in their fund-raising efforts; the Belfast staff raised £48,000 – more than any other store.

The centenary projects further strengthened the ties between our stores and the communities in which we trade, to our mutual advantage.

Mutual interests, both in the need for good human relations at work and in the need for free enterprise to be actively and constructively involved in the communities in which it operates, have brought us into contact with the Prince of Wales. His Royal Highness is also interested in 'sourcing' in the United Kingdom – that is, developing production here and thus reducing unemployment. In our initial discussion he asked how he could hear more about the importance of good human relations at work, so I arranged for a dinner at which the chief executives of six of our suppliers, ranging from large to small, who implemented such a policy were present. Prince Charles asked many pertinent questions and, on leaving, asked where he could see such a policy being implemented. I told him he could do so at one of our suppliers' factories or at one of our stores. He chose to visit our stores. We went to Brixton and Croydon, not long after the first Brixton riots in 1982. At Brixton he talked to at least thirty members of the staff and an equal number of customers, and went through the store from top to bottom. The fact that he was going to visit the store became known; when he got there it was crowded. On our way from Brixton to Croydon he told me that he had learned a good deal. When we arrived at Croydon the store was jammed with people and we had to push our way through the crowds; again he went through the store in great detail. This took him longer, as Croydon is a much larger store than Brixton. He asked questions and chatted with everybody; he even visited the ladies' hairdressing section, talking to some pensioners who happened to be there.

As I have said, the Prince of Wales also appreciates the importance of developing production at home, about which he has spoken publicly. I am grateful because I believe his interest will stimulate further action in implementing such a policy.

CHAPTER SIXTEEN

{   }

I CONTINUED to visit Israel regularly, to maintain contact with
Marks & Spencer's Israeli suppliers, who were making good progress,
to keep myself *au fait* with the Weizmann Institute, and to see if I
could be useful in other fields. I was in touch with Israel's political
leaders, continuing in a different way the work I had started over
twenty years before. Lily came with me on nearly all these visits,
because not only has she many friends from her schooldays in Israel,
but also, following in my mother's footsteps, she is keenly involved
in the UK with the Women's Zionist Organization, of which the
world headquarters are in Israel.

We were in Israel in November 1971, both for the international
board of governors' meeting of the Weizmann Institute and for the
opening of the Rebecca Sieff Hospital, which had been built in the
north, in Safad, in memory of my mother. Golda Meir, who was then
Prime Minister, was to open it. I first met Golda before the state was
created; she was Minister of Labour in the first Israeli government,
and amongst other things had to deal with the flood of refugees.
Among Golda's problems were training, housing and finding work
for the immigrants. Marks & Spencer's experience in training proved
useful. Flora Solomon, who had done so much to develop the Marks
& Spencer staff management and welfare policy, spent considerable
time in Israel in those early days and made a valuable contribution
to Golda's programmes.

Over the years since then I had become friendly with Golda. For
the opening of the Rebecca Sieff Hospital, the day after our arrival,
Lily and I flew from Tel Aviv to Safad with Golda by helicopter.
During the journey I said, 'Golda, what are you going to say in your
speech?' She replied, 'I never prepare a speech in advance unless it is
a political speech or a formal statement of policy or something of
that nature, about which one has to be careful. Otherwise I speak off
the cuff.' I said, 'How am I going to reply?' She replied, 'I'm sure it
will be all right; between the two of us we ought to be able in a
relatively short time to pay tribute to your mother and her achievements.'

I was glad to hear Golda say she would talk only briefly, and I congratulated her on the increasing brevity of both parliamentary and public speaking in Israel, a blessing when compared with the inordinately long speeches of the days before Israel's birth, and the early years of the state's existence, when even the best speakers could become very boring. At one early Zionist congress, as the day wore on the speeches became longer and longer, and by late evening two people were left in the hall, the speaker and a member of the congress, who sat patiently and listened. At the end of his speech the speaker thanked the sole member of the audience for his courtesy in staying to hear him out to the end. His brief reply was: 'I had to stay, I'm the next speaker.'

Golda told me that in her early days in America a Jewish summer camp was held annually for youngsters. On the final day a Jewish leader always came to talk to them. These were the days of the long speeches. This particular year Golda, already a leader in the Jewish world, was to give the address. Her daughter, who was at the camp, came to collect her. On their way to the assembly she said, 'Mother, do you know what you're going to talk about?' Golda replied, 'Yes, darling, I do.' Her daughter said, 'For how long are you going to speak, Mother?' Golda said, 'Thirty to forty minutes.' At which her daughter exclaimed, 'Good God, Mother, if you have nothing to say, why did you accept the invitation to speak?'

In 1973 the Yom Kippur War erupted. Israel was caught unprepared and in the first few days suffered grievous losses in men, arms and other materials; at one time it looked as though Israel would be defeated and the state destroyed. In the end Israel was victorious, but at a high cost. It was at this time that I first got to know that remarkable man, Henry Kissinger, by then the US Secretary of State. He played a role of great importance. When Israel had recovered from her initial defeats and driven both the Egyptians and the Syrians back, Kissinger began his shuttle between the combatants, and was largely instrumental in bringing about a ceasefire, and eventually an armistice.

Regrettably, the British Government did not behave well at the time; as soon as hostilities started, they put an embargo on the sales of arms to the Middle East. The Israelis, who had bought a number of British Centurion tanks, had also bought and paid for spare parts and ammunition for them. The tanks had taken a severe battering in the early days of the war. The ammunition and spares had been loaded into a ship and were urgently needed, but, despite the fact that they had been bought and paid for, and loaded, the Government would not agree to their despatch. I went to see Mr Heath, the Prime Minister, and asked that they should be released; he would not agree.

It was during this time that I began to have talks with some leading Arabs who wanted to find a *modus vivendi* and ultimately to establish peace between Israel and her Arab neighbours. A major problem was Israel's control of the West Bank, with its one million Arabs, which the Israeli government was certainly not prepared to return until Israel's neighbours had recognized its right to exist and peace had been established. Even then it would have been essential for Israel to have certain guarantees of security: a hostile force occupying the West Bank was a threat to Israel's existence. The Arab governments, except, ultimately, Egypt, refused to make peace; Israel refused to hand back any of the territories it had occupied during the Six-Day War. King Hussein had wanted for a number of years to find a *modus vivendi* whereby Jordan and Israel could work out a peace agreement, but for this he felt he must have the support of the Arabs on the West Bank, and of the PLO, to whom the Arab rulers had given authority to act on behalf of the West Bank Palestinians. The PLO, which had become a wealthy organization, refused to recognize Israel, continually talked about its destruction, and continued to make terrorist attacks, both inside Israel and at other places in the world with Jewish connections; a large number of people were murdered. This refusal of the Arabs to negotiate, and their continuing policy of terror, led to the development of a growing hardline group in Israel who refused to contemplate handing back the West Bank, or, as they called the area, Judea and Samaria.

Meanwhile the Mapai Party, which had been the leader of various coalition governments with moderate left policies, was becoming tired, having been in power for over twenty-five years. There were scandals in high places. Some of the original idealism which had done so much to prevent the state being destroyed at birth, and had then led to its remarkable development, was waning; the Mapai coalition was defeated in the general election of 1977. A right-wing government, the Likud coalition, was formed when the Herut Party, headed by Menachem Begin, took power. There was a considerable difference

in the policy of the Likud coalition from that of the previous government. Begin was, in his way, a leader, but his approach to that role
was fundamentalist, autocratic and nationalist. He had little respect
for the traditions of Western Europe, where as a young man he had
suffered at the hands of the Poles and the Russians. He had been the
leader of the stop-at-nothing Irgun assault on British rule in Palestine
after World War II, and had launched many extremist operations,
which Ben Gurion and his colleagues did their best, often unsuc-
cessfully, to prevent. Initially, given his knowledge of Old Testament
history and his experience of the holocaust, I thought he was ready
to see Israel go it alone and perish rather than give up an inch of
territory or rely on the promises of so-called friends. I was wrong.

From his Irgun days Begin had cultivated the support of what he
sometimes referred to as the down-trodden oriental Jews. He promised them relief, equality, justice and jobs. The Labour party had tried,
since the inception of the state, to create a society much on western
lines, sophisticated, secular, technologically educated, socially mobile,
skilfully employed – whether on the farm or in the factory – ready
to move faster so as to obtain a higher standard of living and enjoy
an enhanced quality of life. Many oriental Jews (Sephardi) had not
shared fully in these higher standards of living and were looked down
upon by a section of the European, westernized Jews (Ashkenazi).
The Sephardi were conservative; but they still wanted a greater share
in the increasing prosperity and also in the government of Israel.
Begin promised to rescue them from their inferior social and economic
position.

When Jimmy Carter became President of the United States, one of
his objectives was to become known as the man who had brought
peace to the Middle East. To that end he put considerable pressure
on the Prime Minister of Israel, Yitzhak Rabin. Relations between the
United States and Israel soon became tense. Rabin resisted Carter. The
Israeli Government, and Israel's friends everywhere, were shocked by
Carter's pronouncement that Israel's forces should retreat behind the
Six-Day-War lines. Carter then switched Israel from the top of the
list of USA's allies for the supply of arms and equipment to a lower
position. All this alarmed the Israelis, particularly as the American
Democratic Party had hitherto been considered as Israel's greatest
ally in the United States. Carter was tearing holes in the policies

established by Presidents Nixon and Ford, and implemented by Henry Kissinger, who had helped to initiate these policies.

All this increased support for Begin. When he became Prime Minister he was helped by the participation in his coalition of a new party, the Democratic Movement for Change, led by my old friend, Yigael Yadin. Begin started by announcing a tough foreign policy, although fears of what might happen were somewhat alleviated when he asked Moshe Dayan, who was fundamentally a man of peace, to become Foreign Minister.

Six months after Begin came to power, President Sadat of Egypt made the famous speech in which he said: 'Israel will be stunned to hear me tell you [the Egyptian parliament] that I am ready to go to their home, to the Knesset itself, to argue with them, in order to prevent one Egyptian soldier from being wounded. . . .' Like many others, I would say most others, inside and outside Israel, I was sceptical about this. Four years previously Sadat had publicly stated that he would sacrifice the lives of a million Egyptian soldiers to regain the territories that the Israelis had occupied. Within a few days, however, it became clear that Sadat meant business. Begin responded decisively with admirable speed. Just as the ill-fated Rabin administration deserves credit for contributing to the steps which led to Sadat deciding to make his move, Begin deserves some too. His uncompromising do-or-die stance – no surrender, perish rather than yield an inch of territory – must have convinced Sadat that this was his only course of action.

Like everybody else I was elated when Sadat went to Jerusalem. He arrived on 19 November 1977, and, after meeting the Prime Minister and his cabinet, toured the Old City and addressed the Knesset. In his speech he invited Begin to visit Egypt. Though nobody misjudged the tremendous importance of Sadat's visit to Jerusalem, in itself a form of recognition of the State of Israel which he had sworn never to give, it was noticed that the President had reiterated all the Arab demands for the return of occupied territories, and had offered to concede nothing in return. There was a sense of disappointment. At Christmas Begin went to Egypt, meeting Sadat at Ismailia. Their meetings yielded nothing. There was now a sense of anticlimax. There followed eight months of negotiation, inspired by the Americans, who could not bear the thought of the state of affairs in the Middle East reverting to what it had been after the Yom

Kippur War. They found Begin difficult to deal with, stubborn and inflexible. But Dayan, whom they knew of old, was pragmatic, experienced and a skilful diplomat. His position on the future of the West Bank was liberal – unlike Begin he did not demand that Israelis be allowed to settle there – and he was prepared for Israel to negotiate. That terms were agreed between Carter, Sadat and Begin at Camp David in 1978, and that the eight months' search for peace did not end in failure, was, in my view, more to the credit of Dayan's skill and patience than to anybody else. In some respects I think it was his finest hour. At the same time credit must be given to Begin; under the terms of the Camp David agreement, and in exchange for peace, he returned to Egypt the whole of Sinai, which, I suspect, was considerably more than the Egyptians had expected.

I asked myself what I could do to help. After discussing the matter with my friends in the UK and Israel, I made a speech to the Anglo-Israel Association in London in December 1978, in which I said that it would be impossible to conceive of Israel's giving up the West Bank for it to become an independent state under PLO leadership. 'The PLO's national convention', I reminded my listeners, 'still calls for the destruction of the State of Israel.' There would be no security for Israel if at her very centre she found herself restricted to a strip of land nine miles wide, with the sea on one side and hostile armies on the other. I said that if a peace agreement was signed, Marks & Spencer would offer the Egyptians help in developing their textile and food industries, based on our experience in Israel over the past twenty years. I expressed the hope that the meeting at Camp David would lead to a peace treaty being signed, which could be a turning point for the Middle East. I described how the lessons learned and applied in industry and agriculture by the Israelis could be useful to the Egyptians. 'Israel', I said, 'has been able to transfer her know-how to developing countries in different parts of the world, particularly in Africa, where her advice has been profitably accepted in, notably, Zambia, the Ivory Coast and Kenya. I hope that similar help can be given to, and similar developments can take place in Egypt, creating employment for many and helping to raise the standard of living of those involved, and providing a base for exports.' The fact that a prominent Zionist was ready to try to help Egypt as soon as a peace treaty was signed attracted quite a bit of publicity.

The peace treaty was signed in March 1979. Carter had had to work desperately hard on both Sadat and Begin, and must have heaved a colossal sigh of relief when they signed at the White House. As a treaty it was far from ideal, but the miracle was that it had been signed at all. His great work done, and conscious of the differences between Begin's reading of the terms and his own, Dayan resigned the following October, to be followed in November by Ezer Weizman, who found that there were many Likud policies which he could not support.

In the autumn of 1979, when I was staying at the Tel Aviv Hilton, I received a visit from an American called Fell. He was a big supplier of grain to Egypt. He had heard of the offers I had made to Egypt of help and advice from Marks & Spencer if a peace treaty was signed. Did the offer still stand? 'Yes,' I said. As a result of my talks with Fell, two of our senior staff went to Egypt early the following year – Nathan Goldenberg, who by now had been our chief food consultant for twenty years, and Martin Mendoza, one of our textile executives. They spent several weeks there and were well received.

Later in 1980 I received a visit from an Egyptian named Sayed Salem. He asked me whether I would accept an invitation to visit Egypt as the guest of the government. Lily, who was included in the invitation, and I went in November. Goldenberg and Mendoza came with us; so too did David Frost, who is a good friend and had become a governor of the Weizmann Institute. We were going from Egypt to a governors' meeting in Israel. Lily and I were installed in the Cairo Hilton's presidential suite, with three security guards on duty twenty-four hours a day. The programme began with an intensive tour of some of the country's textile and clothing developments. I was accompanied by a number of Egyptian ministers. I saw some remarkable manufacturing plants, one of them at Mehala, in the Nile delta, where over 20,000 people were employed in one complex. The complex contained magnificent gardens, playing-fields and a hospital, and living accommodation for about 5,000 workers. The machinery was modern, much of it provided by financial assistance from the Americans. What the Egyptians wanted from us was advice on what best to produce with it for world and domestic markets. In other delta towns I had meetings with several ministers, and we also had discussions with the Minister of Agriculture and senior members of his staff. It was a hectic week.

While I was working hard in Cairo, the delta and Alexandria, Lily and David went down the Nile to Luxor to visit the tombs of the Pharaohs and the magnificent temple of Karnak. On the Saturday morning we went to Sadat's house on the Nile a few miles outside Cairo. This was my first meeting with him. We had a long and friendly discussion, during which he told me about his ambitions for peace and closer co-operation with Israel. He had much charisma, warmth and charm, and was uncomplicated. I was impressed by his understanding of Israeli problems, by his realism, and above all by his evident resolve to establish peace and to cement it by co-operation. He was optimistic, even though after the signing of the peace treaty in 1979 Egypt had been suspended from several Arab organizations by the other Arab states. Sadat spoke well of Navon, then President of Israel, who had visited Egypt a couple of weeks previously. 'I know,' he said, 'that Israel's President has little or no political power, but as an ambassador for Israel to the Egyptian people you couldn't have a better person than President Navon. It's not only that he speaks good Arabic, and was able to talk to the Egyptian people in their own tongue, it's that his whole approach to our problems is right.'

Before I returned home from Egypt the President arranged for me to visit the then Vice President, Hosni Mubarak, now President. Mubarak spoke to me mainly about the problem of Egypt's increasing population and said that if the birth rate continued at its present rate the outlook for Egypt was grim. He said they were doing what they could to control it, but it was very difficult: even if the Egyptians found a method to control the birth rate the population would rise from forty million in 1980 to sixty million by the year 2000. Even if they could keep it down to that level it would be difficult to develop a reasonable standard of living; if the increase was greater, heaven help them. At the time of writing, the Egyptian birth rate will mean a far greater population than sixty million by the year 2000; the result can only be major economic and social problems for the country.

Marks & Spencer was able to offer some worthwhile advice to Egypt, much of it based on what we had learned in Israel, but the problem was to get it implemented. Many of the problems, in fact, were similar to those which Israel had faced and overcome, but progress there had been based to some extent on scientific and technological developments, and on a labour force that had become progressively better trained. Egypt's problem was that, though they had manpower and water – the two most vital elements for developing agriculture satisfactorily – technological progress and trained manpower were lacking. I met President Sadat several times, and on one occasion, after he had recently visited Israel, he told me: 'When I cross the border between Egypt and Israel in my plane, I know instantly when I have gone from one country to the other – when I look down and see a great stretch of arid yellow desert suddenly stop and green fields begin.' (Some modest progress was in fact made in farming in the Nile delta with the aid of Israeli experts, who went to help the Egyptians, and in this particular activity the Minister of Agriculture was most co-operative.)

As well as from a lack of trained manpower and of technological development, Egypt suffered from excessive bureaucracy. It so hampered what we were doing to try to help the country that I sent a memorandum on the subject to the ministerial department concerned. Some time later I heard that President Sadat was passing through London on his way to Washington; I phoned the Egyptian ambassador and said I would like to see the President. I was told that Sadat was only going to be in London for twenty-four hours and would not be having any private meetings. However, two days before his arrival I received a message that he would like to see me. When I arrived at the embassy he thanked me generously for the help we were giving Egypt. 'We could do a great deal more, Mr President,' I said, 'but there are problems.' He replied, 'If you think I have not seen your memorandum on our bureaucracy you are wrong, but we have spent one hundred years or more building up that bureaucracy – neither you nor I, even working together, will break it down in one or two years, but if we work together we shall at least make progress.' He then went on to Washington. Three months later, in October 1981, he was assassinated. I believe that Sadat's murder was a great tragedy, not always fully appreciated, and that, had he survived, peace in the Middle East today would be far more advanced.

Menachem Begin retired in August 1983. I came to know him a little better during his premiership, but we never established the sort of rapport that I had enjoyed with previous Israeli Prime Ministers, and I had little contact with most of the members of his cabinet. One person, however, whom I did get to know moderately well was Arik Sharon, though he and I had differing views. Although I appreciated Israel's need for a security zone in southern Lebanon so that terrorists could not launch attacks into northern Israel or fire their rockets from just across the border, and understood why Israel decided to obtain that zone by war, I was opposed to the extension of the war into the major part of Lebanon. I said so, both verbally and in writing, which did not make me popular. The war in the end turned out disastrously for Israel, despite the initial advances. Beirut was bombed in support of Israel's Lebanese Christian allies; then Israel was blamed, after capturing Beirut, for the massacre of Palestinians by the Christian Phalangists in the Sabra and Shatilla camps. This provoked an international outcry. In the end Israel has largely pulled out from the Lebanon under Shimon Peres's leadership, having gained little from the campaign there which she could not already have obtained from her initial forty-kilometre advance. Her former Christian allies, now disunited, are under constant attack, and Lebanon, apart from the Israeli invasion, has been in a state of civil war for ten years, with tens of thousands of casualties; this civil war is still going on at the time of writing.

The Likud government's economic policy was a failure. Before the fall of the Roman Empire in the third century AD, history records that its leaders introduced a policy of bread and circuses, meaning that the mass of the people were fed and entertained to keep them quiet. They became demoralized, conditions deteriorated, and eventually the Roman Empire was destroyed. Despite Israel's economic problems, the Likud government introduced the modern equivalent of bread and circuses in the shape of cars, television sets and videos, which were imported in large numbers and caused a damaging deterioration in Israel's balance of payments. Huge wage increases were granted to keep up with inflation, which, of course, led to further inflation. Industrial production was stagnant, exports declined and imports soared. Israel's foreign debt increased enormously and by 1983 she was in the grip of a major economic crisis. Had the policy continued for much longer then, in so far as a country can go bankrupt, Israel would have done so.

I remember going with Lily and the MP Hugh Fraser in November 1983 for three or four days to Eilat, where we stayed at a hotel in what is now the disputed Taba area. As we drove the few miles from the airport to the hotel we saw thousands of Japanese cars, which had been discharged from ships in Eilat, parked on the quays and adjoining land. We returned to Israel again in May 1984. On the night after we arrived I was asked to talk to the Israel-British Chamber of Commerce, the sister chamber in Israel of the British-Israel Chamber of Commerce in the United Kingdom. As I was told it was a private meeting, I decided to speak my mind. I based my talk initially on the theme of the Roman bread and circuses syndrome, and predicted that if the car, television and video imports were not controlled and if the Israelis did not tighten their belts, the economic and social damage to Israel would be enormous. I then went on to describe and praise what had been well done in Israel, and to suggest where Israel could make further economic progress. The following day we went to lunch with the President, Chaim Herzog, and his wife, Aura, who are old friends. I thought that it would be just a private family lunch. However, when we arrived, the first person I saw was Eli Hurvitz, the chairman of the Manufacturer's Association, and his wife. He said, 'Very good talk you gave last night, Marcus.'

'How do you know?' I asked. 'You weren't there.'

He said, 'It's prominent in the papers this morning.'

I must say that, had I known my words would be reported, I'm not sure I would have said what I did.

I then turned round and saw, standing behind me, Yitzhak Shamir, who had become Prime Minister after Begin resigned, and whose government I had criticized in my talk.

As a result of the 1984 Israeli elections no party had a majority; the only possibility for any form of effective government was a coalition of the Labour Party and Likud. Agreement was reached that Shimon Peres would be Prime Minister for two years, with Shamir as Foreign Secretary, after which — that is half way through the parliamentary term — they would change posts. In early discussions I had with Shimon about the economic situation, he told me his intentions; they seemed eminently sensible, but I saw little evidence in the first six months of them being implemented. When I talked to cab drivers, waiters, and those of my friends who were not involved in government or politics, they all said that they had thought they would be asked to tighten their belts and had been ready to do so, but the call had not yet come. Inflation continued to be rampant. I believed that great economic and social deterioration would ensue, but I was wrong.

It is fortunate for Israel that Shimon Peres headed the government at that time. I have known him for more than thirty-seven years, and at various times during those years we have worked together. His contribution, firstly as a young man, to the creation of Israel and since that time to its development has been a great one. He presides over one of the most disunited cabinets in any democracy anywhere — disunited because in many areas the views of the two major parties in the coalition differ substantially. Nevertheless, in the seventeen months (at the time of writing) that he has been Prime Minister he has, with determination and ability, tackled Israel's two greatest problems — peace and economic stability.

On the economic front Peres prepared his plans skilfully and, with the co-operation of some able and intelligent ministers from the Likud side, particularly Modai, the Finance Minister, initiated a policy which for several months had a considerable measure of success. Inflation in July 1985 was running at a level of over 500% per year; six months later it had fallen to a level of 20% per year. The majority of Israelis finally tightened their belts, accepted a substantial reduction in their standard of living and co-operated with the government. In less than a year there has been a remarkable improvement in Israel's economic performance and situation, and many Israelis have rediscovered their sense of dedication.

At the same time, Shimon Peres, despite some opposition from his Likud coalition colleagues, has made it clear that he is prepared to make substantial concessions to obtain peace with his neighbours. The tragedy so far is that, although King Hussein would like to reach an agreement, he feels he cannot do so without the agreement of the PLO and the support of some of the neighbouring Arab states. Israel refuses to have the PLO involved in any negotiations, certainly so long as they refuse to abide by UN Resolutions 242 and 338, which give recognition to Israel, and so long as they refuse to denounce terrorism as a weapon and to agree, genuinely, to work for peace.

I hope that when Shimon Peres hands over the premiership to Shamir in October 1986, he is able as Foreign Secretary to continue his policy of seeking and eventually obtaining a constructive peace with Israel's Arab neighbours; and that Shamir, when he becomes

Prime Minister, continues with the present economic policy, which is revitalizing Israel's economy. At the time of writing the 'peace' ball rests in the Arab court; regrettably there is little evidence that they are prepared to seize it.

Because of my activities in Israel during the period that I have covered in this chapter I have, from time to time, sought the advice and help of our Prime Ministers and Foreign Secretaries. I have already referred to my meetings with Edward Heath. I had a number of discussions, both with Harold Wilson and James Callaghan; both were constructive and helpful, naturally always taking into account British interests. They looked at the problems as objectively as they could and took what action they thought was right. They gave me some sound advice. Over the years I found some senior Foreign Office officials far less objective; they generally supported Arab views without fully taking into account the Israeli position. The bias towards the Arab countries of the Foreign Office as a whole is understandable; after all, we have twenty ambassadors to Arab countries, against one ambassador to Israel, and Israel is a very small country. Many of these ambassadors, at one time or another in their careers, become senior members of the Foreign Office staff. They have been exposed to Arab influences, and know the Arab problems; some have indeed never visited Israel. I am glad to say that it seems to me that, today, senior Foreign Office officials are taking a more balanced view of the situation in the Middle East.

Prior to his visit to the Middle East in 1982 I had several discussions with Lord Carrington. He wanted to improve our relations with Israel. His visit went well, but while he was in Israel the Falklands War broke out. Because he was out of Britain at the time of the Argentinian assault on the Falklands, and being a man of high principle, he resigned. We lost a formidable Foreign Secretary and an important and constructive political leader.

In 1974, when James Callaghan was Foreign Secretary, he asked me to go and see him at the Foreign Office. When I got there, he said, 'Marcus, I want to ask you a question, but I don't want a reply for two days.'

'Go ahead, Foreign Secretary,' I replied.

He said, 'I would like you to go as Her Majesty's Government's ambassador to Israel.'

I couldn't believe my ears. I said, 'Jim, am I hearing you correctly?'
'Yes,' he said.

'Well,' I said, 'I'm very flattered, but everybody knows of my long and close relations with Israel and no one would believe that if I went there as ambassador I would put the United Kingdom's interests first, even if I was doing so. They would think I was prejudiced.'

'You are wrong,' said James Callaghan. 'That is not what we think.'

'It's out of the question.'

He said, 'I asked you not to give a hasty answer. Think about it and reply in two days' time.'

I thanked him, but my reply forty-eight hours later was the same.

When I asked him recently if he minded my recounting this episode, his jocular reply was, 'As this was one of my better ideas, I have absolutely no objection to you referring to it in your book.'

{   }

CHAPTER SEVENTEEN

{   }

THIS IS the last chapter of my book. In it I want to give an up-to-date account of my various activities and interests, of the causes I have worked for, and of the family I have loved. The chapter will, therefore, probably strike the reader as somewhat disjointed. I am sorry for this, but I cannot avoid it.

I retired as chairman and chief executive of Marks & Spencer in July 1984 but remained as president, and as a member of the board, until October 1985, when I ceased to be a director and became honorary president.

On the night preceding our annual general meeting in 1984, just before I relinquished the chairmanship, the Marks & Spencer board was entertained to dinner by the Dewhirst directors to celebrate our centenary of trading together. Alistair Dewhirst, the chairman, spoke about our one hundred years of friendship and co-operation and presented me with a beautiful antique clock. I replied to his warm words to the best of my ability, and then presented him with a £5 gold coin, not 1884 vintage – we couldn't find one – but 1887, in repayment of the £5 his grandfather had loaned my grandfather one hundred years before. The following day at our annual general meeting, the last I was to chair, I was able to tell the assembled shareholders that finally, after one hundred years, Marks & Spencer was out of debt.

When I retired from the board of Marks & Spencer fifty-seven years had passed since the day in 1928 when I entered the store in Brewer Street, Soho, to do my first day's work for the company. The reader will understand, I am sure, that the weeks following my retirement were a somewhat emotional period for me. The change in my life was, however, made much easier for me by my successor and his colleagues. I retained my office in Michael House, our headquarters, and was encouraged to keep up my contacts, both in headquarters and in the stores. I continue to look, listen and learn; when I have something that I think worthwhile passing on I report it to Derek Rayner or to one of the other senior members of the board. But though I make suggestions I am careful to avoid anything that might be construed as interference with the running of the business. I would not be allowed to interfere even if I wanted to, but I don't: it was right for me to retire and for younger people to take the lead. I still go to the office most days, and my relationship with my long-time colleagues is warm.

I had looked forward to my retirement as a period in my life in which I could relax, spend more time reading, fishing and on the farm, and generally take things easy. So far this aim has not been achieved — something always seems to come up which I am asked to do or want to do.

On 4 October 1984 I went to lunch with Harold Lever. He and his wife Diane are close friends of Lily's and mine, and our discussions have always covered a wide range of mutual interests. This lunch was an all-male affair; the other three guests were the senior executives of three very large businesses. Towards the end of lunch we got on to the subject of unemployment and I said that the result of Marks & Spencer's policy of seeking always to source (that is, buy our merchandise) in the UK, providing the products represented good quality and value, had been the creation of over 60,000 jobs in industry and agriculture. One of Harold's other guests, whose organization was considerably larger than ours, said, 'Yes, Marcus, but what is 60,000 against 3 million unemployed?' 'Not much,' I replied, 'but what if one hundred of the larger firms, through a similar policy, were each able to create between 3000 and 4000 jobs? Instead of unemployment rising, unemployment would be falling. I'm sure there are many people in top management who do not understand how much of what they import could be equally well produced at home.'

On my return to the office I decided that, as I had stuck my neck out, I had better do something about it and over the next few weeks I invited in, one by one, the chief executives of sixteen of our greatest companies, covering a wide range of industries and retailing. I asked each of them the same question: 'What is your policy towards sourcing in the UK?'

The majority said, 'Of course, Marcus, that *is* our policy.'

I said, 'Well, how do you do it?'

They said, 'What do you mean? It's our policy.'

I then asked, 'When did you last see the senior members of your buying team and re-emphasize the policy to them, ask how they were getting on, what problems they were meeting, what success they had had in replacing imports with British products just as good or better, or in creating exports?'

'Well,' each of my guests said, in more or less the same terms, 'we don't do it quite like that, but it *is* our policy.'

In fact, the majority of them did not carry out such a policy seriously or dynamically; and some didn't really carry it out at all. Three of the men I talked to *do* have such a policy, and carry it out with vigour: Hector Laing of United Biscuits, Eddie Nixon of IBM (UK), and David Alliance of Coats-Viyella. That IBM does so is all the more creditable because they are a subsidiary of an American parent. It is interesting that IBM's exports from the UK increased from £1.1 billion in 1984 to £1.580 billion in 1985.

Of the sixteen executives I talked to, three said, with total frankness, that the idea of a sourcing policy had never crossed their minds, though they emphasized with great unanimity that they were not anti-British. I said, mildly, 'I hope not.'

Three or four months later two of the sixteen executives came back to me and said that they had started on a sourcing policy and met with some initial success. The chief executive of a major food-processing firm told me that, having hitherto bought all their packaging in Scandinavia, they had decided to see if some of it could be produced in the UK. They had made a trial, which had been successful and had created more than 200 new jobs. He added that until then his firm had imported refined sugar, but they had now experimented with importing raw sugar and refining it at home, had been successful, and had created about one hundred new jobs. Good news came to me also from the chief executive of a major retailing group. He told me that hitherto some 30% of what his firm sold had been imported. They had decided to experiment with the home production of three items which they had previously bought abroad. The experiment had been successful and, even in its early days, it had resulted in 600 new jobs.

At about this time I had discussions with Norman Tebbit, who was then in charge of the Department of Trade and Industry, and also, at his suggestion, with Norman Fowler, in charge of the Department of Health and Social Security. Some of the senior permanent civil servants attended these discussions. As a result, it is clear to me that there is a great deal of scope for more government purchasing at home. I am glad to say that this opportunity is now being better pursued. In all my activities on this front I have had the full support of the Prime Minister, who is genuinely concerned to reduce the level of unemployment. Whenever I have sought Mrs Thatcher's advice and help in areas relating to the well being of people, I have found her sympathetic, active and helpful. She has not always agreed with me, but her advice has been sensible, constructive and to the point. She is a woman of vision whose drive and determination will achieve much for our country, though not always appreciated at the time.

In November 1985 I gave a Friday evening 'discourse', as it is termed, at the Royal Institution. These discourses are mainly on technological or scientific subjects, but the title of mine was 'We Can Increase Employment in the United Kingdom: Here's How'. I have spoken to conferences of the British Institute of Management and the CBI on the same subject. I believe that more leaders in industry and government are now trying hard to get more of the goods we buy produced in this country. But there is much to do; unless many more industrial leaders become imbued with the idea and implement it dynamically and persistently it will remain little more than an idea.

In my so-called 'retirement' I continue to preach the gospel of 'good human relations at work'. To further this cause I talk to business conferences, political gatherings, academic seminars and schools. But development of the production of goods here in Britain, to reduce our import bill and increase employment are now my first priorities.

When President Mitterrand of France made his state visit to Britain in October 1984, Lily and I were invited first to the banquet for him, and then to the lunch which the Prime Minister gave in his honour the following day. The two of us were the only people for whose presence at both occasions I could not find a justification. Lily sat next to the French ambassador, Monsieur de Margerie, and told him that she wondered why the Sieffs had been asked. The ambassador made a polite but unconvincing reply. After further thought Lily said to him: 'I know why we were invited. Napoleon called Britain a nation of shopkeepers – we are here representing the nation.'

I was delighted when, in 1966, my father became a life peer and even more delighted when I myself was made a life peer in 1980, particularly as we were the first father and son to become life peers. My father chose the title of Lord (Baron) Sieff of Brimpton in the Royal County of Berkshire. As I also live in the same area, I said that I too would like to call myself Lord Sieff of Brimpton in the Royal County of Berkshire. However, those in authority at the College of Arms told me I could not do so because it would be similar to establishing a hereditary peerage, which was against the principle of bestowing life peerages. We eventually found a compromise and I took the title 'Lord Sieff of Brimpton, *of Brimpton* in the Royal County of Berkshire'. Father could sign letters and documents 'Sieff'; my signature is not valid unless I sign 'Sieff of Brimpton'. Thus a satisfactory solution was found to a very serious problem!

I was delighted too when my old college, Corpus Christi, made me an honorary fellow some years ago, and extremely flattered that St Andrew's, Sterling and Reading Universities, Babson College, USA and Manchester Polytechnic awarded me honorary degrees. The Royal College of Surgeons, to which Marks & Spencer and my family have given long and continuing support, made me an honorary fellow. I do not ask if I deserve such honours; I just say that I am grateful for them.

In my later years, to my surprise, I have become involved in a number of activities which I had never anticipated. One such was the Police Foundation. Some time in 1979 Lord Goodman asked if I could join him for a meeting at the Home Office; he did not say what it was about. On arrival I found Lord Goodman, Sir Robert Armstrong, then permanent under-secretary at the Home Office, Lord Harris, who had been Minister of State there, and the Metropolitan Police Commissioner, Sir David McNee. They explained that it was their intention to set up the Police Foundation, a body that was to be totally independent of government, the police or any other authority, the main aim of which would be to study methods of policing, police training, police relations with the communities in which they operate, and a number of allied subjects. The foundation was to be an independent body, both physically and financially. Arnold Goodman said that those who had advocated the setting-up of the Police Foundation would like me to be the first chairman of the trustees. I replied that I would be happy to be a trustee, but not chairman.

He then said, 'No one connected with the law can be chairman; that eliminates me. No one connected with government or the civil service can be chairman; that eliminates John Harris and Robert Armstrong; obviously no one connected with the police can be chairman. That leaves you.'

I repeated that I could not accept the position. An appeal was made to my sense of duty; I then agreed to become chairman but only for a year. That year stretched to five years. In 1984 I said it was essential that I should be replaced by a younger man. I was delighted when John Harvey-Jones, chairman of ICI, agreed to succeed me.

In the early days of the Foundation I asked the Prince of Wales to become a patron; he declined but offered to become president. He delivered the first of what is now an annual Police Foundation lecture. The foundation's task has grown in importance as problems of relations between the police and many communities have increased; it plays a valuable role. Its reports have been most constructive and, if implemented, should help to ameliorate, if they do not solve, some of the growing problems in this area.

My involvement in Israel and with the problems of the Middle East continues. I resigned as chairman of the international board of governors of the Weizmann Institute last year, but was delighted to be elected chancellor, my only regret being that this coincided with the resignation of Michael Sela, an eminent scientist, who had been an excellent president throughout my term as chairman. Michael made the move so that he could concentrate more on his scientific work. He and his very attractive wife Sara did a great deal for the institute, which, notwithstanding his departure, continues to expand its scientific activities.

I worked closely with Morry Levinson, who succeeded me as chairman of the international board of governors and who, had as head of the American committee, given considerable support of every kind to the institute. The Weizmann Institute also brought me in close contact with David Ginsburg, one of Washington's most eminent lawyers and a man of rare qualities, whose advice on numerous occasions, has been of great value. In Canada the institute led to friendships with Murray Koffler, a vice-chairman of the international board of governors, and Jimmy Kaye, chairman of the Canadian committee. Both of them have made an important contribution to the work of the institute.

In 1972 I was succeeded as chairman of the Weizmann Institute Foundation, the supporting body in Great Britain, by Derrick Kleeman. He did a splendid job for eleven years, and was in turn succeeded in 1983 by my son David, who is also doing well. The institute today has up to one hundred visiting scientists working there from all over the world, non-Jews as well as Jews. I believe that when better relations are established between Israel and her neighbours, the Weizmann Institute will be one of the bridges over which real peace will pass.

At the beginning of 1985 all of us connected with the Weizmann Institute were delighted when the Prime Minister, Margaret Thatcher, agreed that a chair in chemistry, the subject she had studied at Oxford, should be established at the institute in her name.

I have been associated with the Prime Minister in a number of fields and have found her most helpful and co-operative, whether about the problems of British industry and unemployment or about relations with Israel and the Middle East. I have developed both affection and respect for her, though I do not always agree with her views. That the recent visit of Shimon Peres in January 1986 – he was the first Israeli Prime Minister to visit Britain officially – was a success, was in large part due, not only to the constructive and sensible policies which Peres expounded, but also to the warm and co-operative reception he received from the Prime Minister and her colleagues.

Then, in May 1986, Mrs Thatcher in turn paid the first visit to Israel by a British prime minister in office. I was with her there on a number of occasions and was delighted to host a luncheon in her honour at the Weizmann Institute. From my observations, this exchange of visits by the two prime ministers and their colleagues has already improved relations between their countries.

As I have said earlier, Lily and my sister Judith, who lives in Israel, are active members of the Women's International Zionist Organization, and Lily is a leading member of the British Federation of Women Zionists, which supports in Britain the work which Mother initiated in the early 1920s in what was then British mandated Palestine. Mother died in 1966. She was buried in Tel Mond, not far from her house. She enjoyed a full life. Appreciation of her work through WIZO, for the old and infirm, the young and the sick, Arabs as well as Jews, could not have been better demonstrated than by the many hundreds who walked behind the coffin at her funeral, including some hundreds of Arabs. She was not an easy woman to succeed, but would be delighted that today's world president of WIZO, Raya Jaglom, is a woman of outstanding ability and great dynamism, who has further expanded the organization's remarkable work.

One of my more recent involvements in Israel has been to take an active interest in a settlement near the monastery of Latrun, called Neve Shalom — 'Oasis of Peace'. This was established in 1973 by Father Bruno, a Dominican monk of great energy and vision. He wanted to create some means whereby members of the Moslem, Christian and Jewish clergy could live and work together to help bring about peace. In its early days Neve Shalom did not make much progress; Father Bruno decided its character should be changed, so, under the leadership of Pinchas (Wellesley) Aron, a former 8th Army officer, it has been developed into a joint Arab/Jewish settlement in which some sixty people now live and work. Half are Jews, half Arabs; all are bilingual. Neve Shalom runs four-day courses for young Jews and Arabs from the same neighbourhood, twenty from each denomination. I have attended some of the courses, and was very interested to see what happens when the two peoples are brought together. On the first day the Arabs and Jews keep their distance and are suspicious of each other, but by the fourth day, as a result of being together and because of the joint training, contacts are made and friendships are being formed, a number of which continue after the youngsters return home. Some 7000 young Jews and Arabs have been to Neve Shalom; it is a modest but worthwhile effort. Over the last five years, during which I have visited Neve Shalom half a dozen times, I have seen remarkable progress. Recently the settlement opened a kindergarten for the children born there, who are bilingual from early days. It is also a school for peace. Sam Lewis, who, until he retired, was the United States ambassador to Israel and the longest serving ambassador there, called it the brightest hope for peace in the strife-torn Middle East; he is right. I must not exaggerate the hope for peace that Neve Shalom brings, but it is, at the very least, a gleam of peace on the horizon, and an important one.

One of the most most pleasant evenings I have spent in Israel was in April 1983, when I attended a dinner given to celebrate my seventieth birthday. A number of people spoke in the most flattering way, but what moved me most was the speech made by Abba Eban, the former Foreign Minister, who ended with: 'So we do not leave Marcus Sieff tonight in any mood of valediction or release. On the contrary, now that the years of his apprenticeship have passed it is time for him to get down to some serious work.'

Earlier in this narrative I have mentioned several people who have tried to help Israel and to bring about a stable and permanent peace in the Middle East. Some years ago Lily and I were staying with our good American friends Esther and Walter Schoenfeld in Seattle; they asked whether we would like to meet their friends, Senator 'Scoop' Jackson and his wife Helen. The four of us hit it off well. Scoop was a member of important committees of the Senate, covering a wide field, a man of power and influence. He was always concerned with the security of Israel and with peace in the Middle East. He was equally concerned with the implementation of the Helsinki Treaty on Human Rights and sought, under the treaty, the release of those Russians, including Jews, who wished to emigrate but were not permitted to do so. The determination with which he pursued his objectives was phenomenal; his motive came from conviction, not from calculation of political gain. He was senator for the state of Washington, where few Jews live. Talking with him at the time he was seeking the Democratic Party nomination for presidential candidate, I suggested that it might be better for his prospects if he played down a little his views about Jews, Russian Jews, Israel and the Middle East. He replied, 'Marcus, I cannot, nor am I prepared to try to, compromise my beliefs for any political advantage.' Tragically he died in 1983. He was a friend, sorely missed. His charming widow, Helen, carries on some of the work he began.

Professor Guido Goldman of Harvard, an expert on European, in particular German, affairs, is another American whose political advice I have found of particular value. He and I share gourmet tastes and an appreciation of fine wines, of which he has an excellent range, and which I sample with pleasure!

In 1984 I was elected president of the Royal Agricultural Society of England (RASE). I did not believe that I was the right person for the job, but Francis Pemberton, my friend from Cambridge days, and Charlie Smith-Ryland, of Barbados holiday days, both of whom have been long and actively involved with RASE, convinced me that I should take on the presidency for a one-year term. I did what I could and had the opportunity at the Royal Show in 1985, in my opening talk, to put over again my views on the importance both of producing what the consumer wants and of quality and value – never more so than today, when farming in the Common Market is going through an economic crisis because of our mountains of grain and beef and our lakes of wine. However, as a farmer myself, I know that it is far easier to say what should be done than to do it.

A sad event in 1986 was the death of Michael Sacher, my cousin and my friend. He was also my colleague in the business for over forty years and made an important contribution to its development in many fields, particularly in his insistence on high quality. We did not always agree, but this in no way affected our close and warm relationship. I greatly valued his opinion and will miss him very much.

None of the events I have recalled would have meant so much without the presence of my wife Lily, who has put up with me for twenty-four years. Not only is she a great support and an outstanding hostess, but she has also over the last ten years acquired a considerable knowledge of fine art and built up a successful business in modern prints. I was proud and pleased for her when her last annual exhibition received very good reviews in the major national newpapers. Lily has been my most consistent, but most constructive, critic – I hope she will always remain so.

As it says in *The Ethics of the Fathers*, 'It is not your responsibility to finish the task, nor are you permitted to desist from it.' Now, in the September of my life, there are three things which I shall continue to strive for. The first is to make progress in solving our socio-economic problems by the creation of more employment in the United Kingdom. The second is the improvement of good human relations in the workplace. The third, and perhaps the most important, is to make at least a modest contribution towards greater stability and peace in the Middle East.

INDEX